ILLUSION OF LIFE AND DEATH

KYABJE DZOGCHEN PEMA KALSANG RINPOCHE

TRANSLATED BY CHRISTIAN A STEWART

MAHASANDHI PUBLISHING

Mahasandhi Publishing
5 Corinthian Court
West Hill Road
Cowes
Isle of Wight
PO31 7SF

www.dzogchen-monastery.org

Design and typeset by Mahasandhi Publishing
Printed in the U.K.

ILLUSION OF LIFE AND DEATH
Kyabje Dzogchen Pema Kalsang Rinpoche
Translated by Christian A Stewart

ISBN: 978-0-9568596-0-0

CONTENTS

ILLUSION OF LIFE AND DEATH

TRANSLATOR'S INTRODUCTION

'Illusion of Life and Death' examines the transitory nature of life and the need to make careful preparation for our future. Kyabje Dzogchen Pema Kalsang Rinpoche engages in thought-provoking discussion of the uncertainties faced by everyone, and using insightful observation, encourages us to reflect more deeply on what is truly important in life.

These discussions are followed by more traditional presentations of Buddhist teachings, including detailed instructions for the Dzogchen Preliminary Practices. Here, Kyabje Rinpoche draws from his deep knowledge of the tradition to guide the reader through each step of practice. Throughout the text, Kyabje Rinpoche does not shy away from confronting the reader with challenging questions in order to evoke genuine feelings and understanding of the Dharma.

In later chapters, Kyabje Rinpoche introduces some advanced and secret practices of the main Dzogchen teachings, including subtle body visualisations, rushen or dividing samsara and nirvana, and Jigme Lingpa's no-thought meditations. Many of these have not been previously made available in English.

Throughout the translation process, I have worked closely with Kyabje Rinpoche and his nephew Mura Rinpoche to ensure the meaning of the text is conveyed accurately and in keeping with the true spirit of the original. I have deliberately avoided embellishing the text with any of my own notes or explanations. Specifically, in some of the more advanced chapters, it was Kyabje Rinpoche's wish to avoid the inclusion of any additional material. The reader is therefore expected to use these teachings as part of a wider programme of study, supported by the guidance of a suitably qualified Lama.

May this virtue enlighten all beings!

Christian A Stewart
May, 2011

Pema Tung Retreat Centre
Dzogchen Monastery, Tibet
www.dzogchen-monastery.org

A Brief Introduction to the Life and Work of
Kyabje Dzogchen Pema Kalsang Rinpoche

Having received an intense and enlightening education with some of the most eminent masters of the 20th century, Kyabje Pema Kalsang Rinpoche became twelfth Throne Holder of Dzogchen Monastery. Throughout the bleak period of the 1960s and '70s, he managed to maintain and practise Dharma in secret. As soon as circumstances permitted, Kyabje Rinpoche spared no effort in undertaking to completely rebuild not only Dzogchen Monastery, but also Shira Sing Buddhist University; and more recently Kyabje Rinpoche established Dzogchen Pema Tung Great Perfection Retreat Centre. His untiring efforts have resulted in a great revival of the Dzogchen tradition and Dzogchen Monastery is once again an unrivalled example of both scholarly excellence and meditative realisation.

Kyabje Pema Kalsang Rinpoche was born on 6th June 1943 in Dzachuka, Eastern Tibet, the homeland of many exceptional masters, including the great Bodhisattva Patrul Rinpoche and the incomparable scholar Mipham Rinpoche. Kyabje Rinpoche's mother was the sister of accomplished master Dzogchen Adro Socho, and she bore many signs of a dakini, including a naturally occurring AH syllable on her tongue. It is said that when Rinpoche was born the surrounding area was filled with blossoming flowers which had never been seen before, tents of rainbows appeared and water miraculously turned into milk. Rinpoche's maternal uncle, the fourth Mura Rinpoche Pema Norbu, named the child Pema Kalsang.

When Pema Kalsang reached the age of five, Dzogchen Kontul Rinpoche, who had been very close to the second Pema Banza, travelled to Dzachuka and arrived at the family camp. As soon as the young Pema Kalsang saw the Rinpoche, he went to sit on his lap very joyfully, as if he was a good friend. He also recognised the knife strapped to Kontul Rinpoche's belt, saying, "That's mine!" The knife had belonged to the second Pema Banza. The names of Rinpoche's parents, his place of birth and other details were found to correspond with the prophesies of Jamyang Khyentse Choki Lodro, the sixth Dzogchen Rinpoche and other genuine masters, and Pema Kalsang was identified as the third incarnation of the Great Khenpo Pema Banza.

In that region the first Dzogchen Pema Banza, also known as Padma Vajra or Pema Dorje, was considered the most learned master of his time. He presided as head Khenpo in Shira Sing Buddhist University for many years, and in the latter part of his life lived and taught in Dzogchen Pema Tung. He was amazingly realised and in particular, in visions of the wisdom body of All-knowing Jigme Lingpa, attained indications of realising the ultimate lineage, thereby receiving transmission of luminous secret Heart Essence. Khenchen Pema Banza had many eminent students including Mipham Rinpoche, Jamyang Khyentse Wangpo, the fourth Shechen Gyaltsab, Do Khyentse, the third Dodrupchen, Adzom Drukpa, the fifth Shechen Rabjam and the treasure revealer Lerab Lingpa. The second Pema Banza Daychog Dorje (born 1898) was also a very learned Khenpo. At the age of thirty-eight he took over as tenth Throne Holder of Dzogchen Monastery for over seven years following the fifth Dzogchen Rinpoche's passing.

Pema Banza is in turn considered to be the emanation of Zurchen Choying Rangdrol (1604-1669), who was the Tantra master, root guru and Dzogchen master to none other than the Great Fifth Dalai Lama. He is a very important and precious figure in Tibetan Buddhism, numbering many eminent masters of the seventeenth century among his students. The Great Fifth Dalai Lama wrote a biography of Zurchen Choying Rangdrol which shows the profound devotion he had for his master:

> "By the power of these virtuous actions,
> Until I have directly realised the expressivity of rigpa,
>   Samantabhadra,
> In all lives, may you, my guardian and spiritual mentor,
> Hold me inseparably in your care."

At the age of seven, Kyabje Rinpoche went to Jangma monastery to study reading, writing and arithmetic with Dzogchen Khenpo Chogyur. He was an amazingly bright child and mastered his subjects quickly without any effort. Then, at the age of ten, together with Mura Tulku Pema Norbu, his parents, and a group of more than twenty others, Rinpoche was ceremonially brought to Dzogchen Monastery. Several thousand Lamas, monks and lay people rode out for three days to Dzachuka to welcome him. There were twenty or thirty incarnate Lamas in Dzogchen Monastery at the time, but none of them received such a huge welcoming party as this.

While he was growing up, Kyabje Rinpoche lived and studied with his root guru Khenpo Gonre and the sixth Dzogchen Rinpoche for many years in the Lama Palace of Dzogchen Monastery. During this time he received what must have been the most profound and complete spiritual education possible, with highly realised masters as his teachers and companions. From Khenpo Gonre, Kyabje Rinpoche received many profound teachings including those of Longchenpa, Jigme Lingpa and Patrul Rinpoche, together with Khenpo Gonre's own writings.

In addition, Dzogchen Rinpoche gave Kyabje Rinpoche many key empowerments. Together they travelled to the monastery of Dzongsar Khyentse Jamyang Choki Lodru a total of three times, for two or three months at a time, to receive empowerments of the old and new traditions, Sutras, Tantras and treasure texts. In all, there were very few teachings, empowerments and transmissions which Kyabje Rinpoche did not receive during the course of his education.

At the age of thirteen, Kyabje Rinpoche took the vows of a novice monk from Khenpo Gonre and later received the vows of a fully ordained monk from the master Khenpo Wangde Rinpoche; he was given the ordination name Tupten Longdok Tenbe Gyaltsen. In 1955, Kyabje Rinpoche, together with Khenpo Gonre and the sixth Dzogchen Rinpoche, travelled to Central Tibet and Tsang on extensive pilgrimage and met many great Lamas including His Holiness the Fourteenth Dalai Lama. Following their return, from the age of fourteen to sixteen, Kyabje Rinpoche lived in the Long Life Retreat Centre above the Dzogchen valley with great Khenpo Pema Tsewang, who taught him personally. This was to be the last opportunity Kyabje Rinpoche had to study with his masters.

In the autumn of 1958, when Kyabje Rinpoche was seventeen, Dzogchen Rinpoche took him to Gyalgi Drakkar, the retreat centre of Great Khenpo Tupten Nyendrak. With tears in his eyes, Dzogchen Rinpoche requested the Khenpo to give Kyabje Rinpoche seventeen long life empowerments corresponding in number to the years of his age. Dzogchen Rinpoche said to the Khenpo, "Very soon the Buddhist tradition will face great obstacles and destruction. At that time don't worry about me, focus your attention on this young one"; and he pointed to Kyabje Rinpoche. It was only a few days later the political situation deteriorated into violence.

During the winter of the following year, Kyabje Rinpoche, Dzogchen Rinpoche and Khenpo Gonre were imprisoned in Dege for political re-education. At one stage Dzogchen Rinpoche and Khenpo were forced to return to Dzogchen to undergo sessions of criticism and confession. When they were leaving, Dzogchen Rinpoche implored Sonam Gyaltsen, the supervisor of his residence who was with them, to look after Pema

Kalsang Rinpoche especially well. Dzogchen Rinpoche promised Pema Kalsang, "We'll meet again in the not too distant future." At that time, Sonam Gyaltsen thought Dzogchen Rinpoche was instructing him to look after the young Rinpoche for a few days while he was away; only later did he realise what he had been told was prophetic. This was the last time they saw either Dzogchen Rinpoche or Khenpo Gonre. Kyabje Rinpoche himself recalls a brief exchange which happened several years earlier:

> "One day, as we were sitting together, Dzogchen Rinpoche turned and said to me quite emphatically, 'I have no heir but you. Do you understand?' I didn't know it at the time, but later I realised what Rinpoche said to me that day was prophetic."

The next twenty years brought terrible suffering, even before the turmoil of the Cultural Revolution began. Dzogchen Monastery and Shira Sing Buddhist University were completely razed to the ground and Kyabje Rinpoche was forced to live in Dzogchen village.

From the start of 1959 to the end of 1980, under extreme duress and with no personal freedom, Kyabje Rinpoche was allotted the heaviest manual labour, forced into all kinds of physical exertions including moving earth and stones, making roads, and building houses for the Chinese. Not only was this work extremely exhausting physically, but the persecution resulting from the socio-political struggle was mentally even more debilitating. During the worst years, not only was he forced to do heavy labour during the day, but the evenings were filled with the mental torment of political education sessions. Every so often, Kyabje Rinpoche was arrested and threatened with imprisonment, or even death, if he did not conform, and this would last for several months at a time. He was often singled out as an object of intimidation, repression and struggle. During the years of the Cultural Revolution, Kyabje Rinpoche was accused of various anti-revolutionary crimes, and forced to live in conditions worse than anyone else. It was only many years later that he was given the less demanding work of tailoring.

In the words of Kyabje Rinpoche himself:

> "More devastating than all of this was the complete waste of the crucial time when my youthful mental faculties were developing at their clearest. My progress in studying general areas of knowledge and science, and in particular the traditions of Tibetan Buddhism, came to an abrupt end under the Chinese regime. The little

4

knowledge I have of Dharma does not extend beyond that which I had when I was sixteen years old. If I had completed my education, I believe I would certainly be able to write a few dozen Dharma-related books and leave a positive legacy which would benefit many future generations. However, the lives of my parents and family were taken when I was young, and my holy tutors, spiritual companions and master Khenpos were separated from me by force, leaving me alive but orphaned from their wisdom and love."

During this time, Kyabje Pema Kalsang Rinpoche prayed day and night for the revival of the precious Buddhist teachings. He risked his life to store secretly even the smallest piece of scripture or representation of the Buddha which came into his possession. He did not waste any time resting from the exhausting daily labour, but tirelessly practised the approach and accomplishment of the yidam, and the practices of generation, perfection and Great Perfection. In this way he embraced the bad conditions into the path of Dharma, and facilitated enhancement of realisation. In Rinpoche's own words:

"Despite all the physical and mental hardship and suffering that I endured, I also realised many beneficial aspects of these experiences, true teachers which cannot be found in the words of books. These included true renunciation of samsara, realisation of the impermanence and unreliability of worldly pursuits, the way to find inner happiness from undefiled samadhi, and non-separation from the Lama which resides in the centre of the heart."

During the years 1978 and 1979, limited freedom to travel was allowed, and Kyabje Rinpoche took the opportunity to travel to almost all the important holy sites of the Central and Tsang regions of Tibet. He did this mostly on foot and managed to recover many extremely important texts and statues which had escaped destruction. These he saved, and often carrying them on his back, brought them to Dzogchen. In this way he managed to preserve many sacred items which otherwise would have been lost or sold.

Returning to Dzogchen, Kyabje Rinpoche cleverly saw an opportunity to reinstate one of Dzogchen Monastery's important traditions. At that time, although religious practices were still strictly outlawed, the Chinese authorities had deemed the Legend of King Gesar of Ling to be suitable reading material. Kyabje Rinpoche managed to persuade the Chinese into allowing performances of the King Gesar Lama dance. The tradition of dancing the Legend of Gesar originated with the fifth Dzogchen

Rinpoche, who saw the dance in sacred visions. To reinstate this tradition, Kyabje Rinpoche personally crafted the masks which were traditionally used by Lama dancers in Dzogchen Monastery, and also managed to gather together basic materials for costumes.

Following this, Kyabje Rinpoche gathered resources to build a small mani wheel house. This was barely permissible at the time, but he managed to complete its construction and it still stands today, at the upper side of the monastery. At the time only a few collapsed earth walls remained of what used to be the glorious monastery of Dzogchen. Kyabje Rinpoche was finally able to move back into the monastery where he lived in a tent. Small pujas and spiritual services began to be held in makeshift buildings, and monks were permitted to wear robes once again.

In 1981, with the support of a good connection among the officials in charge of the region, Kyabje Rinpoche proposed to build a storehouse for the Gesar dance masks he had made. This was a tactical move to begin reconstruction of the ground floor of the Dzogchen Lama Palace. He based the design on the original building and began construction on the original site, managing to finish it the same year. This was the crucial first step in the revival of Dzogchen Monastery.

In the same year, Kyabje Pema Kalsang Rinpoche, together with Zankar Rinpoche, managed to get permission to establish the first Tibetan Language College of Sichuan Province on the site of Shira Sing Buddhist University. Kyabje Rinpoche made great efforts, and travelled great distances to invite senior non-sectarian masters, chief holders of the Dzogchen teaching lineage, to give instruction on Tibetan language and other core subjects. Because Dzogchen is historically such an important seat, these eminent Lamas and Khenpos were willing to act as school teachers in the new Tibetan Language School.

At first the school was merely a few tents pitched on the site of the original university. Only later was it possible for basic classrooms and accommodation to be built. The school served as a lone outpost of learning and culture to educate a generation of Tibetans who otherwise would have had no opportunity of receiving an education or even studying their own language. At that time, becoming a monk or nun was prohibited, so the school also served as a refuge for young men and women, where they were able to dedicate themselves to concentrated study. Later, the Tibetan Language School was moved to Da'u, and finally to Dartsedo, where it continues to provide comprehensive learning opportunities to young Tibetans; opportunities which are very hard to find elsewhere in the region.

After that, with the slightly improved political climate and the support of one regional official, permission was granted to rebuild the main temple of Dzogchen Monastery. However, at the time money and materials were in scarce supply, so Kyabje Rinpoche expended tremendous effort and went through numerous hardships to gather resources, travelling far and wide to distant communities to garner support. A few other Tulkus also lent their support to the efforts, and as political rule gradually loosened its harsh grip, others joined in the reconstruction efforts, including people from the village.

In 1982, at the age of thirty-nine, Kyabje Rinpoche set out to travel to India, but was tragically involved in a terrible car accident. He was seriously injured and almost died. In Kyabje Rinpoche's own words:

> "I managed to survive all the obstacles that threatened my life. I was the only one left of all the Lamas and monks who had lived in the Lama Palace of Dzogchen. That I was able to continue to work for the Dharma at a time of extreme decline was certainly due to the power of Dzogchen Rinpoche's prayers, and the blessings of Khenpo Tupten Nyendrak's seventeen long life empowerments."

Kyabje Rinpoche was forced to spend a year in hospital where he underwent multiple operations to pin together broken bones, some of which had to be repositioned over and over again. Not disheartened, Kyabje Rinpoche recovered his strength, and relying on two walking sticks, travelled to India and Nepal, working for the teachings and making pilgrimage to all the major holy sites. During this time he once again met with His Holiness the Dalai Lama. From India he visited Europe and the United States, where he gave teachings to many fortunate Westerners.

Having returned to Tibet, Kyabje Rinpoche took responsibility for the completion of the Lama Palace, as well as the reconstruction of the Grand Temple of Dzogchen Monastery. Despite the physical hardships, he once again joined in the manual labour on the construction site. Pooling all his resources, Kyabje Rinpoche built a golden reliquary stupa to enshrine the relics of the sixth Dzogchen Rinpoche, which he had risked his life keeping for twenty-five years. The stupa is now enshrined in the Temple of Great Perfection in Dzogchen Pema Tung Retreat Centre.

From a prophesy of the Great Treasure Revealer Pema Namdrol Lingpa:

"On the supreme fearless lion throne
Of Shira Singha Dharma centre,
Padma's mind emanation, named Pema,
Will illuminate like the sun
The excellent and enlightened qualities
Of all the conqueror's teachings,
And the thousand-petal lotuses
Of many young Pemas will bloom."

This prophesy was fulfilled when reconstruction of the great Buddhist University of Shira Sing began in the fortunate Dragon year of 1988. Kyabje Rinpoche used the small amount of money he received in compensation from his road accident to start the building work. In the past, the university was a highly specialised establishment accommodating only fifty of the most exceptional and promising Tulkus and monks, together with the most eminent Khenpos and Lamas. Kyabje Rinpoche saw the opportunity for expansion, and constructed buildings to accommodate five hundred monks, and a large temple which could hold one thousand. Again, Kyabje Rinpoche worked personally on the construction work to the extent that the soles of his feet split open.

When the building was complete, he invited many of the surviving senior and most learned masters from all schools of Tibetan Buddhism to revive the teaching lineages, and so Shira Sing Buddhist University attracted students from all traditions. This was a very fragile time for the Dharma in Tibet, but Kyabje Rinpoche managed to bring up a new generation of monks, Tulkus and Khenpos in the true Dharma, educating them to the highest possible standard. Kyabje Rinpoche spent the next ten years living in Shira Sing focusing on educating the younger generation, so there would be qualified teachers to spread the Dharma in the future. The basis of the Buddha's teaching, the ordination tradition, including the lineage of vows, was also revived from the foundations upwards by Kyabje Rinpoche.

In 1998, Kyabje Rinpoche began the construction of the Dzogchen Pema Tung Great Perfection Retreat Centre in the secluded grassy meadow of Pema Tung, the site of his previous incarnation Pema Banza's retreat centre. In 2003, the stunning Temple of Great Perfection was completed, and it became time for Kyabje Rinpoche to accept the throne of teaching. Despite his education coming to an abrupt end when he was only sixteen, everyone was amazed at the lucid and realised teachings he began to impart on the most profound and subtle topics of the Great Perfection. Now, every summer, large numbers of Tulkus, Khenpos, monks and nuns come from all over Tibet to attend his profound teachings.

According to a prophesy by Apung Terton:

"In tattered times, around Rudam snow-mountain,
A crystal boulder will unfurl in the Lotus Ground."

Kyabje Rinpoche considers the reference to the crystal in this prophesy not to refer to shining boulders of temples or buildings, but to the crystal used to indicate rigpa awareness in the Great Perfection tradition. This prophesy, therefore, accurately foretells a revelation of the Dzogchen teachings in Dzogchen Pema Tung or Lotus Ground, after a serious decline.

Kyabje Rinpoche is the main holder of one of the closest and most pure Dzogchen Longchen Nyingthig lineages in the world. Only five lineage holders connect All-knowing Jigme Lingpa with Kyabje Rinpoche, all of whom were truly eminent masters. The heart son of Jigme Lingpa was Jigme Gyalwe Nyugu, root guru of Patrul Rinpoche, who bestowed the Longchen Nyingthig lineage to the fourth Dzogchen Rinpoche Migyur Namkhar Dorje. He then passed it to Khenpo Orgyen Tenzin Norbu, who was the uncle and guru of the incomparable master Khenpo Zhenga, Shenpen Choki Nunwa. He, in turn, was root guru to great Khenpo Yonten Gonpo, who was the root master of Kyabje Rinpoche. This is the close lineage which brings tremendous realisation and blessings to all the teachings, empowerments and transmissions Kyabje Rinpoche imparts.

Kyabje Rinpoche has been invited to the great monastic seats of Dorje Drak, Mindroling, Palri, Jigme Lingpa's seat at Tsering Jong, Samye and Drigang, as well as over fifty of Dzogchen's branch monasteries to give teachings and empowerments. He has sent financial support, as well as Tulkus and Khenpos, to these and many other monasteries and universities all around Tibet. Kyabje Rinpoche was the first master to give the vows of ordination in Samye Monastery after the Chinese take-over, in the same temple where the first seven Tibetans became monks. He has also established extensive community aid programmes through his charitable organisation, the Kalsang Foundation. He has recognised over fifty Tulkus of the younger generation and is the root guru to tens of thousands of Tibetans, Chinese and Western students.

More recently, in Dzogchen Pema Tung, Kyabje Rinpoche has begun to give regular teachings to the lay community on the Preliminaries and Pure Realm practices. Traditionally, the lay community would support the monastery's activities and receive occasional empowerments and blessings, but this is the first time in Dzogchen that Dharma teachings have been given to the wider community. To enable the community to receive these teachings, as well as to accommodate large gatherings of monks and nuns, the temple in Pema Tung was extended in 2009. The result has been tremendously positive, with many lay people becoming active in studying and practising the Dharma for the first time.

Despite being very active in teaching, writing and travelling to many centres of Dharma, Kyabje Rinpoche spends most of his time in retreat, rising early every day to engage in full practice sessions of prostration, sadhana practise and meditation. Despite all the tremendous hardships and challenges he has faced throughout his life, Kyabje Rinpoche has always remained happy and content, with a vast and spacious outlook. He embodies activities of Buddha body, speech and mind. With his body he has rebuilt Dzogchen Monastery from the foundations up. With his speech he teaches the enlightened view of the Great Perfection, and with his mind he never ceases in his efforts to benefit all sentient beings.

Undoubtedly, Dzogchen Monastery, now full of life and Dharma, is almost entirely the result of the intense and prolonged effort of one single master, Kyabje Rinpoche. Without his efforts, Dzogchen would probably still be empty and lifeless. He is the vital force and embodiment of Dzogchen the monastery, Dzogchen the teaching and Dzogchen the realisation.

In Rinpoche's own words:

> "From 1980 to the present day, I have been busy with many activities of Dharma, reviving the continuum of previous teachings and practice, and further developing them. For the sake of one Dharma journey, I was involved in a car crash which resulted in the physical problems I continue to suffer from. However, with the joy and happiness that comes from reviving the life of the precious Dharma teachings and practice with my own warm blood, I make prayers of aspiration that all my journeys and activities may benefit the mind. For as long as I live, by uniting and training with the Dharma, I pray this may never cease."

ILLUSION OF LIFE AND DEATH

KYABJE DZOGCHEN PEMA KALSANG RINPOCHE

ONE

THE FIRST YESTERDAY AND THE LAST TOMORROW

To begin, I would like to consider where all of us living on this spherical planet came from, how we exist, and ultimately what we will become. But firstly, in order to do this, we must address the question of the nature of time. The moment in which we began to think about this topic has now passed, along with a few more moments of our lives, so let us take a look backwards and ask: Where have these moments disappeared to?

What we call 'time' is a vast ever-flowing river, a great demon that consumes everything. If I were to trace back this morning to yesterday, yesterday to the day before, and so on, I would eventually reach the day I first appeared in this world. The day before that I was not yet born, but there were certainly many other people who were. If we go back further along this stream of endless yesterdays, we will eventually come to the point when the first living creatures appeared. Before these single-celled creatures came into existence there was only physical matter. Physical matter, despite lacking consciousness, undergoes formation and disintegration in the same way as the living creatures of the world come into existence and die. If we trace even further back in time to before the earth existed, we are able to infer that there were other planets in existence at that time, but who can say how many of these planets there were? The most advanced telescope cannot see even a fraction of the universe, so currently it is impossible to determine exactly how the stars and galaxies came to be formed.

The enlightened Buddha taught that the cycles of the universe are endless and have no beginning. It is also taught in the Buddhist scriptures that in one single atom an unimaginable number of universes exist. These profound concepts are important to consider, no matter how limited our world view may be.

Again, if we trace time forwards from tomorrow, we inevitably find another tomorrow. Even if tomorrow is my time to die, it is most probable that there will be other humans still alive who will experience even more tomorrows. Through such a process of analysis we may reach the conclusion which the Buddha asserted, that the cyclic existence of samsara is endless.

Where did we come from? We all came from our parents. Where did they come from? They came from their parents. If we trace backwards in time in this way we will come to the moment when a creature produced the very first offspring. Where did this creature come from? It could have evolved from a similar species, it might have come from a different planet, or perhaps it came into existence miraculously. These are the only possible options.

If we suggest the creature came from another planet, we assume there are living creatures on other planets in the universe. We cannot see these planets and we do not know how many there may be. It may be stretching our imagination, but we cannot be certain that alien worlds and extraterrestrial creatures do not exist. Even if we trace time back in this way to an ancestor from another planet, we are still unable to determine the beginning of time.

If humans and other types of creature are the result of evolution, or even came into being through miraculous birth, all of them depend on the basis and interaction of the four main elements: earth, water, fire and wind. However, a living creature does not come to life from a mere arrangement of these elements. Regardless of the type of living creature or the place where they come into existence, each one is, to a greater or lesser degree, conscious. The continuum of consciousness is determined by propensities and their results, and this is known as karma.

Two thousand five hundred years ago the Buddha taught that multitudinous kinds of universes come into existence through the action of interdependent connection and karma. These two concepts, together with the unimaginable true nature of phenomena, which is beyond the normal comprehension of ordinary beings, must become the main focus of our attention if we are to understand the nature of our existence in this world.

There is a point, known in the scriptures of the Dzogchen Great Perfection as the 'ground where samsara and nirvana divide'. It marks the very moment when, through the creative power of interconnectedness, the four elements and karmic winds unite together, and a consciousness becomes associated with a physical body possessing the five sense faculties. It is through examining this crucial event that I believe the investigations of materialists, religious believers and impartial scientific researchers will find common ground.

There are three periods in the time cycle of a universe: formation, abiding and destruction. This cycle of change is the essential nature of every material object. In the Buddhist scriptures the period of time when a universe is formed is called the 'aeon of formation'. The time it abides is the 'aeon of remaining', and finally, when the universe disintegrates, it is known as the 'aeon of destruction'. This is one way in which we can understand the changes of our world system.

Alternatively, by examining ancient rocks and fossils, we can learn about the gradual formation of our universe over hundreds of thousands of years, and how it changes. However, ultimately it is certain that this world system will reach a point of disintegration. At that time it is not certain if other world systems will also disintegrate. This planet that we live on will be destroyed eventually, but other planets may not.

According to Buddhist understanding, consciousness exists separately from the four elements, and is able to change its physical basis. Should our planet be destroyed, we can infer that consciousness would be able to transfer to another planet or world system. For this and other reasons, researchers should at least develop clear understanding of what consciousness is in essence, from where it arises, and finally how it can change.

According to the Buddhist scriptures, there are six or eight different modes of consciousness, but none of these is understood to transcend the illusions which appear to the mind as reality. This means that in everyday life, the natural clear awareness of the mind is shaken up by karmic winds, which cause all kinds of discursive thoughts and feelings to arise. If we are continuously driven by these karmic winds, we experience unstable feelings of pleasure and suffering throughout rebirth after rebirth.

However, if we engage in particular practices and conditions are favourable, our experiences can change. The senses of the mind can become separated from the disturbing winds. This will cut their continuum and the mind will come to rest in its natural state. In Buddhism this is understood to be the special state called 'attainment of liberation' or 'enlightenment'. It is also known as 'separating from' or 'passing beyond suffering', Nirvana in Sanskrit. This is nothing more or less than entering a state of permanent and fully satisfying happiness.

If this is so, the question arises: when did consciousness first appear? Other than the aspect of consciousness which has been confused from time without beginning by the power of ignorance, there are no newly appearing consciousnesses. If new consciousnesses were to appear, we could discover the beginning of cyclic existence. This is not to be found, so in the same way, a beginning of consciousness is undiscoverable.

'Time' is the name given to the division between past and future. No one is able to say, "This is the start of time." For this reason, the esoteric Dzogchen Great Perfection scriptures epitomise the conclusion of all Buddhist analytical traditions: the true state is understood to be timeless, beyond the three times, and known as the 'fourth time of equality'.

Due to our ignorance, or the external influence of unknowing, we take on all kinds of physical forms continuously, and experience bouts of happiness and suffering. In this present life we have taken birth in this world to parents with whom we have karmic connections. If we continue to create more karmic propensities, we will have no choice but to follow their resulting influences, just as a dream unfolds uncontrollably while we sleep.

Billions of people who currently live in this world are ceaselessly busy every day and unable to relax at night. They keep themselves occupied with countless tasks right up until the moment they die. We have never met and we will never meet anyone who has managed to accomplish all the tasks they think they must complete in their lifetime. We are all born in different places, our fates are different, the level of comfort and status we enjoy varies, but we all spend our entire lives chasing after happiness and comfort. Ultimately we all end up the same. We have to leave everything behind and depart empty-handed. Both the vulnerable and exhausted beggar wandering around the outskirts of a town and the silken-robed king living in a wonderful palace full of jewels are equally powerless in front of the Lord of Death.

Modern people are becoming expert in engineering and science, and we witness daily advances in technological development. The force of competition ensures this will continue with even more impressive developments in the future. However, with the rapid proliferation of external material objects, disturbances to our internal state of mind also increase. Positive tendencies are not encouraged, and the result is imbalance. One person's pursuit of pleasure harms others. This kind of selfish motivation results in misery, both for us and others, and these ripples extend out into the wider world, influencing matters beyond our comprehension.

Analysing the limits of yesterday and tomorrow, we see that time does not stay still for one moment but passes away continuously. An entire aeon and a single moment are identical when they are over. We consider living for a hundred years to be a long life, but in another world system it may pass with just a click of the fingers. Our lives consist of sleeping, waking, eating and sleeping again. We may occupy ourselves with trivialities, like children at play; but after what seems like no time at all it is as if a switch is suddenly turned off. Between one beat and the next our heart stops and we are powerless to get up from what has become our deathbed.

Like last night's dream, the time of childhood and youth flashes by without us even noticing, in the same way as the sun passes over the western mountains. When we suddenly come up against the great door of death, we see that all the things we rushed around busily achieving are useless. It confirms that everything we do in life is like the dance of a madman. Therefore I consider it very important for us to examine our current situation carefully.

At present there are billions of people living on this planet. The previous generations also contained similar numbers of people. The total number of people who have set foot on this earth is beyond calculation. Like us they all ran around, frantically trying to achieve things in their lives. Ultimately they did not achieve anything permanent and at last even their names have vanished from memory. This is both comical and depressing. Among these trillions of people there were certainly many intelligent and far-sighted people, but none of them found a way to live forever. Only a few of them were truly unafraid of death, having realised and investigated the happiness and suffering that follows it. What is the reason so few people investigate and realise the nature of life and death?

It is a terrible shame that throughout all ages various false religions and cults have exploited countless people for political and financial gain. Through instilling ignorant philosophies, blind faith and fear, these false religions have ruined the lives and minds of many generations of people. However, to consider the importance of the future, in terms of rebirth for example, as some religious cults do, is much better than never addressing such concepts at all. In this way, a mistaken path can promote the urge to find an authentic one, and through gaining experience of opposing points of view, this situation has helped create a legacy of experience for future generations. If people of the past and present were as concerned with questions of death and what lies beyond as they are with concerns of this life, this would certainly result in benefitting everyone.

Some exceptional masters, by spending their entire lives in meditation on profound truths, have actually transmuted their physical bodies into light. However, it is my guess that if they had concentrated their attention and effort on the mundane pursuits of one lifetime, they would probably have achieved even greater scientific advances than the most pioneering modern scientist. But these Buddhist masters, using the opportunity given by what they considered to be the borrowed body of one lifetime, contemplated deeply and with great insight on how their suffering and the suffering of others could be overcome, once and for all. Understanding the implications of future rebirths, these masters sought a method to enable them to abandon the afflictions that are the cause of, and main factors involved in, all our problems. They sought the answer to the crucial question: how to put an end to suffering forever. These masters established a new path for achieving this goal which is a million times more useful for everyone than, for example, establishing a human colony on Mars.

To illustrate the importance of a far-sighted attitude with regards to our current situation, let us look at the Legend of the Supreme Steed:

Long ago, before his enlightenment, Buddha Sakyamuni was born as the son of a sea merchant. He was named Singala and was very handsome and strong. As a boy he was extremely intelligent and he studied all areas of learning and became very wise. When he grew up, after pleading with his father, he finally obtained permission to equip a ship and together with five hundred men, set sail to find wish-fulfilling jewels.

To navigate the great ocean they knew they would have to face grave danger and risk their lives many times, but they were determined. Singala thought, "If we don't encounter any obstacles, we'll be able to cross the great ocean and find what we desire, but if the boat sinks we'll be eaten by sea monsters. If we're driven off course by unfavourable winds we won't be able to return home and we'll all lose our lives." Singala captained the ship, with a crew of five hundred other merchants.

Having set sail, a powerful easterly wind drove the ship off course towards the shores of the southern Copper Island where, unknown to the sailors, lived flesh-eating demonesses. On the island were two fortune-telling banners; one indicated fortunate events, the other predicted disasters. As the merchant ship smashed against the island's rocky coast, the banner indicating fortunate events shook. This alerted the attention of the demonesses who knew immediately that a ship had been wrecked.

The demonesses transformed themselves into beautiful women, dressed up in fine clothes, adorned themselves with gorgeous jewellery, and ran down to the seashore. When they saw the merchants swimming towards the island, the demonesses called out to them. "Handsome men, come here!" they cried. "We have the best food and clothes, delightful accommodation and villas, pleasure grounds, forests, parks and bathing pools. We have wish-fulfilling jewels, gems, pearls, right-spiralling conch shells, and many more riches. Take these for yourselves, we have no men folk here, become our husbands and look after us." All this was promised to the merchants on one condition; they were forbidden to venture down the path which led to the south of the island.

The men, seduced by the demonesses, fell in love with them and fathered many children. A long time passed. The merchant leader Singala began to think over what had happened and wondered why the women were so protective about the southern path. He decided he must discover the secret. One night he gently left his wife sleeping in bed, strapped a sharp sword under his arm and set out to the south.

After walking for some time, he began to hear the cries of many men echoing out of the darkness. Listening carefully, he heard the lament: "We're forever separated from our families, our children, and loving friends... We'll never return to the wonderful human world in this lifetime..." Terrified by what he heard, Singala stopped in his tracks. At last, overcoming his fear, he made for the direction where the cries were coming from and swiftly reached a huge iron city surrounded by a high wall. Thinking there must be a few windows in the wall, he searched the perimeter but could not even find a hole big enough for a rat to enter. However, close to the northern edge was a very tall tree. Singala climbed the tree and was able to look down into the city.

Inside he saw a group of wretched men cowering in houses made of metal. Calling out to them, Singala asked, "How did you end up in here? Why are you weeping?" The men replied, "We were merchants from the human world. We were sailing across this ocean when sea monsters destroyed our ship. By clinging to spars and broken wood we survived and swam to this Copper Island. But when we arrived we were deceived by a group of demonesses. They transformed themselves into beautiful women and seduced us into becoming their lovers and fathering their children. Not long after this, more traders were shipwrecked and arrived on the island. When the demonesses discovered that new merchants had arrived, they revealed their true terrifying forms to us. They devoured most of us immediately, down to the last hair and nail. They even licked up the drops of blood which had fallen on the ground. The few of us they didn't eat were thrown into this metal fortress to be eaten later."

Singala asked the prisoners if there was any way to escape. They replied, "We have no way out. However we try, the metal walls double or treble in size so we can't escape. But there is a way out for you. Gods once passed over in the sky and called out to us, "Hey, childish traders from the human world! On the fifteenth day of this month at full moon, follow the northern path. There the king of horses known as Powerful Cloud lives on wild Salu rice. He is free of illness, and has great strength. When he extends his head and asks three times in a human voice, 'Who wants to travel safely and easily to the world across the ocean?' approach him and say, 'We want to travel across the ocean, take us safely to the human world.' Then he will carry you across the ocean."

Hearing this, Singala memorised the exact instructions of the gods and returned to his house, slipping into bed without waking the sleeping demon-woman. The next day he got up early and secretly assembled the other merchants in a secluded park. He told them exactly what he had seen and heard the previous night. Everyone agreed to go to the north on the fifteenth day, and Singala forbade the traders to speak of the plan or bring their children or wives.

On the full moon night the merchants followed the path to the north, found the king of horses and begged him to take them back to the human world. The king of horses spoke to them, saying, "Do not be even the slightest bit attached to your women, your children, or your houses or riches, and do not look back. If you are attached you will fall from my back like a ripe fruit from a tree and the demonesses will eat you alive. Those without attachment, simply hold onto my mane and you will escape easily." Saying this, the great horse stooped down and allowed them to mount.

Some of the merchants clambered onto his back, some onto his hind quarters, and they all held onto his mane. Using all his strength, the king of horses named Powerful Cloud soared up into the sky. Below on the island, the banner which predicted disaster suddenly shook violently and the demonesses immediately knew that the merchants were escaping. They quickly transformed their faces to seem beautiful, adorned themselves with the finest jewellery and, carrying their children, called out with heart-wrenching cries, "Handsome men! Have you no consciences? Stay as our lovers and protectors, this is your home, these are your children, and we are your wives!" Some of the merchants felt attachment towards their partners, children and possessions and so slipped from the mighty horse's back. As they fell to the ground and ran to their wives, the demonesses revealed their true repulsive form and devoured them completely, even licking the last drops of blood from the ground. Singala and the remaining merchants felt no attachment and returned safely back to the human world.

Like the merchants in the legend, if we are attached to our identity and our possessions we will never be free from cyclic existence. If we do not experience attachment we will become liberated forever. So we need to think like this: We are merely a wandering consciousness from some unknown place. This consciousness has conjoined with the sperm and ovum of our parents to produce a solid body of flesh and bone, but it is through this that we experience all the suffering of this life, without the slightest true happiness.

Everything desirable in cyclic existence is certainly deceptive, no different from the island of demonesses in the legend. At the end of life there is not one living creature that does not have to go screaming into the mouth of the demoness of impermanence. If just one person could manage to refrain from seizing onto essence-less deceptive phenomena and find a method to escape permanently from this place of suffering, cyclic existence, he or she would become a leader of many people, like the merchant chief Singala. Everyone would consider them wise, intelligent and more exalted than others.

We consider the length of our human lives to be very long. The time we spend running around attending to mundane concerns can be divided into past, present and future. However, we are unable to separate the present moment from the past and future. Because of this, the past and future cannot be determined either. Therefore everything that depends on the continuity of time, which does not exist inherently, is either grossly impermanent, obviously changing continuously, or subtly impermanent, but still changing moment by moment.

If this is the case, then, whether we consider the past or the future, even the nature of great mountains and the earth itself is changeable and unstable. Obviously our small and feeble human body is even more unstable. Made of fragile flesh, blood and bone it can be destroyed by just small changes in heat and cold. Compare photos of yourself when you were a child to those taken when you were grown up, or in middle age, and now perhaps, when you are old and decrepit. Looking back at past events that happened yesterday or the day before it is hard to believe the months and years are now gone forever.

The changing appearance of our face and body can be compared to a soap opera on television. It is almost as if the suffering of human life experienced by one person from childhood to old age is condensed into a single episode, just an hour or a half hour long. But this is our own real TV show, a living tragedy of human life. The way to end the script of this brief programme depends on you, the writer and director, and it is connected with the future path you take in life.

The path in front of us has many turns. From the crossroads of uncertain paths, which direction we choose should depend on our new eyes of wisdom, otherwise we will be confused by lack of awareness. If we do not even have a plan for tomorrow, we will be left to be jostled along by others. If we let this happen and the unseeing group we follow jumps into a great ocean, will we also follow then? Think about this.

We pass through the appearances of childhood, youth, adulthood and old age which are accompanied by the sufferings of birth, ageing, sickness and death. Eventually we will come to the end of our human life. However, we presently have enjoyments and happiness and we assume that we will live a long time, so we strive to increase our wealth and possessions, cope with adverse circumstances, and look after our loved ones. Jobs that need our attention keep on appearing, one after another, like the ripples of a stream. If these tasks do not cease appearing then we will never reach an eventual or definite goal. Therefore, if we do not have a guarantee that we are going to live forever, the way we live our lives is no different from that of the most ignorant animal. Having been rounded up for slaughter, a yak still munches grass unaware of the fact that its life is about to end.

In the time since the formation of the earth many billions of years ago, there has not lived one single being that has not died. In one hundred years time everyone on this earth will almost certainly be dead. If we had clairvoyance or foreknowledge of the exact day, month, year and cause of our death, we would have no appetite for food today. However, we are like stupid yaks in many ways. We know that one day we will die, but we do not know when or how, so we laze around carefree, cheating ourselves, as if we could sit around like this forever. Is this not incredibly dangerous?

Now, I am going to push the nib of my pen to record the memory of events in my own life:

Into the arms of my parents were born five treasured spirits, like five feathers blown together by the winds of karma. These were my elder and younger brother and sisters. During the period when we were together, our family situation was wealthy and harmonious. We lived in nomadic pastures like gardens, where wild deer, donkeys and other forest animals wandered peacefully. We ate fresh and nutritious food, wore clothes of soft white lamb fleeces, and spent our time playing and enjoying life. When I think about it now, this life was as wonderful as that of the gods. But this vision of a happy and pleasurable human life disappeared like mountaintop mist, a summer rainbow, or the dream of last night; just another example of impermanence.

My younger brother was a kind-hearted and intelligent young monk with a tanned face and rosy cheeks; everyone liked him. In August of 1959, when he was just thirteen years old, he was forced to flee his home and leave his playground behind. Surrounded by the bodies of the relatives who had brought him up, his father, uncles and aunts, and the gentle horse who was his constant companion, his maroon robes were torn to pieces. Among bombs that struck like lightning, just as a flower is destroyed by hailstones, a hail of bullets that knew no compassion stole his cherished life, and his warm blood fell onto cold ground.

My younger sister was also thirteen when we were separated forever. She had a light complexion with rosy cheeks, and teeth like rows of pearls. Like all girls of the nomadic meadows, she was always kind and happy, dressed in her soft lamb's wool clothes and hat. Sometimes she would go out with a thousand or more of our family's sheep to the high park-like meadows of the mountains. There she would enjoy picking flowers with petals which looked like red silk tassels, and playing with the little lambs. After her elder brother and entire family had gone together down the path of impermanence, she did not wander very long in the barren plain of suffering. In the darkness of night the howls of a wolf merged with the wailing northerly wind across the wilderness, and a lone girl, radiant in the prime of youth, suddenly fell.

My youngest sister, lovely, and complete with all the beauty of youth, was orphaned at six. After being left without friend or protector she suffered great misery and yearning, with no chance of enjoying any feelings of happiness and pleasure in this world. Not long after, the fragile spirit of this little one also travelled, once again, down a future path.

In summer, young lotus blooms in a flower garden are beautiful in every way and emanate natural fragrance. The smooth surfaces of fresh petals are more beautiful than any painted by an artist's brush. Some are beginning to blossom, some are fully developed, some buds are just forming. All of them have grown from the same root, their gorgeous petals and leaves attractive to everyone. But suddenly black storm clouds cover the sky. Lightning, thunder and hail stones crash down, and the delicate flowers are destroyed to the root.

My tear drops of terrible sadness rain on fierce flames of yearning. Feelings of unbearable pain well up in my heart. Urged by the force of sadness and yearning, I use my tears as ink to draw the following picture:

> Alas! Sun above! Can you see
> upon the ground your beams embrace
> vague reflections of my sisters and brother?
> Please send out warm rays of kind light
> to care for each of them.
>
> Full white conch moon!
> In your orbit have you seen
> three wandering, unsupported spirits?
> Please illuminate their lonely path
> with your brilliant light.
>
> Vast earth! May the fresh blood
> of my cherished, precious siblings
> dissolve into your soil and revive you.
> May the essence of their radiant flesh
> merge into your great expanse.

Keep them forever safe
in your loving kindness.

Sometimes I visit their mournful graves,
cold, encircled by wandering spirits.
But the high craggy cliffs,
piercing the thin air
and wrapped in hail and thunder,
are still vengeful.

Alas! Lord of Death!
Will you not grant
three innocent wandering spirits
freedom to go as they please?

Ah! Three Jewels of the sky!
Will you lead my siblings
with pure aspirations
to a pure divine land?

Small white easterly cloud!
Did you welcome my siblings
with a rain of flowers and rainbow light
scattered from within your heart?

Three beautiful spirits, my beloved siblings, listen! We had only a short opportunity to meet in this life but, with indestructible confidence and unyielding armour, may we find a way to protect other timid and frightened children like us. By generating true confidence and strength, may we come to protect all sentient beings, our mothers in countless lives, threatened by the three sufferings of the boundless ocean of samsara. This is my true heart-felt aspiration, may it also be yours!

It might be better if, when we die, there was nothing left to experience any pleasure or suffering; if we were to disappear naturally and completely, like an extinguished butter lamp, or a wolf's paw print in melted snow. However, there is no reliable logical argument or authoritative assurance that this will be the case. So, if we are not careful from this point on, there is a danger that we will make the mistake of incorrectly focussing our energy and effort forever.

Some people do not believe in the relationship of karmic cause and effect. They decide that there will be no future lives. Having come under the influence of ignorance, they think that just because they cannot perceive future lives, therefore they do not exist. This illogical view cannot be defended indefinitely. Some people, so long as they are alive and well, are happy to believe in the non-existence of future lives, but at the time of their death they suddenly become afraid and cry out, "Help me!" Others in their youth are lucky in their endeavours and proudly believe there is no one better than themselves in the whole world. Only when they encounter negative circumstances which force them to lower their heads, do they begin to consider karmic cause and effect. These short- sighted attitudes are foolish.

To wise up to our human predicament we should first gain an understanding of some essential points. For example, we should understand the basis of past and future lives, and karmic cause and effect. We need to understand where we came from, where we are going, and how long we will remain here. Once we have achieved this, and when we have settled our minds by assimilating these ideas, we should live a comfortable, happy life. But we should not sit around blindly accepting whatever happens to us and occupy ourselves with minor distractions. This is dangerous, just like the way a pig lives; a pig bends its head down to the ground searching for food with its tough snout. It never looks up at the sky. A pig sees the sky only once in its lifetime, and that is when the butcher, getting ready to stab a knife into its heart, turns the pig over onto its back. By that time it is too late.

To start with, we have become deluded, and therefore we wander in cyclic existence, the root of which is ignorance. In this life we constantly come under the influence of emotional afflictions and accumulate all kinds of negative karmic propensities. We live our brief lives in a state of tension and anxiety. Finally, we go helplessly down the path of impermanence and death. At this time we experience the undesirable results of the negative karmic propensities which we have accumulated, and once more we must wander endlessly in cyclic existence. This is such a shame! How chilling to the heart!

In fact, right now we have a rare opportunity to discover true happiness. We should not waste the time that we have in this life; we should make our lives meaningful. Having found a way to accomplish the goal of ultimate happiness, we should certainly do so without delay.

In Buddhist understanding, to gain a human body, complete with all the freedoms and advantages, is very rare. While we have this short human life, we should not end up dying empty-handed, having wasted all this freedom and opportunity. We can make our lives meaningful. We should find the unmistaken path which results in happiness and fulfilment, not just for now but also for our entire future. We should engage determinedly in the great practices that result in everlasting happiness and achieve our true potential without delay!

TWO

THE MYSTERIES OF LIFE

In the ancient Tibetan Buddhist tradition, life is understood to be the period during which a physical body is united with vital energy or life force. In the subtle life channel, the wind element and subtle essence combine into something akin to saliva. Within this are two elements: the basis for consciousness, which produces the warmth of life, and the subtle essence of breath, which resembles a single hair of a horse's tail. If this 'hair' cracks, twists or bends, this creates a predisposition for numerous adverse physical conditions. If there are no cracks, twists or breakdowns of integrity, and additionally it is long, then so too will life be long. When this combination of factors is active this is what we call 'life'.

The term 'life force' refers to consciousness residing in a body or, in other words, when the five aggregates of form, feeling, perception, formation and consciousness are combined. This is the continuum of life, or the continuum of a living being.

'Consciousness' is the collective name given to the perceptions of the five 'doors': eyes, ears, nose, tongue and skin. The traditional example for explaining this concept is by using the metaphor of a monkey in a room which has five windows. Perceptions (the windows) are facets of consciousness (the monkey), but these facets of consciousness do not perceive anything other than the delusions of the unenlightened mind. This example illustrates that the stream of consciousness is the dominant factor in the perceptions of the six senses: sight, hearing, smell, taste, touch and mental consciousness.

The state of being alive is defined as the combination of 1. the physical body, 2. the sense faculties and 3. awareness, which is a union of life, life force and consciousness.

A body from which the life force has departed is called a corpse. An unsupported consciousness without a body is called a 'sentient being in the intermediate state', between death and rebirth.

A body is the result of the fusion of the male sperm and female ovum, which go through a process of growth and division, and become a combination of 'the thirty-six unclean substances', in other words the numerous physical components detailed by modern biological science. In this way, the cells of the living embryo multiply and the form of this new life can be seen clearly on an ultra-sound scan. There is no need to discuss this in more detail.

However, the mysterious entity known as 'mind' or 'consciousness' seems to lie hidden within life and the life force. We cannot detect it anywhere, inside or outside the body, in either the upper, middle or lower regions. This formless, indescribable, elusively-existing entity we term consciousness has a nature of clarity and awareness.

The deep complexities of the mind veil the true nature of consciousness, which is untainted by discursive thoughts or mental reflection. It is the mode of being of 'uncontrived absolute nature'. Shimmering out from uncontrived absolute nature are our delusions of divine and hellish realms, our consciousness that experiences pleasure and suffering, and the karma of accumulated causes and effects. It is very important that we investigate rigorously all the secret depths of our minds.

We can postulate that our body and consciousness develop together, like a butter lamp and its flame, so that, when the body breaks down, the consciousness also vanishes, like a butter lamp which has run out of oil. However, if that were the case, as our body was formed from our parents' sperm and ovum, we must accept that our consciousness was formed in the same way. So, if we accept this premise, we are faced with a situation that requires our parents to have many consciousnesses, or consciousnesses capable of fragmentation, dividing into many parts. This kind of explanation suggests a result without a cause and is logically impossible, in the same way as it is impossible for a lotus flower to appear randomly in the sky.

From similar causes come similar results. Therefore, the cause of a formless consciousness must logically be the continuity of a similar consciousness, and this has to be the continuity of consciousness from a previous life. The problem with an argument which posits that no previous consciousnesses exist is that, when the bodies of sentient beings break down, the number of consciousnesses would therefore become less numerous, so when more beings come to take rebirth, because the previous consciousnesses no longer exist, sentient beings would become fewer and fewer, and eventually cease to exist.

If we actually knew the number of beings with consciousness we could calculate whether or not new consciousnesses are in fact appearing. However, because of our limited knowledge and awareness, we cannot make such a calculation. We do not know the number of universes and planets that exist, except for those in proximity to the earth, or the number of planets that constitute a galaxy. Not only that, but the number of universes which, it is taught, exist on a point the size of the tip of a hair, is incalculable and immeasurable. These things are not only beyond the limits of our deductive capabilities, but even beyond the limits of our comprehension. We simply have no way of knowing these things.

If we employ faulty logic, or accept mere postulation as truth when there is no proof, it is as if we look at the world upside-down and see everyone else as being upside-down. If we continue to do this, we will eventually believe that everyone else is actually the wrong way up.

So, we conclude that there is not one conditioned phenomenon that is independent of causes and conditions, and phenomena always arise in reliance on and connection with each other. The ultimate cause of this indicates the inconceivable nature of phenomena.

We are all born from our mother's womb. We all experience mundane phenomena, in the aspects of other living beings, and inanimate objects such as the ground, rocks, hills, valleys and our houses. It is important to investigate whether or not matter, comprised of the four elements, and multitudinous living creatures, based on the continuum of consciousness, both arise from causes and conditions.

Why does the external world arise solely from matter, but living beings come into being due to the action of consciousness? This is because consciousness possesses a quality that is self-perpetuating, so consciousness, by its nature, brings about future rebirths. When the body perishes, the continuum of consciousness does not. This continuum definitely exists, and when it is associated with a body, that body possesses life force, and is called a living creature. It is alive; it moves and has clear memory. If consciousness is separated from the breath or 'wind', which is traditionally likened to a horse, it dissolves into the inner sky, or may enter another body. The body left behind becomes inanimate matter, just like earth or stone. By the force of this argument, consciousness, or the basis on which karma is deposited, must exist separate from the body.

The body is like a pile of stones which is on the point of collapse, and consciousness is like a bird which has landed on it, and is about to fly away. When the requisite conditions are fulfilled, the pile of stones collapses and the bird flies away. However, if the conditions necessary for the pile to collapse are not fulfilled, but the bird encounters other determining conditions, it will still fly away. So, when a body perishes from old age or sickness, the consciousness goes on to find another body; but if the conditions causing the body to perish are not fulfilled, for example while the body is still young and healthy, traumatic occurrences, such as accidents, can also cause the consciousness to move on to another body.

Has consciousness a cause? The answer is yes. The previous moment of consciousness is the perpetuating cause from which the next moment of consciousness arises. The original cause of consciousness is co-emergent ignorance. Originally, from the ground of all, the wind of wisdom residing in the life force was agitated, and instantly sentient beings of the three realms became dependent on self-grasping discursive thoughts of 'I', or attachment to self, and 'my', attachment to things. Due to this cause, sentient beings wander continuously in cyclic existence in utter confusion. Under the influence of confusion, discursive thoughts of attachment and aversion cause gross afflictions to arise, karma is created, and consequently suffering is experienced.

What is known as 'karma' is that which appears as the various results of actions. The Buddha taught that multiple kinds of worlds arise due to karma. In this manner, myriad causes produce myriad results. Happiness is the result of accumulated virtuous karma. Because negative karma is accumulated, resultant suffering occurs. We can observe this clearly in our own lives.

There have been and will be many people all over the world who remember their previous lives. Some people are able to recount exact details, for example, "In my past life I was born with such and such a body. Now in this life, I'm like this." These testimonies can help us validate the existence of past and future lives. Contemplation on the existence of past and future lives clarifies our understanding of karma and its results: from previous lives come subsequent lives.

The Buddha taught eight analogies to explain how a previous life gives rise to a subsequent life. The first analogy is of a teacher reciting a text and a student learning it. Both the teacher and the student are in possession of all their faculties, and the teacher reads the text. The student listens to the text and memorises it. If these three factors are complete, then the process of transmission will occur. The teacher symbolises the current life. The student symbolises the next life. The text represents the consciousness bridging the gap between lives.

The second analogy is of one butter lamp being lit from the flame of another. The butter lamp is composed of butter, a wick and a container. The first lamp represents this life. The second lamp represents the next life. The fire of the first lamp lights the wick of the next. This analogy demonstrates the non-transference of permanent things, in that the lamp does not perpetuate itself; only the flame can be transferred. The analogy also shows that things cannot come into being without a cause, because the fire of the second lamp was lit from the fire of the first.

The third analogy is of a reflection appearing in a mirror. When something is in front of a mirror and there is light, a reflection appears. This analogy demonstrates that, although objects themselves cannot be transferred, that which we have in this life, indicated by what is in front of the mirror, also appears in our next life as a kind of reflection.

The fourth analogy is of a mould for making tsa tsa (small clay images). This analogy indicates that the nature of the activities we engage in in this life dictates the form of our future rebirth, as a mould shapes its contents.

The fifth analogy is of a magnifying glass concentrating the sun's rays in order to start a fire. A fire starts when the magnifying glass, sunlight, dry grass and twigs, are all assembled. This analogy demonstrates how different kinds of lives, in this example the objects for starting a fire, give rise to different rebirths, the fire, which differs in nature from the objects that started it.

The sixth analogy is of a seed from which a shoot grows. A shoot grows from the coming together of a seed, earth, moisture, and so on. This indicates that when the continuity of something stops, in this case the seed, it does not disappear but changes, for example into a shoot.

The seventh analogy is how the mere mention of something sour makes us salivate. If we have had experience of drinking something sour, when we hear the word 'sour' spoken, our glands produce saliva. This is an analogy of how our experiences give rise to rebirths.

The eighth analogy is of an echo from a cliff. When a sound is made and there is a cliff face close by, unless other loud noises distract us, we hear an echo. This shows how rebirth occurs from an appropriate combination of factors.

These analogies indicate how rebirth occurs if the causes and conditions are present, and there are no other disrupting conditions. These analogies also demonstrate how present and future lives are neither the same as, nor different from, each other. The limitations of the earlier analogies are clarified in the latter examples.

These eight analogies not only illustrate the way in which lives follow on, one from another, but also demonstrate the mechanism of conditioned existence; how beings continuously circle round the twelve links of interdependent connection: ignorance, compositional factors, and consciousness, through to birth, ageing and death.

In this present life, which results from the propelling force of karma, we can see people in all states of wealth and poverty, happiness and misery. In the same way, the kind of future we can expect is also dictated by karma. Generosity will bring us wealth and valuable possessions, but if we steal or are miserly now it will cause us to suffer poverty. If we maintain a high standard of moral conduct, we will have a good physical body, but abandoning moral conduct results in an unattractive, unhealthy body.

Therefore, although we are human beings in this life, in the future there is no certainty that we will again be born human. The same applies if we are poor now, in our next life we may be rich. This is why we all know of people who indulge in many negative activities, such as dishonesty and fighting, but who seem to be happy and comfortable. And yet there are others, no matter how many righteous and meritorious deeds they accumulate, whose lives only become more and more difficult.

We may think, how can this happen? The ramifications of karmic actions and results are beyond our comprehension; but we do know the force of karmic actions can never be lost. We may experience the results of our past actions in this life or the next, or we may not experience these results for several lives to come, but we can be sure that the results will catch up with us sooner or later. In addition, there are various kinds of karma: propelling karma and completing karma, as well as many divisions of karmic result: the fully ripened result, the dominant result, the conditioning result, and so on.

Those who behave in a negative way can be seen to be happy because they are experiencing the result of previous positive karma. Later, they will inevitably experience the result of their negative karma. Those who engage solely in virtuous behaviour in this life but still experience suffering, are purifying the remains of previously accumulated negative karma, and the results of their positive actions will certainly ripen in the future.

For example, when a bird flies high into the sky, we cannot see its shadow, but at some point when it comes down to land, its black shadow is visibly connected to its body. The karma we have accumulated cannot ripen for anything inanimate, for example earth or stone; it must ripen through our physical body, which possesses a consciousness.

The continuum of one consciousness experiences the pleasure and suffering of many bodies. We can see that the bodies of different lifetimes have no connection, they are always separate. In the same way, the gross consciousness of different lifetimes also differs, for example the consciousness of a dog and a human. The consciousness of a dog or a human is steered by the ordinary awareness of their individual body, and therefore their behaviour is different.

For this reason, we can see that the living being which accumulates karma and the living being which experiences the results are separate. Not just dogs and humans, but the thoughts, actions and perceptions of the six kinds of sentient beings are separate. The reason for this is that virtuous and non-virtuous karma infuses a tendency or pattern of behaviour into the consciousness, and that tendency continues on within the consciousness through rebirth. The power of positive or negative karma causes all the various kinds of bodies of beings in the higher and lower realms to come into existence. When rebirth occurs, the character of the consciousness also changes. For example, when the body of a rat is taken up, its instinct is to steal, and when the body of a cat is taken up its instinct is to kill.

In addition to this kind of association, the tendencies which we develop in our past lives continue on into our future lives. Consider a woman with six sons, each one with the same parents, but each one having taken rebirth from one of the six realms of existence. All six sons would experience perceptions in accordance with being human, but in addition they would also display karmic tendencies from their previous lives. The son whose previous life was as a god in the god realm would be handsome and gentle. The son reborn from the demigod realm would be jealous and vicious. The one previously in the human realm would be intelligent and feeble. The son reborn from the animal realm would be stupid and hardy. The one from the hungry ghost realm would be of bad colour and full of longing, and the son transferred from the hell realm would appear repulsive and suffer constantly.

Humans share the same perception and connections of flesh and blood, but our history, modes of thinking, behaviour and characters are obviously very different. Perception arises from the power of causal resemblance, and has as its basis the continuum of consciousness between earlier and subsequent lives. However, through the influence of karma, our characters change.

The Buddha taught that beings reborn as forest animals like eating grass, and rebirth as a wild animal brings the desire to eat meat. In the case of a being in the intermediate state, during the first half of this period its body and perceptions are similar to those of its previous life. During the latter half this changes, anticipating the body and perception patterns of its future rebirth.

The actual details of the effects of propelling karma, completing karma, and so on, are incredibly complex. Only with the all-knowing wisdom of enlightenment can we understand all the varying divisions of causes, and the way in which cause and effect operates in its entirety; so until we become a perfect Buddha, we are only able to speak generally on this subject.

Does the continuity of a consciousness which accumulates all kinds of karma, and experiences various results, one day cease and die? Because the consciousness does not have a form its continuity cannot be broken; however it does transform. Ultimately, consciousness will attain the level of buddhahood and then its continuity transforms. In other words, that part of consciousness which was confused ceases to be. In other terms, it is taught that the consciousness becomes free from obscurations.

Speaking from the perspective of the aspect of consciousness that is perfect in enlightened wisdom, separate from negative emotions and mature in enlightened qualities, it can be said that in general there is no beginning or end to cyclic existence; but for an individual sentient being there is an end to confusion. The reason for this is that in the mind stream of the lowest tiny insect all the way up to the utmost perfect Buddha, there is the same seed of Buddha nature.

This essence of Buddha nature pervades a being as oil pervades a sesame seed. The more we analyse and investigate this true nature, we will eventually come to understand what the Buddha taught: Buddha nature is an empty, unelaborated and inconceivable way of abiding. There is nothing to add to this. If we trust these truly spoken immutable words we will definitely not be deceived. Through investigation and analysis we will achieve certainty. By meditating on the inconceivable nature of phenomena, the unelaborated inner sun of wisdom will rise from our hearts and we will be able to enter the deathless unchanging holy kingdom of enlightenment in this lifetime.

In the sutras, the Buddha Sakyamuni taught karmic cause and effect:

> Whatever kind of action one does,
> in accordance, the fully ripened result will come about.
> After ten million aeons it will not change at all.

And again:

> If one engages in virtue, one will achieve happiness.
> From non-virtuous actions comes suffering.
> In this way, the karmic results of virtue and non-virtue are
> clearly demonstrated.

The following is a list of the ten virtues. See them as a chariot which will take us to a happy state of existence:

* If we *stop killing* the result will be a long life free from illness.
* If we *do not take things* that are not given to us we will have great wealth.
* If we *refrain from sexual misconduct* we will meet a beautiful partner who will not turn against us.
* *Stop lying* and we will be praised and achieve fame.
* *Refrain from speaking contentiously* and we will be liked by everyone and our associates will be amiable.
* If we *avoid using harsh words* we will always hear pleasant speech and thus be happy.

* If we *do not gossip* we will achieve a position in which we are respected and people believe what we say.
* *Stop being covetous* and we will attain everything we want.
* If we *stop thinking malicious thoughts* we will appear attractive and help others feel calm.
* *Abandon the wrong view* of life and in all our future lives we will maintain the correct view.

Alternatively, if we engage in non-virtuous activities then, depending on the strength of negative motivation behind our actions, this will inevitably cause us to be reborn in one of the lower states of existence: the hell realm, the hungry ghost realm, or the animal realm. In addition to these karmic results, there is what is known as the 'result of experience' which resembles the cause. For example:

* Killing causes a short life.
* Stealing brings poverty.
* Sexual misconduct creates numerous enemies.
* Lying encourages others to disparage us.
* Contentious talk causes separation from good friends and turns everyone into enemies.
* Speaking harsh words means we will always hear unpleasant words.
* Gossip makes our speech disrespectful.
* Covetousness causes our hopes to be left unfulfilled.
* Malicious thoughts make us continually nervous and afraid.
* Wrong views cause stupidity and confusion.

Another function of karma is called 'action resembling its cause'. This refers to a habituation of actions in rebirth. For example, if someone incurred a karmic predisposition by frequent acts of slaughter in a previous life, they would enjoy killing in their next life.

The dominant result of karmic actions also ripens in our environment, and the results can come about in this and future lives:

* Killing lessens the efficacy of medicine.
* Stealing prevents our wealth from increasing.
* Sexual misconduct causes our environment to be unclean.
* Lying causes our environment to be smelly.
* Contentious talk results in a region with many precipices and ravines.

* Harsh words cause thorny deserts.
* Gossip causes the seasons to be very changeable.
* Covetousness causes our efforts to yield little or no result.
* Malicious thoughts cause our food to taste bad and have low nutritional value.
* Wrong views cause our crops to fail.

Committing non-virtuous actions is like consuming a deadly poison which will ruin and destroy us. Knowing this, if we desire happiness we should abandon negative actions, engage in the ten meritorious virtues, and gradually practise the liberating root virtues. If we engage step by step in the paths of beings of lower, middling and higher capacities we can pursue the path of liberation. This brings the permanent happiness of the peace of enlightenment, as is told in the legend of Latshamma:

In a region of ancient India, there once lived a king named Rabsal who had a brother known as Topkyi Grogpo. Topkyi Grogpo's daughter was called Latshamma, a girl both wise and truthful. In a neighbouring kingdom, one of the king's ministers named Ridags had seven sons; Latshamma was given to Ridags's youngest son as his wife, and she became head of the family.

One day, a bird from an island in the ocean flew overhead carrying an ear of rice and dropped it on the palace roof. The King Rabsal ordered his ministers to plant the rice grains to produce medicine. Obeying this order, a few ministers planted some of the rice, but it did not grow at all. However, Latshamma planted a few grains and there was an abundant crop. King Rabsal's wife was cured of her sickness by medicine made from Latshamma's rice.

At another time, the ruler of another kingdom challenged the King Rabsal to attempt certain trials in order to test his wisdom and authority. First, this rival sent the king a pair of horses, a mare and her foal, who looked exactly the same. The king's test was to identify correctly which was the mare and which the foal. No one could tell the difference, but Latshamma separated the mare from her foal, and gave a handful of grass to one but not the other. Rather than eat the grass herself, the mare went to give it to her foal, and so Latshamma knew at once which animal was which.

Next, the rival ruler sent two identical snakes. The task was to decide which snake was male and which one female. Latshamma knew that if she placed both snakes on a smooth cloth, the male would thrash about uncomfortably but the female would remain still. As a final test, two logs were sent, identical in length and thickness, but one cut from the top and one from the bottom of a sapling. The task was to tell which log was cut from the top and which from the bottom. Latshamma put the logs in water, knowing that the one cut from the bottom would sink and the one cut from the top would float. Because all the challenges were successfully completed, King Rabsal and his rival became reconciled and, pleased with Latshamma's ingenuity, she was rewarded generously.

After some time, Latshamma became pregnant and nine months later gave birth to thirty-two eggs. When the eggs hatched, each one contained a beautiful boy. The boys grew up, each with the strength of a thousand men. At that time, the Buddha went to Latshamma's home to teach the Dharma. Everyone present achieved the fruition of stream-entry, except the youngest boy who rode away on an elephant.

Crossing a bridge over a great river, the youngest boy met the son of another minister riding in a chariot and neither of them would give way. The boy born from an egg became angry and threw the minister's son, together with his chariot, into the water. Upset and depressed, the minister's son went crying to his father and told him what had happened. The minister became angry and thought up an evil plan. He went to the place where the thirty-two boys were living and gave them a toy staff covered with jewels, but inside the staff he had hidden a sharp double-edged sword.

Latshamma's thirty-two sons enjoyed playing with the staff and took it with them wherever they went. The following day, the thirty-two boys happened to choose King Rabsal's garden as their playground. The minister whose son had been thrown into the river approached the king and muttered in his ear, "Latshamma's children are plotting to kill you. If you don't believe me, look inside their staff." When the king found the sharp sword hidden in the staff, he became furiously angry, and cut off all the boys' heads. He put the heads into a wooden box and sent it to Latshamma.

That day Latshamma had invited the Buddha and his retinue to her home. When the box arrived she thought King Rabsal had sent some offerings for the Buddha. As she went to open the box, the Buddha said, "Don't open that yet, first serve the food." When they had eaten, the Buddha gave teachings and Latshamma attained the result of a non-returner. After the teachings, she promised to supply some sick monks who accompanied the Buddha with all the provisions they needed, and also to give whatever was necessary to those who were caring for them and the other monks. Latshamma also gave provisions to a party of monks who were preparing to set off on a journey. In response to this the Buddha said, "Excellent! The merit of your four offerings is great, as great as making offerings to a Buddha."

When the Buddha had left, Latshamma opened the box and found the heads of her sons. However, as she had been liberated from attachment, Latshamma was not disturbed; but those around her became angry, mustered an army and set out to kill King Rabsal. The king managed to escape and sought refuge in the Buddha's camp in Jetavana Grove. When the army surrounded the camp, Ananda, the Buddha's attendant, asked the Buddha about the karmic cause of the situation. The Buddha gave the following teaching:

"A long time ago thirty-two people decided to steal a cow. In the vicinity lived a poor old lady with no children, nephews or nieces. Having stolen the cow, the thirty-two thieves took it to the old lady's house. They killed the cow and divided up the flesh and blood between themselves and the old lady, who was pleased. However, aware of its imminent death, the cow had taken an oath, vowing, 'Because you intend to kill me now, in a future time, even if I attain realisation, may I keep this oath and kill all of you!'

The cow was eventually reborn as King Rabsal. The thirty-two thieves became Latshamma's thirty-two sons, and the old lady is now Latshamma herself. The fully ripened karmic result of this negative action has been for the thieves to be killed five hundred times over five hundred lifetimes. As the old lady, Latshamma was pleased about killing the cow. Because of that she has suffered from being the mother of the thirty-two thieves and experiencing their deaths over and over again."

The Buddha also taught on the cause of the positive karma which allowed Latshamma and her sons to be reborn into a noble family, enjoy power and great riches, and actually meet the Buddha:

"When the previous Buddha Kasyapa was in this world, a faithful old lady bought some incense and butter lamps and offered them to a stupa beside the road. Thirty-two people came along and helped her. Together they made a prayer of aspiration; they prayed that as a result of the merit they had created, wherever they were subsequently reborn, they would never be separated, but always be mother and sons. They also prayed that they would always be reborn in the highest caste with strong, healthy bodies and plenty of wealth and possessions, and that they would meet with the Buddha and receive teachings of the holy Dharma."

Upon hearing the Buddha's teaching, Latshamma's supporters and their army understood that the current situation was the result of previous karma, so they calmed their anger and harboured no ill feelings towards King Rabsal.

From this legend we learn that if we kill and rejoice in killing, or any other negative action, the unpleasant fully ripened result is unavoidable. The same applies to positive actions, especially if they are done in relation to a holy object. Also, we see that aspiration prayers made at the moment of death are very powerful, and that the law of karmic cause and effect is never-failing.

THREE

IMPERMANENCE OF HUMAN LIFE

At some stage our universe came into existence; at the present time it remains in existence, but eventually it will disintegrate, leaving empty space, just as it was before it formed. In the same way as the external world is subject to disintegration, so too the bodies of its inhabitants are destructible. In the case of mind, first, from the natural state of mind which is sky-like, ignorance and the wind of all-consuming concepts form the basis of conceptual mind. This mind remains for a period, and finally will come to destruction. This happens because all conceptual things are compounded and must therefore separate, in the same way as all things born must die and all things formed must disintegrate.

When the time comes for us to die, the four external elements dissolve into the four internal elements. The internal elements then dissolve into luminosity, and there is a moment when this experience becomes equal to the sky.

Through the workings of karma all kinds of universes come into existence; in the same way, once we postulate the existence of a previous life, the existence of a future life is naturally established. In this way we come to understand that at death we will discard our current body, like a suit of clothes just borrowed for an instant. If we take time to think about where we may take rebirth, it is a frightening and formidable prospect.

If we could gather up the bones of all the various bodies of countless higher and lower rebirths which we have taken in the past, the pile would certainly be as high as the highest mountain. Or, if we collected all the tears we have cried in all our lifetimes, the pool would certainly form an enormous ocean. This being the case, the number of times sentient beings have been each other's parents, children, friends and enemies is beyond reckoning. Based on these truths, we recognise sentient beings are totally unaware of their plight, and under the complete control of karma. We are continuously led along by our karma, experiencing nothing but suffering, like a bee trapped in a jar flying round and round, unable to escape. We mistake the suffering of samsara for happiness. What could be more miserable than this?

I am sure some of you reading this are young, healthy, attractive and well off, so you may be thinking, "The world is so enjoyable! How come he's saying it's suffering? That's crazy - he doesn't know what he's talking about!" My reply to you is, "Have a think about it!"

How did you first arrive in this world? Before birth you struggled to survive and grow, cramped in your mother's dark womb. Then, turned upside down by karmic winds, you suffered the pangs of being born. As you arrived into this world, you endured harsh sensations as if you had fallen into a pit of thorns. Next, you were totally unable to take care of yourself; inability to control your body, heat and cold, movement, bladder and bowels and so on, all caused great problems. You could not even communicate with others. You have no recollection of these and other sufferings which you experienced during the first one or two years of this life, in just the same way as you are unable to remember the events of your previous life.

If we really think about our predicament from birth until we learned to speak and move, we can see that childhood too was full of suffering, being completely dependent on others. Similarly, the time we studied at school was full of suffering when we could not understand what we were taught. Playing with our peers, we suffered from rivalry; fights, bullying, anger and hurt feelings all caused us suffering. Now we are adults. If we are wealthy, we torment ourselves with worry over losing our wealth. If we are poor we are constantly anxious that we will not be able to afford enough food or clothing. Not only do we continually suffer from heat and cold, hunger and over-eating, but we suffer when we do not get what we want, and when undesirable things are forced upon us. Each hour of every day our human life is never without suffering.

We do not realise that our meagre, tainted enjoyments are suffused by the suffering of change and the pervasive condition of suffering, and we mistake them for happiness. If someone has never tasted sweetness, they do not know what sweetness actually tastes like. We are just the same. We have never experienced true happiness free from suffering, so we take suffering to be happiness. Because our perception is tainted, the pleasure we gain from our attachments and desires is just the same as the pleasure a maggot gets from wallowing in excrement.

From the time when we were children, and even now if you happen to be in the prime of youth, we will not stay like this; time continues to pass day by day, stealing away all the qualities of youth we may still be holding onto. Before very long, your face will be full of wrinkles, your hair will be as white as a bunch of withered grass, and your limbs will become stiff and dry like wood. This decrepit appearance is sure to bring you great grief. Loving friends who once enjoyed your company will gradually grow distant. Moreover, all your faculties will degenerate. Your sight will become hazy, your hearing will become less acute. Your once beautiful, even, closely-spaced teeth will loosen and fall out, and the taste of delicious food will become lost on you. With this physical decline your mind will also degenerate and become childlike. Approaching senility will bring despair. Everyone will call you 'old biddy' or 'old fogy', and you will be excluded from the lines of the living.

However, while we remain in samsaric suffering, we should consider it fortunate to live a long life. In Tibet, instead of saying 'goodbye' people wish each other 'long life', saying "May you live to be one hundred!" However, until we have attained the deathless immutable body of enlightenment, it seems improbable that we will always remain full of youthful vigour.

In the shadow of old age and sickness is our great enemy death, gnawing away right now, mouthful by mouthful, at our human lives. In view of this, dare we laze around nonchalantly? Knowing that the confusion of cyclic existence is an illusion, we should begin early and practise the holy Dharma to liberate our mind from this confusion. For those who do so, the sufferings of old age, illness, death, or whatever happiness or misery we encounter, all become like friends on the path to liberation, and appear as instructions to enhance our practice.

As Milarepa said:

> No one asking if I'm sick,
> no one weeping when I die.
> To die alone in this charnel ground
> completes the wishes of the yogi.

And also:

> What is known as death
> is a small enlightenment for a yogi.

When we reach this stage of realisation, bliss arises naturally from our hearts; so all external happiness and suffering which arises serves only as a support for this. So continues my rambling discourse...

Now, to illustrate further: on this sphere, our earth, the species we call 'homo sapiens' is the most advanced species of all living creatures and, because of our superior intellects, we are able to control powerful, savage, carnivorous creatures like tigers, lions and so on. We have no wings, but the achievements of scientists and engineers have enabled us to fly in the sky, and even into space. We have become masters of our world in these and many other ways, but still a means to avoid death eludes us. We do not possess any methods of reversing the dying process, any means to avoid rebirth in the lower realms of existence, or even a way to ensure future rebirths without suffering. We have not found one solution to escape any of these threats forever.

Having said that, there are a few people who really do know how to accomplish such things, but those of us who actually turn our minds towards these concerns are very rare. How foolish that there are so few of us! As we already discussed, nothing could be better than having the certainty that there is definitely no such thing as future rebirths. However, there are no real logical arguments or reasons which disprove the existence of future rebirths, other than their seeming imperceptibility. Therefore, because of a lack of viable alternatives, it is suitable that we place greater confidence in the truth of the Buddha's teachings.

At the moment, we find it unbearable if our precious, cherished body is damaged in even the slightest way, so there is no need to mention how we will feel when our body is disposed of after death. However, we are all wearing the noose of the Lord of Death, and the year, month, day and minute of our death has already been decided. Do we dare just sit around? From the moment we were born the time of our death has been coming ever closer. Even if someone has the strength to live for a hundred years, from the first evening of their birth the years and months of their life become one night shorter. Our life becomes shorter with every day that passes.

According to Tibetan theory, we take twenty-one thousand, six hundred breaths every day. Each breath we take, or every second we live, we come closer to death; the time ticks by ceaselessly, like a waterfall cascading down a steep mountain side. As the setting sun gradually disappears, so we approach our death. Our life is like the setting sun approaching the western mountains, while the shadow of the Lord of Death creeps ever closer. How chilling!

Let's say you are at present thirty years old and you have a life expectancy of eighty years; you would still have fifty years left to live, which seems quite a long time. About one third of these fifty years will be spent sleeping, which, except for some subtle differences, is just like a small death into which we drift unconsciously. Of the remaining thirty or so years, half you will spend busily working to supply your need for food and clothing, and it is hard to say exactly where the time goes. Now fifteen years are left. Five days of each week you are busy at work, and the remaining two days are usually full of distractions, so it is very difficult to actually find any free time at all. So we see, however long our human life may seem, it is still very short.

We cherish what we call our body; we give it tasty food to eat and adorn it with good clothes and beautiful accessories. We conduct rituals to keep it clean and hygienic and are careful with what we let it do. We strive in hundreds of ways to protect ourselves and preserve our lives. Some people even kill without a second thought in order to nourish themselves. We dislike it when others criticise us even mildly, or give us a brief unpleasant glance, but some people in positions of power imprison and beat those who are innocent and helpless, even though they cannot bear to be pricked by a thorn themselves. They do not know how to feel compassion for others. When the Lord of Death suddenly arrives for these selfish people, all their power and status, possessions and wealth, bravery and vigour, will be no match for death. As they are lying down in their last bed, they experience visions of their next life and tears well from their eyes. When it is their time to depart, suddenly these people are very pitiful.

If we had a definite fixed lifespan we could feel a little better, but we have no certainty as to the length of our lives. We could die tomorrow, or the day after tomorrow. We do not know if we may die now or later this evening. Not only that, but we do not even know the conditions which will cause our deaths. What on earth can we do?

We might think: "I will be able to bear it when I die. People much more important than me have all gone down the path of death; it is nothing to be surprised about. However, even more dear to me than my own body are my children, my life partner and my friends. They are bound to feel more grief and anxiety at my death than if they actually died themselves. How will I be able to bear that?"

"And what if I were to die first? Later, when my loved ones traverse the dangerous defiles of the Bardo, there will be no one able to protect them from fear. I will be powerless to provide company in their despair, a bright lamp in the darkness, or show them the path to liberation. If a child is killed in front of its mother, she experiences the most terrible suffering. My inability to provide protection to my loved ones is equally agonising."

If the elements which constitute our body become even slightly out of balance, our physical condition deteriorates; if we become terminally ill, our body becomes our own worst enemy. Suffering terrible aches and pains before death, it is as if we actually experience the hell realms before dying.

We consume delicious sweet foods and drinks in order to nourish our body, but these can easily harm us, causing health problems and eventually resulting in death. Additionally, there are many potential hazards: disasters, accidents, conflicts and so on, and relatively few conditions that promote life. Some beings die in the womb without seeing this world. Some die as babies, without having time to enjoy the pleasures of this world. Some die in their prime, suddenly separated from their life companion. Some die when they are old and decrepit, without friends, having endured all the suffering of old age.

In short, manifestations of impermanence known as the 'coarse continuous impermanence' and the 'subtle momentary impermanence' of time, are like great destructive enemies, gobbling up the three realms of existence. No one escapes their power.

The fragile continuum of our feeble life force depends on the small movement of air in and out of our lungs. Suddenly, without finishing our meal, our work, or fully enjoying anything we have, we leave behind our relatives and loved ones, like a hair pulled from butter, and depart alone and powerless. How very pitiful!

After the body we cherished so much becomes a corpse, its living radiance ceases and people are scared to look at it. Our relatives, friends and children that we cherished and protected all our life leave us, and our body gets crammed into a black hole, or is burnt in blazing fire and becomes a mere fistful of ash. Whichever way our body is disposed of, from that day on we become excluded from the company of the living and ranked with the dead. At this time it is doubtful if the smoke of burnt offerings or the flowers laid on our gravestone will benefit us as we venture unprotected and without refuge into the intermediate state of the Bardo.

Among the people living on this planet, those who accept the existence of past and future lives are in the minority. A large percentage believe there are no future lives, and some are uncertain as to whether past and future lives exist or not. This latter group can be divided into four kinds of people: 1. Those who have never investigated the subject. 2. Those who are naively narrow minded. 3. Those who dare not think about death. 4. Those who do not wish to talk about it.

There are two kinds of people who accept the existence of future lives. The first group believe in future lives not because others do, but because they have conducted their own analysis and investigation. They determine through authentic instruction and logic that future lives do exist, and they make up their own minds. The second group think that because such and such a holy person has taught this and that, or perhaps because the existence of future lives has been accepted in a particular place since ancient times, it must be true; so they automatically and blindly accept that future lives exist without a hair's-breadth of doubt.

It is difficult for those who think there are no future lives to find persuasive research or firm logical support for their argument. There are several major religions in the world, plus many other smaller sects, and there are many additional systems of belief. Each claims scriptural authority and apparently valid theories to support their dogma. If one of them is actually correct, then it follows the others are necessarily false. Over the centuries widely differing individuals have propagated religious theory, some for their own selfish ends, some striving to benefit humanity, and still others with differing motivation. We may feel baffled by all these conflicting religious theories, and for these reasons some people come to the conclusion that all religions are false.

Those who argue there is no cause and effect can also be divided into two kinds. The first group consists of those who follow the traditional doctrines of certain philosophical schools which assert that anything which is not an object of the five senses does not exist. The second group are those who follow the ideas of persuasive individuals who promote, in accordance with a personal agenda, a belief in the non-existence of virtue or sin, or cause and effect. However, if the majority of people were to believe in cause and effect, the position of this second group would become less tenable.

Uncertain about the existence of past and future lives, many people are willing to consider the idea, but ultimately remain undecided. Others, who are of more limited intelligence, do not even consider such a proposition as future rebirth after death. They are even afraid to talk about death, and do not dare to think about death at all. To use an analogy, it is as if, travelling along, we encounter an unavoidable abyss on the path in front of us. People afraid to contemplate death cannot bring themselves to think about what the terrible experience of falling down the abyss might be like. Not only that but, knowing that there is an abyss ahead, knowing there is no alternative path and no other option but to continue travelling on, these people close their eyes and try to pretend there is no abyss looming ahead!

Whenever they experience mental suffering, some foolish people drink alcohol or take drugs to numb their body and mind in order to relieve the pain for a little while. This immature kind of person acts under the influence of ignorance and cheats only themselves. They too are included in this second category of people.

At this time, there seems to be wide division between schools of thought which conform to modern scientific theory, and those which avoid such conformity. In my opinion, it would be useful to conduct some research into the terminology employed by each school of thought, in order to clarify the precise meaning of various terms. People's mental outlook, their individual viewpoints and ideologies are always at odds because of differences in understanding or explanation of terms and textual references. In my opinion, whichever frame of reference is used, whether of materialism or idealism and so on, it should stand up to scrutiny by scientific method.

It seems to me, whichever object or knowable phenomenon is examined, an authentic, unmistaken, undeceiving, correctly-concluded understanding of its nature determined from all sides is actually ultimately reached by investigating and realising the ultimate or so-called true nature of all phenomena, the true actual way of abiding. I think this search for the true nature of all phenomena is the real purpose of pure science research, and putting this kind of research into practice can therefore be considered to be in firm accordance with true scientific principles.

Basically, pure science purports to discover unmistaken truths; however it is very hard to find an expert scientist who has actually reached the supreme goal of comprehending ultimate truth. Today's scientists have identified particles which cannot be seen by the naked eye, and have developed methods to manipulate their forces. It is more than probable many things scientists cannot see or have not discovered today will be detected and identified by scientists in the future. Not only that, but many things which cannot be detected or conceptualised by the eyes or minds of humans from this universe could perhaps be conceptualised by beings in other universes. Many things which our human corporeal eyes cannot see are sure to be perceived by non-corporeal eyes.

Materialists say that anything that cannot be seen instantly in front of our eyes exists only in the fantasy world of the idealists. So it was that if, two or three hundred years ago, an inventor gave a lecture on the possibility of constructing a machine which could fly in the sky, this would have been dismissed by the scientific community as a figment of the idealist's imagination. Now, as we can actually see aeroplanes in the sky, can we accept that the view of idealists has become that of the materialists?

If we believe the view of the idealists to be false, and mind, which is not a gross object, to have no power or influence, than we should begin to investigate some rare but still manifest phenomena, like the powerful effects of concentration meditation. If done effectively, as a sign of power and accomplishment, meditation can result in the physical body actually vanishing into a 'rainbow body' of light; meditation can also revive recollections of past lives, and so on.

At least we must admit that if our mind is happy we laugh, or if it is unhappy we cry. With regard to body, speech and mind, the mind is like the king controlling the body and speech. We are all aware of this, so to hold the opinion that anything beyond our ordinary perceptions does not exist cannot actually accord with pure scientific principles. On the other hand, when something does not accord with the correct and obvious situation, then that is also in opposition with scientific view.

To take the example of an unbiased researcher who honestly resolves to find for themselves and all humankind a correct path leading to an end to human discomfort and suffering: If they have not had the benefit of meeting Buddhists, have not been influenced by followers of other religions, nor met others with opposing points of view, then they would need to adopt an impartial outlook and thereby carefully differentiate the correct path themselves.

The earliest human civilisations believed with blind faith that everything beyond their control, for example: the elements, the sun and moon etc., were all gods. Gradually, new religions were created to fulfil individual, social or political needs. Some of these different religions thrived and today have followers all over the world. Each individual religious teaching offers reasons to support belief in each of its doctrinal principles; however it is very unusual for these principles to withstand logical analysis or be able to offer evidence in corroboration. Therefore I consider it inappropriate to have confidence in every religion.

However, to suggest that religions are only concerned with achieving worldly profit or spiritual reassurance, and are therefore entirely false is also deceptive and untrue. To say such things only highlights an overall lack of understanding. Regardless of the tenets of whichever religion we examine, if we analyse carefully, we realise that each tenet has many facets of inner meaning which are authentic, and each path is sure to have an ultimate goal supported by reasoning. If we wish to choose one religion, we definitely want to choose the best and most authentic, one without error which is one hundred percent reliable. This is the most important thing for our happiness, both in this life and the next.

The way to examine a religion is through the three kinds of intellectual reasoning: clear, unapparent and ultimate, from which basis we may come to conclusions that accord with our individual understanding. We need to know that whoever the teacher of the religious system is, they are all-knowing, that the path that they teach is unmistaken, and that whatever results can be attained from this teaching, they are everlastingly blissful and completely free from suffering.

Again, whichever teacher we rely on, we must be sure that their teaching is not be a path which is wayward. Sometimes a spiritual path only accomplishes the causes for rebirth in the higher realms of samsara, not the everlasting bliss of liberation. Some paths are ill-considered and they are more harmful than useful, causing all those connected with them to be misled. All these and other factors must be given careful consideration.

I personally consider the ability to analyse hidden phenomena and extremely abstruse phenomena, beyond that which is obvious, to be the goal of pure scientific method. Ultimately, I believe the most rigorous scientific and philosophical investigations of the most highly qualified scientists and learned scholars will one day arrive at a conclusion which concurs with the pinnacle of Buddhist wisdom, and a common understanding of the true nature of reality will be reached.

Furthermore, from a political perspective, supposing the ideologies of world leaders and those who hold mundane power are upheld as true, in contrast the words of others, if two leaders of the same status were to hold different views, which one would we believe in? Faced with this kind of situation, all distinctions between what is correct and incorrect should be decided ultimately by a scientific approach with which everyone is in agreement. To find a true path in this way, through correct analysis, is much better than never turning our attention to religion or spiritual pursuits, or to concepts of this life and the next, good and evil, and what actions we should take up and which abandon.

Based on this understanding, we grasp the importance of finding a good path in the future. When we experience the problems caused by following a mistaken path, we can learn how to select a true path and never go wrong again, as is illustrated by the story of Master Pawo:

Master Pawo (Acharya Vira) was a famous non-Buddhist yogin who engaged in debate with the Buddhists at Nalanda, but could not defeat them. However, he refused to abandon his beliefs and adopt Buddhism, as was the required custom, so he was locked in the library. At first he piled up the volumes of scriptures to sleep on, but slowly he began to read them and realised their authenticity. Finally he became a very learned Buddhist master and undertook many activities of the true Dharma.

Everything will be destroyed and eaten by time, the 'all consumer'. When the time comes, the whole world will be destroyed. The consumer of time is the Lord of Death. He will even consume the gods living in the heavenly realms who have life spans of hundreds of millions of human years. The length of our human life is uncertain. Whether we command a high or low position or are strong or weak, all of us without exception will eventually be destroyed. Therefore the great enemy which all living beings should fear is known as death.

In this world I see two kinds of people who, living their lives, not only do not fear death but actually look forward to it in their hearts. Those suffering in agony with diseases like cancer are one kind. Some suffer from constant physical abuse, and they also want to die. Some people try to escape from suffering by means of suicide. Others however, motivated initially by fearing the horrors of death, practise the holy Dharma and, by the strength of meditation on profound quintessential instructions, determine within themselves the genuine deathless state and true happiness in their hearts. These individuals also look forward to death. They see death as being like the flight of a swan from one lotus pool to another. Leaving the prison-like human body, they look forward to going to the pleasure groves of the divine realms, and long for that much more than any other prospect.

There are also other kinds of people who, when they reach the point of death, may beat their chests and wail and cry. Some grab hold of their family members and friends, begging, "Don't let me die!" But many other people spend their whole life working hard, doing virtuous deeds and so, although they do not look forward to dying, at the moment of death they have no regrets.

There are some Tibetans who are not Lamas or monks, but even so at the point of death, they sit up straight and sound the syllable HIK! Some even pass away in the rainbow body of light whereby, apart from the hair and fingernails, their gross corporal elements disappear into rainbow light. Most Tibetans are seen to pass away like everyone else, but they still put their hands together in faithful prayer to the Three Precious Jewels. There are many Tibetans who have paintings of the Divine Realm of Great Bliss or the Copper Coloured Mountain and gaze at them, with the palms of their hands held together, keeping a vision of a divine realm in their mind as they pass away.

There are also known to be many people who, when dying, experience frightening visions of the livestock and wild animals which they themselves killed during their life, and they cry out, begging for these visions to stop. There are a few people who are so strongly attached to the pleasures they cherished during life: family, friends and possessions, that they obsess over having to leave them. They are also very distraught at the time of death.

Of all these kinds of people, those who die praying to their Lama and Three Precious Jewels have the personal belief they have a reliable unmistaken refuge, a guide to protect them from fear and to accompany them on the journey of death. They have prepared beforehand for death and therefore their suffering is not too bad.

As a common Tibetan saying goes:

'Rely on the Lama and the Three Precious Jewels,
discuss things with one's gracious parents.'

Placing our confidence in the Lama and Precious Jewels is never a mistake, either now or in the future. Good-natured and gracious parents never hold a bad attitude towards us, so it is appropriate to discuss things with them.

Some people, at the point of death, focus on a divine realm and in meditative concentration merge their awareness with the outer expanse. At the moment of death they engage in the actual practice of the quintessential instructions of Phowa transference of consciousness to move onward. Their bodies atomise and they accomplish the observable body of rainbow light. This is the most exalted way to move on. Not only are such people unafraid but moreover enjoy dying; they face death directly, and those left behind remain in a happy state of mind. Such people provide a good example to those around them, and their death becomes meaningful to everyone with whom they have a karmic connection.

Those who engage in negative actions and harm others in life have no place of refuge or object of reliance at the time of death. Weeping and without any Buddhist teachings, they must go empty-handed to death, and so deserve our compassion. Even if, at that time, one hundred compassionate Buddhas holding hooks of compassion came to rescue them, because they are ignorant of any devotion, those with negative karma do not have the ring of faith by which they may be led to freedom. Their vision is impure and so there is no place for them to go other than the steel cities of hell. What terrible suffering!

Generally speaking, when people see a newborn child they are joyful and have a celebration. At the turning of the year we hold a New Year's party. When people die we mourn them sorrowfully. But if we think logically about this, we are doing things the wrong way round. As soon as a baby is born, not only does its death begin approaching, but moreover from that day on the cause and result of suffering begins. So why do we celebrate? Alternatively, we could say the child has come into this world crying, so it would be more appropriate if we were to keep them company by crying too. Human life is short and there is no certainty about the length of life. On top of this, at New Year one year is over, so it would be fitting if we were to mourn its passing; therefore I feel New Year's celebrations are inappropriate.

In the same way, when death comes we cast off our unclean body of suffering. Especially, after death welcome and beneficial opportunities will arise for those who have a measure of confidence in practice. They will experience bliss and incomparable sensations in divine realms and so on; therefore it would be appropriate to welcome death with celebration. People do not act like this because we solidify our hallucinatory experiences as real and we are strongly attached to them. This is the truth expressed in the saying 'We see our home as pleasant, even if it is hell.' This appearance of all the activities of samsara is just like a weird illusory show.

In this way, when we have arrived at the door of the city of death it is useless to cry. We may scream to our friends, "Don't let me die!" but when life is over, even if the Medicine Buddha himself came to our aid, he could not help us. Thinking carelessly, "Everyone must die, I am no exception, so whatever happens, happens..." does not help with regard to the negative karmic results of our actions. Those who doubt whether or not there will be an 'I' in the next life to experience suffering become even more miserable at death.

At the time of death we need to meditate on the six recollections:

* The Buddha
* His teachings (Dharma)
* The spiritual community (Sangha)
* Generosity
* Moral conduct
* Our personal deity (yidam)

As well as this, we should remember what the Buddha taught:

> The nature of all things is pure,
> therefore meditate on the cognition of intangibleness.
> With Bodhicitta, meditate on cognition of great compassion.
> Everything is naturally reference-less and luminous,
> therefore do not fixate on anything.
> Mind is the cause of enlightened wisdom,
> so do not search for Buddha elsewhere.

Also, bring to mind the ten cognitions as taught in the sutras:

* Remember not to be attached to this life.
* Think of loving kindness for all sentient beings.
* Completely abandon all resentment.

* Completely abandon all laxness in discipline.
* Engage in all modes of pure discipline.
* Consider that all serious faults committed become lighter in karmic force.
* Generate fearlessness towards all future lives.
* Meditate on the impermanence of all compounded phenomena.
* Remember that all phenomena have no self essence.
* Recall that nirvana is the pacification of all suffering.

We should also contemplate over and over again the array of Buddha divine realms; and also dedicate the completion of the two accumulations and all the roots of merit of the unexcelled Mahayana generation of Bodhicitta, so this may become the cause for us to be reborn in the divine realms.

FOUR

SACRED FUTURE DESTINY

Regardless of whatever karma and emotional afflictions caused us to take rebirth, once we have taken up our present body, there is no quick way of reversing the process. However, our body is no more substantial than a bubble in water; it has no lasting essence. In the same way, all the gratification we gain from the appearances of this life is as impermanent as a rainbow in the sky. The pleasures of our senses fool us like a magician's tricks; deceptive as a mirage, they are illusory and false. Because this is the nature of phenomena, the individual karmic visions of migratory beings are irreversible in the short term, so the antics of wandering beings are, from a certain point of view, nonsensical and absurd. Considered from another perspective, their experiences are so sad we want to shed tears for their suffering.

All our parents, relatives and friends of this life are totally unaware of having had any previous connection with each other. A few wandering consciousnesses in the intermediate state have come together in this physical basis, the human body, like independent travellers who lodge together in a hotel. Why should we have attachment to one another? It could be that these people were our enemies in the past. Think about this situation; isn't it ironic? Think of those who have gone down the final path and died: your parents, beloved in your heart, your dearly-loved siblings, or perhaps the partner you adored. Among which of the six kinds of beings are they now? Are the phenomena manifesting in their perceptions the same as yours?

According to their karma, regardless of whether they have taken rebirth in a high or low realm, if our parents, relatives and friends of this life transferred to another realm they would have passed through the intermediate state; so, have the apparent phenomena manifesting in their perceptions changed or not? Is it possible that they have taken rebirth in this world which you see? Have they been reborn in your vicinity as some person or animal or insect that you can see or hear? If they have taken such a rebirth and you happened to meet, you would not recognise each other. Even if you did know it was them, you would not necessarily be able to help them if they had taken rebirth as an insect, for example. Understanding the truth about our situation can be hard to bear.

In the Tibetan heroic epic based on the life of King Gesar of Ling, the episode known as 'The Conquest of Hor' tells the following story:

While King Gesar was absent from his kingdom, subduing the horrifying Violent Naga King in the place called the High Northern Lands, the army of Gurdkar, King of Hor invaded Ling, marching into the upper region of the Wholesome District of Khramo. Before this, Bumpa'i Gyatsha Zhalkar, the elder half-brother of King Gesar, and Tshazhang Danma Zhangkhra, together with thirty other warriors famed throughout the land, had defended and protected Khramo for many years, each warrior fighting many times in single-handed combat, always victoriously.

But while King Gesar was travelling in the north, he was tricked by demons into consuming enchanted food and drink, the effects of which caused him to forget his kingly duties entirely, so he was prevented from returning to Khramo for nine years. Eventually, being greatly outnumbered by King Gurdkar's army, the son of a general's advisor called Nangchung Yustag and other cherished sons of Ling were killed. Representations of the Buddha, the Dharma and the Sangha were stolen, the king's castle was destroyed, Gesar's elder wife, Senglcam Drukmo, was kidnapped and Hor was victorious.

By this time the hero Gyatsha, who had no equal for bravery and skill with his sword, had slain seven of Hor's princes and spilt the blood of one hundred thousand Hor soldiers. Eventually, Gyatsha killed his half-brother from his previous life, and the Hor prince Lha'u Legspa, with his sword. As he severed the prince's head from his body, white blood gushed out, which showed that Lha'u Legspa was in fact bound in allegiance to Ling. Discovering this, Gyatsha was distraught. At the same moment a rainbow-shaped cloud appeared in the sky, and a single white cloud floated towards the north. Cool rain mixed with sunlight fell, a white-breasted vulture circled overhead and Gyatsha thought of his younger brother Gesar. He was overwhelmed by sadness.

Impulsively, Gyatsha threw off his impenetrable armour and prayed that it might fall into the hands of his brother Dralha. Then he mounted Peacock, the dead prince of Hor's horse, drew his sword named Yazi Karphran, and swiftly rode off in pursuit of the evil Shenpa Meru of Hor. Because he could find no means of escape, Shenba Meru had hidden himself in a deep hollow in the ground. Here he waited, wedging the haft of his spear into the ground and holding it upright. As Gyatsha approached, the horse Peacock, swerving to one side of the hollow, reared up and threw him. This caused Gyatsha to fall directly onto Shenpa Meru's rigid spear point, and so he died. This was as much a tragedy as if the full moon of the fifteenth night had fallen to earth.

Not long after this, King Gesar, finally free from the enchantment of forgetfulness, set out from the land of demons towards home to subdue Gurdkar, King of Hor. On the journey Gesar encountered ninety-nine enemies, some of whom he defeated skilfully, some with magic, some with physical strength and power. While Gesar was returning home, the hero Gyatsha had taken rebirth as a young hawk and was busy in pursuit of some of Hor's soldiers who had taken rebirth as small birds. Suddenly, Gyatsha saw the crest of King Gesar of Ling's helmet and was overjoyed. He landed for a moment on Gesar's white bow. Thinking that Hor had sent the hawk, Gesar was filled with rage. He snatched an arrow from his quiver and drew back his bowstring. Just as he was about to shoot, his wild chestnut-coloured horse recognised the hawk and bucked, so Gesar's arrow went wide.

Afraid, the young hawk dared not approach Gesar again but could not bear to leave, so he circled in the sky above. Gyatsha began to sing a sorrowful song in a human voice, which caught Gesar's attention:

> "Younger brother, Lord Gesar,
> While you were away in the Northern Lands,
> The invading forces of Hor
> Directed their troops against Ling.
> General Danma rustled many of Hor's horses,
> Gouged out Shenpa of Hor's skull, so his brains spattered on
> the ground.
> I, Gyatsha, leader of warriors,
> Victorious, single-handed won many battles.
> From Hor, four million men advanced on us,
> Only ninety-thousand remained to retreat;
> But to no avail: we were betrayed.
> The hallowed land of Ling was occupied by enemies.
> The long Ja Stronghold was levelled,
> Our young brother's neck was bloodied,
> And your wife, Senglcam Drukmo, snatched away by force.
> Seeing this, I, Gyatsha, would rather die and go to the hell
> realms

Than remain alive and powerless.
I stabbed the nine princes of Hor,
Not to mention the hundreds of thousands of Hor troops I
destroyed,
But in the end I fell on Shenpa's spear.
My consciousness was carried like a feather on the wind,
And the intermediate state of death was wretched indeed.
I had sworn that if I did not taste the heart's blood of the Hor
White Tent Tribe
I would no longer be Gyatsha.
Due to the negative consequences of breaking this, my vow,
And as I was willing to become a hawk,
Look – now I have a hawk's form!
All the Hor troops I killed also became birds,
So I chased them over the hills all morning;
In the afternoon I chased them in the valleys.
Each large bird I killed,
I considered I'd killed a chief Hor butcher.
Each small bird I killed,
I considered I'd killed a Hor soldier.
Still this hallucination is not ended…

But younger brother, Gesar, Great Tiger Leader,
When you went to the Northern Lands,
Why was it you took so long returning?"

The hawk Gyatsha continued:

"This morning, sitting on my nest in the wooden shelter of the
Hundred Thousand Deities of the Pass on Mt. Yakla Sebo, I was
overwhelmed by sudden joy. When I flew out to chase the Hor
troops who had taken rebirth as birds, I saw my younger brother's
crest. You appeared in my vision and I was overcome with joy, and
so I came to perch on your bow."

Gesar saw that his elder brother had been reborn as hawk, but that his
awareness had not changed. He realised that the consciousnesses of his
younger brother, Rongtsha Marleb, and others who had died would also
have changed their physical form. But Gesar knew if he met them he
would not recognise them, and even if he did recognise them, they would
not recognise him.

Gesar's elder brother, Gyatsha, then had the wish that he might aspire to take rebirth in a divine realm, and he sang a song about his aspiration. Having completed the song, it became clear to Gyatsha that the time had not come for him to go to a divine realm. Due to the vow he had taken, only drinking the heart's blood of Gurdkar, King of Hor, would free him to be reborn wherever he wished.

Gyatsha explained all this to King Gesar, and together they made a plan. They decided that Gesar would capture King Gurdkar of Hor, at which time Gesar's magical horse would emanate a vulture to summon Gyatsha. Then Gyatsha could drink King Gurdkar's heart's blood and so be free to go to a pure realm.

This episode of the saga concludes with King Gesar returning once again to the Land of Hor and finally defeating his enemies. Gesar converts the whole territory to Buddhism and enables Gyatsha to attain his wish and go to a divine realm.

All living creatures we see and hear around us were certainly our parents in many lives past, however some of them have now become our enemies. Even worse than this, countless numbers of them are killed every day to provide us with food and clothing. Thinking like this can be very disturbing, but who is there that we can beg to help us?

However much we think about it, it is evident that this samsaric life is a huge prison of negative forces, the upper limits of which are called the 'three higher states': the realms of gods, demigods and humans, where for an instant the conditions of imprisonment are slightly more bearable. The lower limits, called the 'three most unfortunate states', are those of the hell realm, the ghost realm and the animal realm where the conditions of imprisonment are harsh, and beings live in overwhelming misery and suffering.

If there were a way to escape from this vast prison then we should certainly do so now. We have already been imprisoned for far too long. If we are mistakenly occupied in striving for the trivial happiness and comfort of this current life then we disregard the great meaningful goal, considering our petty ambitions as all-important. We are no different from children building castles in sand.

Samsaric activities cease as soon as we stop pursuing them, but once we engage in them, there will never come a time when they are all completely finished. We may spend our whole life preparing to live comfortably, waking up early, going to bed late, however before we have completed all there is to do, our life ends, and the noose of the messengers of the Lord of Death is round our neck. There is not a moment left to look back; it will be time to go.

When we are children we are under the control of our parents and so life is miserable. As adults we go along with the wishes of our friends and partners, and suffer because of the importance we place on the accumulation of money and possessions. We are concerned with maintaining what we have, and anxious about losing anything, so life is miserable. When we are old and frail we fall under the control of our children, partner, in-laws etc., and suffer unhappily from the failing heath of old age.

Even though this is all true, actually this realm, which is known as the human realm, is the best of the three higher states of cyclic existence. In this realm we are obviously among the higher creatures. But, if there is not one of us humans who does not experience the three sufferings, then even more so must the animals we see, and all beings in hell and the lower realms beyond our perception, experience unbearable suffering.

This is the current situation, but what if at some point something changed, and the chance arose for us to avoid having to experience these sufferings? What if we found a path of permanent happiness so that not only our self, but also our parents, brothers, sisters, partners, children and all those we care for never needed to experience any suffering? Wouldn't it be the most amazing discovery! A path to freedom from suffering would be the greatest gift anyone could give, and would bring the greatest possible benefit to everyone. Without doubt this discovery would be hailed as a supreme achievement among all beings.

But living beings are feeble and small-minded, with little power or capability. We may love each other, but we have no way of truly protecting each other. In this sense we are helpless, like a mother with no arms whose child falls into a river and is swept away; or two people, both engulfed by a fast-moving tide unable to help themselves, let alone each other. But if there is a protector capable of providing us with safe and dependable refuge, clearly it would smart for us to try to find them.

Some people accept the philosophical point of view of the materialists but not that of the idealists, who postulate that material objects do not exist independently of mind. If we look at the intrinsic theory of

62

materialism, we see it is science. But we need to make sure that science is true and verifiable, not based on unsound theories. Otherwise how can we call it scientific to say that what I see exists and what I do not see does not exist? You and I and others like us, who rely on the vision of our corporeal eyes, cannot deny the existence of something just because we cannot see it.

Ultimately, for us to investigate whether or not the teachings of Buddha are authentic is like trying to grasp a star in the sky with outstretched hands. To use an analogy, when we examine objects invisible to the naked eye we need a microscope; in the same way, in order to investigate the great mysteries of life, we certainly need an unmistaken mind with valid cognition in order to assess correctly.

In the ancient world, mathematicians and philosophers formulated theories, with varying degrees of accuracy, to explain the nature and function of our universe. They considered the earth was flat, and the sky was like an upturned bowl above them, higher in the middle, lower at the sides, and round in shape. At that time, except for the other people they saw around, they had no real way of knowing, apart from tales brought back by travellers, about other oceans and continents, races of people and animal species different from those with which they were familiar.

All societies in the ancient world formulated myths, in an attempt to explain how the natural world and human beings came into existence. The common theme which runs through all creation myths is that first there was empty space, but within this, explained in mystical rather than rational terms, was some creative force which enabled itself to come into being. This power came to be personified as an all-powerful creator-god, who therefore went on to create more gods and the rest of the natural world. This assumption inevitably led to the belief that all natural disasters are the work of gods, and nature spirits are much more powerful than humans.

The belief was that all mountains, rivers, the sea, the sky, the sun and moon were the manifestations of divine beings, or dwellings of the spirits who ruled them. In the act of surrendering to these powerful forces, superstitions practices developed which people hoped would keep them safe and secure. Because there was belief in many different gods, who were worshiped using many different rituals, various religions evolved. Various views or philosophical schools were formed, many of which remain to this day, including the Eternalists, who believe in the permanent existence of things such as a soul, and Nihilists, who believe that nothing whatsoever actually exists.

Some religions teach that it is their followers' religious duty to harm or even kill non-believers, and others teach that benefiting others is the supreme goal of their religion. It is important for us not to be prejudiced in our support of one religion over another. What we need to do is establish objective truth, and not rely on any wishful thinking. It is important that what we decide to rely on brings benefit both in this life and the next, benefit for ourselves and others. We must be sure that it can actually promote happiness, whatever it is.

We clear-thinking individuals should be without superstition and, having thoroughly investigated different religious ideologies, most certainly need to find an unmistaken refuge or guide for the spiritual path. When we investigate and analyse properly, we may find that some teachers or guides have not freed themselves from the chains of cyclic existence, and are full of the same worldly faults as we are. There may be teachers who have attained some measure of what are known as the 'common accomplishments or powers', but have not completely freed themselves from samsara's chains. Others fabricate a spirituality which has never existed, like the horns of a rabbit. A few, spurred on by political or other selfish motives, even create deceptive belief systems to fool people into following them.

There are so many schools of thought, as numerous as a mushroom's gills. Many of them look very impressive from the outside, but on closer acquaintance we find however much they expound their theories, they really say nothing even slightly resembling the truth. Their previous words contradict what is said subsequently, their terms convey the opposite of what they mean, and their doctrine contains many tenets which directly conflict with each other. If we try to live by such teachings, our afflictions will only become greater; they will influence our mind stream in a negative way because they are not authentic. We must turn our back on all such ideologies.

We should test all ideas as if testing gold. A goldsmith smelts, cuts and rubs gold, examining it a hundred times to make sure it is genuine. In the same way, we should make sure the spiritual path we choose possesses the qualities which will encourage us to make positive changes in our life. It should protect us from suffering and must be truthful, not deceptive.

In my own careful analysis and long experience, I have found the teachings of the Buddha to be both authentic and extremely reliable. It is my conviction that if we desire happiness in this and future lives then we need to go for refuge to this enlightened teacher and practise his authentic teaching of definitive meaning, as summarised in the path of cessation. This is the holy Buddhist doctrine of teaching and realisation, the practise of which is an unmistaken action. This is the entrance way to boundless merit and the basis from which definitive conviction is born.

All living beings are busy running round in pursuit of happiness and pleasure and, needless to say, they are all competing for their own personal happiness and pleasure. Small-minded people only work for the happiness and pleasure of today and tomorrow, or this year and the next. Those more far-sighted work to experience happiness and pleasure before this present life is over. Wiser people know how to think about both now and the future, the short and long term. They understand that short term happiness is of little benefit, so they work to accomplish everlasting happiness. The wisest people renounce concerns of their own happiness and sadness, and work to establish other beings in supreme happiness.

Generally speaking, there are two kinds of joy: physical pleasure and mental happiness. No experience of mundane happiness is able to transcend the underlying and all-pervasive condition of suffering. However, compared to obvious suffering, mundane happiness is the experience of only slight suffering, so we beings in samsara accept that this is what happiness is. We can gain this kind of superficial happiness, for example the fleeting pleasure enjoyed by our physical body through acquiring material possessions. However, inner mental and spiritual happiness cannot be found except by practising the holy Buddhist teachings. If we desire to find unique happiness of both body and mind, in this moment and ultimately, then we need to practise the extraordinary bliss of concentration meditation as taught in the holy Buddhist teachings.

Apart from the holy Buddhist teachings, there is no other way to find this extraordinary bliss which is both temporary and ultimate, physical and mental. The Buddha taught that enlightenment is the result; the cause is practising a pure path. For this reason, first, for someone who wants to attain everlasting happiness, the Buddha is the true holy refuge and object of aspiring accomplishment for oneself and others.

In order to illustrate the experience of the great qualities of enlightenment, forever free from suffering, I relate the following story:

When the Buddha Sakyamuni was residing in Rajagriha in the Bamboo Grove of Kalandaka, six non-Buddhist teachers, Maskari Gosaliputra, Sanjayi Vairadiputra, Ajita, Kakuda Katyayana, Purna Kasyapa and Nirgrantha Jnatiputra had a discussion. "In the past people were very respectful to us," they said, "but now they all follow the monk Gautama. We must hold a contest, competing with him to show off our miraculous powers. And we'll make sure he loses."

They went to Bimbisara, the king of that region, and tried to persuade him, again and again, to allow such a competition. The king told them, "The Buddha knows and sees everything, and his physical body emanates unobstructed miracles based on supernormal powers. Your idea of competing against him is like a firefly trying to outshine the sun, or a fox competing against a lion. It will only cause harm and embarrassment." However the non-Buddhist teachers insisted the competition should be held in seven days' time.

During the next seven days, the Buddha travelled to a place called Nganyid Dusmkhyen, and then he journeyed further away. Eventually he went back to Shravasti where King Bimbisara and his retinue were gathered with tens of thousands and hundreds of thousands of spectators. The six non-Buddhist teachers became even more conceited, boasting, "Gautama suddenly ran away when faced with a contest to compare his miraculous abilities with ours. Now he must compete!" The non-Buddhist teachers made another request to the king, who then said prayers to the Buddha, asking him to consent to the competition. In response, the Buddha said, "I know the time has come." The day was the first of the solar New Year.

Before the king made New Year offerings to the Buddha, first he gave him a toothpick and the Buddha accepted it. When he had used it, the Buddha planted the toothpick in the ground and instantly it began to grow into a tall tree, with branches and leaves extending over two thousand miles. The branches and leaves were precious and covered with flowers and fruit which tasted of nectar, and the fragrance caused everyone to feel blissful and contented. When the wind blew through the branches and leaves, melodious sounds of the Buddhist teachings could be heard and everyone who listened developed pure intention. Together with this emanation, the Buddha gave teachings and many attained the fruit of realisation, or were reborn in the heavenly realms.

On the second day, when King Udrayana made offerings, the Buddha emanated two precious mountains, one on each side of his body, adorned with various plants, flowers and fruit. Excellent tender, sweet-tasting grass grew, and the crowds of people and animals became happy, contented and joyful. Having emanated this, the Buddha gave teachings, and many generated the unexcelled bodhichitta and took rebirth in the higher heavenly realms.

On the third day, when the King Shuntsidala made offerings and the water for bathing the Buddha's feet was poured away, it formed a beautiful lake nine hundred miles in size, filled with the seven precious substances and possessing the eight qualities of perfect water. It was filled with lotus flowers of all colours the size of cartwheels, from which various beguiling scents and lights exuded. Emanating this, the Buddha gave teachings and those listening attained the fruit of realisation, were reborn in the heavenly realms, and generated limitless merit.

On the fourth day, when King Indrawama made offerings, the Buddha emanated eight water channels in each of the eight directions, surrounding and flowing into the precious lake. The sound of the flowing water proclaimed the Buddhist teachings, the meaning of which many realised, and so they attained the fruit of realisation and were reborn in the heavenly realms.

On the fifth day, when King Brahmadana made offerings, a golden light shone out from the Buddha's face, filling the three-thousand-fold universe. All beings touched by the light were liberated from their afflictions and filled with bliss. The Buddha gave teachings and many attained the fruit of realisation as before.

On the sixth day, when the people of Licchavi made offerings, through the blessing of the Buddha, all those present attained higher perception, and they praised the enlightened qualities of the Buddha. The people made prayers of aspiration and the Buddha again gave teachings, and many attained the fruit of realisation.

On the seventh day, when the Sakya clan made offerings, all those present saw, with great respect, an emanation of the Wheel-wielding Universal King with his kingdom and the seven precious possessions, together with his princes and ministers. Then the Buddha gave amazing teachings and many achieved the fruit of realisation.

On the eighth day, when Kaushika, king of the gods made offerings, the Buddha sat upon a lion throne. When the Kings of the Gods, Brahma and Indra, both made offerings, a great sound like an elephant trumpet resounded. Suddenly five huge bloodthirsty demons appeared and destroyed the thrones of the six non-Buddhist teachers. From the Buddha's retinue, Vajrapani struck the six teachers on their heads with a blazing vajra sceptre. The six charlatans became ashamed and ran away; some of them leaped into rivers and drowned. Many followers of the non-Buddhist teachers turned to the Buddha for refuge, received the vows of ordination and later became Foe Destroyers.

Then, from the eighty-thousand hair follicles of the Buddha's body light shone forth and filled the entire sky. On the tip of each beam of light was a great lotus flower upon which appeared an emanated Buddha, together with his retinue, teaching the holy Buddhist teachings. The faith of everyone who saw this emanation increased and they received more teachings. Many aroused bodhichitta and attained the fruit of liberation.

On the ninth day, when the King of the Gods, Brahma, made offerings, the Buddha emanated his body to such a height that he reached the god realm of Brahma and emitted light. Everyone saw this and heard his voice which aroused their faith, and he gave teachings. Many attained the fruit of liberation.

On the tenth day, when the Four Great Kings made offerings, the Buddha emanated his body to touch the peak of existence. From the Four Great Kings' bodies four great lights shone forth and the Buddha taught the entourage, and limitless beings aroused bodhichitta and attained the fruit of liberation.

On the eleventh day, when householder Anathapindada made offerings, the Buddha entered into concentration on great compassion and, sitting on his lion throne, made himself invisible and taught from a mass of light. Countless beings aroused bodhichitta.

On the twelfth day, when the householder Jinta made offerings, the Buddha filled the three-thousand-fold universe with golden light which pacified the minds of all malevolent beings that it touched. The light caused them to develop the mind which enabled them to feel for each other as if they were parents or siblings. The Buddha gave teachings and limitless numbers of them developed bodhichitta.

On the thirteenth day, when King Shuntsidala made offerings, from the Buddha's navel two great lights shone forth, upon each of which was a lotus flower. On each lotus was seated an emanated Buddha from whose navel shone forth two great lights in the same way, eventually completely filling the thousand-fold universe with emanated Buddhas visible to everyone. These Buddhas gave teachings and in the same way limitless beings aroused bodhichitta.

On the fourteenth day, when King Udrayana made offerings, the flowers that the king scattered as offerings became like precious trees and all the beings of the thousand-fold universes saw them. Through the Buddha's teachings, as before, countless beings aroused bodhichitta.

On the fifteenth day, when King Bimbisara made offerings, all the vessels became filled with food which had a hundred different flavours, and the entire entourage was delighted. The Buddha struck the ground with his hand and the limitless beings of the eighteen hell realms became visible. The Buddha explained how in the past they had accumulated negative karma, and how this caused the suffering they were now experiencing, so that the whole entourage became afraid, and developed compassion for the hell beings. The Buddha taught various teachings and some of the hell beings generated the unexcelled bodhichitta. Some attained the level of no-return. Numberless beings generated the root of virtue to be reborn as gods or humans. The hell beings saw the Buddha and, through the condition of hearing the teachings, developed faith; they were released from living in the hell realms, and took rebirth as gods or humans.

This story helps us to understand the significance of the teachings of this amazing teacher. The holy Buddhist teachings, together with the quintessential instructions from a master on the ultimate cause of our hearts' inner joy, contain the supreme method leading to the experience of true bliss, both for oneself and others. By studying, contemplating and practising these teachings, human life is made meaningful, and the fear and panic of birth and death is eliminated. Following the Dharma we become free from fear, and remain so, even if the sky were to collapse upon us. Inappropriate hopes and doubts all become resolved internally.

If we apply ourselves to the Buddhist methods of finding this extraordinary inner bliss of relaxation and happiness of mind, eventually we will gain pure holy bliss. This, among millions of pursuits, is the right one to choose, and is our best opportunity for happiness. Therefore, now is the time for action. If we are distracted by laziness now, later we will develop fierce regret for our procrastination, and will become very miserable.

If we take a close look at the happiness of this life, we see that it has the nature of suffering. Do not be attached to beguiling material possessions, objects of desire, companions, family or relatives. We should practise the Buddhist teachings with as much fervour as a beautiful girl trying to put out the flames when her long hair suddenly catches alight, or the energy of a coward striving to rid himself of the snake which has fallen into his lap; without putting it off to tomorrow or the day after, to next year or the year after that. We must strive from this very moment onwards to gain happiness for ourselves and others.

FIVE

THE UNMISTAKEN ENTRANCE

Buddhism originally spread from India where it was taught that, in the beginning, this world was a great ocean. On this ocean appeared a golden lotus flower with one thousand and two petals. Through this interdependent connection, one thousand and two Buddhas will therefore appear in this age. Of those, the fourth Buddha is our teacher Sakyamuni Buddha. Sakyamuni Buddha was in actuality fully enlightened before he took this rebirth; however, he chose to demonstrate by his life the path which leads to the realisation of enlightenment, in order to teach those capable of understanding. Through his Twelve Deeds, he taught the three spiritual approaches of the Buddhist teachings. Near Varanasi, the Buddha gave his first teaching, the Four Noble Truths, to his five excellent disciples, together with eighty thousand gods.

Next, in the King of Places, Vulture's Peak Mountain, the Buddha taught the section of teachings which explains emptiness to a gathering of Sons of the Conqueror, Bodhisattvas. Additionally, in numerous places, including Vaishali and the Land of Lanka (Sri Lanka), he taught the final section of teachings which precisely and completely defines the absolute nature of all things. The three sections of teachings are known as the 'Causal Vehicle of Characteristics', or Sutra teachings, and each stage corresponds to the abilities of people of modest, medium and greater aptitude. The Buddha taught the section of the resultant esoteric approach of teachings characteristic of Tibetan Buddhism to suitable fortunate beings, gods and nagas, and others not necessarily of the human realm. Due to this, countless unenlightened students entered the path and reached resultant levels of spiritual attainment.

After the Buddha had passed beyond suffering, the collection of the first section of teachings, termed Hinayana teachings, was compiled into three groups; these groups of teachings were named the 'Three Baskets'. Kashyapa and six other heirs of the teachings, and members of the three successive councils carried out this compilation and, supplemented by written commentaries on the Buddha's words, the teachings flourished and spread. The compilation of Mahayana teachings was spread by

Nagajuna and Asanga and flourished as a result of their efforts. Nagajuna and Asanga attained realisation of the enlightened Buddhas Manjushri and Maitreya, together with Aryadeva, Vasubandu, Dignaga and Dharmakirti; these masters are known as the Six Ornaments.

Two hundred years after the Buddha Sakayamuni passed beyond suffering, and in accordance with his prophesy, the Buddha named Vajrapani, Lord of Secrets, came in person and taught the Five Eminent Beings all the Tantras that were taught in the three heavenly realms. These Five Eminent Beings were: God Gragsdan Chogkyong, Naga King Jogpo, Yaksha Meteor Face, Rakshasa Lodro Thupten and Mili Tsab'i Drimed Dragspa. At that time, using molten gold, Rakshasa Lodro Thupten inscribed these Tantras on lapis lazuli, sealed them with the seven abilities of enlightened mind, and blessed them. Through the power of this, King Dza had seven amazing dreams which inspired him to concentrate solely on practice. As foretold in one of these dreams, Tulku Garap Dorje received the Development stage Mahayoga Tantras from Vajrasattva, who visited him in person in the western land of Oddiyana.

The Kriya Tantras were brought to Varanasi. The Yoga Tantras were brought to the peak of the Blazing Mountain. As a result of this, all the outer and inner secret Tantras became renowned in the human world. More especially, Manjushri taught the esoteric inner Tantras to God Gragsdan Chogkyong in the heavenly realms. From there they were gradually transmitted and Indra, King of the Gods, practised them, together with all his retinue of one hundred thousand, and they reached the level of full enlightenment. Araya Avalokiteshvara taught these Tantras to Blackneck, King of the Nagas, in the Naga realm. After this they were transmitted further, and Naga King Jogpo, together with one hundred thousand of his retinue, reached the level of awareness holders. The Lord of Secrets, Vajrapani, taught the Tantras to the Yaksha Samantabhadra, in the land of Yakshas. Following that they were gradually transmitted to others, and Yaksha Meteor Face, together with his retinue of one hundred thousand, attained the level of awareness holders by practising together.

On his deathbed the Buddha prophesied that his teaching would spread north, and accordingly the teachings were discovered in Tibet, Land of Snows, by the Tibetan King Lhathori Nyanshul. At the time of King Songtsen Gampo, the Buddhist teachings became established in Tibet. They spread and flourished during the reign of Trisong Deutsen, who invited one hundred and eight Indian pundits to Tibet; foremost among these pundits were the Second Buddha Master Guru Rinpoche and Abbot Shantarakrhita. One hundred and eight emanated scholars worked together translating the teachings, and the lamp of their holy wisdom burned brightly.

Master Guru Rinpoche was an emanation of Buddha Amithaba who emanated a HRIH syllable from his heart to the Dhanagosha Lake in Oddiyana, where Guru Rinpoche was born. On Lake Dhanagosha, Guru Rinpoche appeared miraculously in the heart of a lotus, untainted by the sufferings of birth from the womb. He was adopted by the King of Oddiyana, but found a way of renouncing the throne and he practised yogic discipline in the eight great charnel grounds. As a result of these practices, Guru Rinpoche attained command over his lifespan and, as an all-conquering victor with miraculous powers, did marvellous deeds for the benefit of beings, staying in India for many years. When the time came, Guru Rinpoche travelled to Tibet and bound hostile spirits and local demons under oath, commanding them to serve the Dharma. Guru Rinpoche blessed many mountains and cliffs as places of practice, and concealed treasures of Buddhist teachings and other precious objects all over Tibet, so they would be rediscovered in time to come. He transmitted his doctrine to nine heart sons, the fortunate twenty-five disciples, including King Trisong Deutsen and his subjects, and many others, establishing all these students on the path of maturation and liberation.

Abbot Shantarakshita ordained the first monks in Tibet, who were known as the Seven to be Tested. Afterwards, many others took monastic vows, and the saffron-clad community and the Buddhist tradition of holy moral discipline were established. Thus the teachings of both the Sutra and Tantra spread.

In this way the precious teachings of the ancient Nyingma tradition were transmitted to Nyag Jnanakumara who had, among others, eight students with the name dPal. These and many others became accomplished. Secondly, the teaching passed onto Nubchen Sangyay Yeshe who had, among others, four students, holders of the intention. Thirdly, the doctrine passed onto Zurchen Shakya bYungnas, who had four senior students and many others. His student was Zurchen Shesrab Dragspa, who had students which included four main holders of the teachings, and eight supporters. Zurskro Phugpa Shakya Senge followed as lineage master who, among other students, had four named the Four Teachers and the famous Zur, Mes and dBon. Next in the succession of transmission was All-knowing Rongzompa Choki Zangpo. Then followed

All-knowing Longchenpa Drime Osal, who passed the lineage onto All-knowing Jigme Lingpa, whose students included the Four Jigmes. From these masters the realised transmission of the Ancient Nyingma lineage of secret Tantric teachings, oral transmissions and quintessential instructions, has continued unbroken to this day.

Among others, the Buddhist scholar from Zahor in Oddiyana, Paldan Mamemdzad, headed the precious Kadampa lineage. This passed to the great pundit Naropa, who had a heart son, or main disciple, Marpa Chokyi Lodro, who in turn taught four main holders of that tradition, principally Jetsun Milarepa, known as the Incomparably Profound and Great One. His main students included the Three Accomplished Ones from Kham, who continued the accomplished transmission of the lineage of realised practitioners, which became known as the Kargu Tradition.

From the great Indian Pundit Gayatara, the great translator Drokmi Lotsa and so on, through the Five Jamyang Gongmas, the realisation of the profound and expansive Glorious Sakya Tradition was transmitted.

Tsongkapa Lozang Dragpa, holder of the entire Sutra and Tantra teachings of the ancient and new traditions, and his students, propagated the Gelug tradition of the three sections of the Buddha's teachings; at this time masters, both scholarly and spiritually accomplished, became as numerous as stars in the night sky.

In this way, teaching and study of the holy Buddhist teachings spread throughout Tibet, Land of Snows. Thousands of monasteries were built, together with many Buddhist universities and meditation centres. The nine spiritual approaches which comprise the entire Buddhist teachings were maintained in their entirety, and integrated the approaches of both Sutra and Tantra. As the unmistaken, undeluded and unsullied teachings of the Buddha became established, Tibet became the great centre for study and practice of the Buddhist teachings.

At the present time, the Buddhist teachings have spread to many countries in the world, but in some places only the Hinayana or lesser spiritual approach is taught, without the Mahayana or greater spiritual approach. In other countries only the Mahayana spiritual approach is taught, without the secret Tantric teachings. There are places where both spiritual approaches are taught, but the continuity of teaching and guidance has been lost, leaving the teachings incomplete and useless, like locks without keys. These days, only the Tibetan Buddhist tradition maintains a complete and pure transmission of the Buddha's teachings. It is evident that in the course of Tibet's history, the teachings have prospered during some centuries and weakened during others, with periods of expansion and decline; however there still remains to this day an unbroken lineage of holy and unsullied Buddhist teachings, and this is due to the power of the positive karma of the beings of this world.

In addition, there are what are known as the 'Four Great Rivers of Transmission' of the secret teachings of the ancient Nyingma school of Tibetan Buddhism. The first Great River is that of common scriptural teaching, which includes explanations and summaries. The Second River is of maturing empowerment, which includes methods of giving empowerments and introduction. The Third River is of experiential advice, which includes expository instructions, and the Fourth River is of putting into practice various activities, which includes working with the protective deities of the teachings and with wrathful mantras. All these teachings are complete and unmistaken.

There are also three or six lineages within the Nyingma tradition.
The Three Lineages are:

1. Mind transmission of the Buddhas
2. Symbol lineage of awareness-holders
3. Hearing lineage of ordinary beings

In addition to the Three Lineages, the Six Lineages include the following:

4. Lineage of written yellow parchment
5. Entrusted prophetic lineage
6. Empowered aspiration lineage

Contained within these lineages are the profound instructions for attaining enlightenment in one lifetime in one body, and therefore they should be considered even more precious than a wish-fulfilling jewel.

Even countless wealth and possessions, gold and silver, emeralds and diamonds, are all like illusions, and are unable to bring us inner mental or emotional happiness and satisfaction, or happiness in our future lives. The happiness which we desire in this life is characterised as tainted, or unsatisfactory, and we need to distinguish the difference between the physical and mental aspects of this happiness; even if all our wealth can bring us physical happiness, it cannot bring us mental happiness.

Furthermore, wealth and riches cannot even prevent the fearful suffering of birth, old age, sickness and death.

Modern science allows travel to other planets, or has the power to bring massive destruction to our own planet in the blink of an eye; however modern science offers no method for attaining the everlasting happiness of liberation and enlightenment. The only thing in this world which is truly unique and has supreme value is the holy Buddhist teachings; specifically the teachings of the Tibetan tradition. Not only does the Tibetan tradition maintain the complete canon of Buddhist teachings, but it possesses the unique experiential methods of realising enlightenment.

Gaining a vague understanding of the teachings by reading a few books and then trying to practise will not bring any results. To gain results, it is necessary for us to have all the complete empowerments, oral transmissions, instructions, personal guidance and experience, plus the unimpaired blessings of the lineage. Being able to make contact with these is the result of previously accumulated karma; having met with these teachings before, the karmic tendency is revived and once again we find ourselves at the doorway of this tradition. Of this we can be certain.

If we think about it from a different perspective, the primary condition conducive to establishing happiness in this world is the Buddhist teachings. These days, we know how to make destructive biological and nuclear weapons and all the machinery of war, and at the same time, motivated by ferocious jealously and rivalry, many countries are competing to build and develop increasingly powerful and horrifying weapons, both openly and in secret. For this reason, hostilities and wars are endemic, like a recurring disease, which causes nothing but misery. Among all the things which bring happiness in the world, wherever we may search, the only lasting cure that can be found for this problem is the holy Buddhist teachings.

If all the people in the world, or even just our political leaders, cultivated in their mind streams the Four Immeasurable Attitudes and bodhichitta, then there would be no need for soldiers, weapons, or border controls, and the world would certainly become one peaceful happy family. Having said this however, even if the Buddha actually appeared in some individual being's karmically-conditioned experience, it would seem to those people as if the Buddha had no actual power at all.

If we turn our minds to the Buddhist teachings and, with the benefit of this human body complete with the eighteen freedoms and advantages which we have attained, take the essence of the freedoms and advantages to accomplish authentically the holy Buddhist teachings, then it would be like travelling to a land of jewels and gold; we would not return empty-handed.

If we do not prepare now to be unafraid when we die, time will not wait. If we leave it too late, then our delay will become the cause of profound regrets. What is known as the holy Buddhist teachings is like a cure for the disease of afflictive emotions. It is not enough to have medicine; if the patient does not take the medicine, it will be no use. In the same way, we cannot merely listen to the teachings, it is necessary for us to integrate them within our mind stream.

If we leave the negative characteristics of our personality unmodified and we leave the Buddhist teachings as words in books, then it would be like a soldier marching out to battle with the enemy and leaving his or her weapons at home. We are wandering like this in cyclic existence, suffering because we have been struck down by the demon of delusion, and we have come under the power of afflictive emotions. By recognising our afflictive emotions as our enemy, we should go into battle against them armed with all kinds of methods and ideas, and carrying remedial weapons. If we can beat this enemy, we will achieve a level of everlasting happiness. Having attained extraordinary attributes of realisation, we will be able to relieve the suffering of other beings, so we must develop firm determination without a second's delay.

What is known as the Buddhist teachings is the key instruction of how to take any suffering or pleasure onto the path, in order to experience the supreme bliss of what is known as our 'inner nectar'. By meditating on the teachings, the suffering of clinging to hopes and doubts will be reduced accordingly, and this in turn will reduce our experience of sickness and pain; one result of this is that we will create the opportunity to increase our lifespan. When the time does come for us to die, we will have made provision, and we will have already created the basis for no more suffering in the future.

Because we are pitiful creatures, the kindest thing we can do for ourselves at this time is to enter the unmistaken path of happiness. If we are lazy about doing so, in the future we will experience irreversible regret. It will be very hard to recover what we have lost, as difficult as it is to retrieve a lost arrow, fired at random from a bow into a thorny thicket.

First, the teachings of the Buddha were spread, at present they remain, and eventually they will be lost. It is said that the Buddhist teachings will remain for five thousand years, but that time is not yet over. Sakyamuni Buddha came to this world and taught three sections of teaching, in order that each would be understood according to the disposition and intelligence of the minds of the three types of being to be trained. The continuity of the Buddha's teachings is unbroken, and still remains in this world, particularly the great spiritual approach of the Mahayana, with complete teachings of unmistaken Sutra and Tantra.

Mahayana teachings spread from the place where the Buddha himself attained enlightenment, Bodhigaya in India, to the northern peaks of the Land of Snows. Today, the only place in this world which holds the complete transmission and practical experience of these teachings, is known as the Buddhist Land of Tibet. Tibet is completely covered from the central heartlands to the furthest borders by the precious Buddhist teaching of instruction and realisation, pure as a soft sheet of white satin, the foundation of happiness and comfort for all the nine kinds of beings.

Whether or not these teachings remain for a long time, or not, depends on the ordinary people who maintain them. Those practitioners living on the snow-mountain plateau, through teaching and practice, maintain, protect, increase and spread the Buddha's teachings of instruction and realisation, and are therefore precious jewels among all people.

Just consider: if all those of us who are afraid of dying, or afraid of the suffering which comes after death, who long for the bad circumstances and obstacles of this life to be mitigated, and who wish to become more and more happy in the future; suppose we were to put new shoes on our horse's hooves and spend our entire life searching in various religious temples in every country around the world, or ask a few million people where this wisdom can be found, we would not find a better place than Tibet, the roof of the world. Think of Tibet: an eastern highland, surrounded by a garland of white snow-mountains, where thousands of people have passed into the rainbow body, and inconceivable numbers of scholars and accomplished masters have lived.

From the treasury of the world's ancient and modern learning, the sole beneficial, lustrous jewel of this and future lives is the Tibetan Buddhist tradition, which I consider has come about due to the extraordinary merit of the beings of the world, together with the gods. At this time, it is not merely uneducated, unintelligent, illiterate and aged people in this world who have faith in Tibetan Buddhism; there are large groups of

Buddhists worldwide, who are young and well-educated and make up a significant percentage of the world's population. The number of Buddhists worldwide is spontaneously increasing every day, a new and unstoppable upsurge of faith.

If we investigate the reason for this, it is simply because everyone in the world longs for happiness and wishes to avoid unhappiness. Let us take an example: if we have to endure poor economic conditions, then we strive to make sure we have enough food and clothes; we try to stave off hunger and thirst, and do our best to keep warm. If we do have enough food, adequate clothing and possessions and a place to sleep, then we turn our attention to finding a way to make sure that the rest of our life, and the lives of our children and their descendants, our relatives and friends, will continue to be happy and enjoyable.

But even if we could suddenly achieve all the infallible predisposing conditions to enable us to do this, all our strenuous efforts would not be of the slightest use in creating happiness in our future lives. Not only that, if one person had control of all the wealth in the world, it would still not guarantee lasting heartfelt happiness for them. Moreover, infinite wealth has no power to take away the inevitability of dying. The suffering after death will not be mitigated; it must be faced.

However, one day, questions of happiness, and suffering after death, are bound to arise in everyone's mind, regardless of whether it is early or later in life, or the capability of our individual wisdom or powers of reasoning. At that time, we wake up completely from the sleep of ignorance and realise that we have wasted our life up to now in pursuing a mistaken path. We realise there is nothing other than the holy Buddhist teachings that can help us in our future life. In other words, we enter the door of the holy Buddhist teachings because of our own self-cherishing. The more we taste the holy Buddhist teachings, the more delicious they become. This is the only reason we engage with the teachings. If we were unwilling to do so and someone in authority forced us to comply, we might obey the instructions outwardly, but our hearts would remain closed.

Having become Buddhists, we learn that all beings have been our mothers in former lives, and so compassion arises within us, motivating us with the spontaneous desire to work for the benefit of others. When this happens, we look on other beings quite differently from the way in which we used to view them, and become more loving. From this turning point, we no longer cause harm to others and others cease to harm us.

We are respectful and considerate to others, open and honest in our actions, words and thoughts, with no hidden agenda, and others naturally respond to us with respect.

All those of us who are Buddhists train our mind streams in the sincere wish that all beings may be happy, and treat everyone with humanity and respect. Gradually, if the number of Buddhists increases, our society will become happy, and if there are enough people practising the genuine Buddhist teachings, then the sun of even greater comfort and happiness will rise everywhere.

However, at the same time, charlatans who are not actual Buddhists are sure to appear. In particular, in hundreds of years from now, or even in ten or twenty years' time, false Buddhists will come, people who appear to be Buddhist but are not. Tibetan Lamas, accomplished masters, and scholars claiming to be lineage students of such and such a master and lineage, will use fake names and a smattering of Buddhist words and terms. They will take a few ideas from other religions, and a few fake prophesies which make sense only to themselves, and mix up the whole lot. They will take the mere sounds of words and write all sorts of books, and be teachers of a wrong path, like an executioner who turns up without being summoned. They will wear incongruous costumes and sully the Buddhist teachings with their ignorant ways. It is inevitable that such people will arrive from both the eastern and western world, all nationalities including Tibetan, without any distinction of blonde or black hair.

The time between one generation and the next is an opportunity for renewal of the Buddhist teachings. In just the same way, a person's body needs to be kept pure, by maintaining healthy diet and conduct, and refraining from everything that may be unwholesome. These preparations are necessary in order to prevent harm occurring in the future. Similarly, we can consider the holy Buddhist tradition as a judge who will condemn false teachers and charlatans, thus preserving the purity of the teachings. This will benefit all races of people. Someone who undertakes this great task is a true holder of the Buddhist teachings, and is without doubt an emanation of the Buddha. I think doing this is of significantly more importance than, for example, investigating whether our planet may be in danger of hazards from other planets. It is even more important than protecting the local or global environment.

We are all heirs to the wealth of the unsullied holy teachings of the Buddha. If we do not protect the teachings, do not cherish them properly, or defend them from damage by blocking all threats, then false teachers will make a show of teaching solely in order to make money, and students will make a show of engaging in the main practices without first training their minds, or completing the preliminary practices. In the end, the secret Tantric teachings will become objects to be bought and sold. If this happens it will be the basis for the ruin of the teachings. Taking offence, the protectors of the teachings will cause treacherous conditions to prevail in this life, and those who commit the negative act of selling the teachings will create the karma of being roasted in the Hell of Unending Torment. Not only that, but lacking respect for the teachings will in itself cause the sun of the Buddha's teachings to set in this world. Better than accumulating this kind of karma would simply be to develop a kind heart and recite the mani mantra of compassion.

Future generations born in the great land of Tibet, the eastern roof of the world, have no need to feel inferior at being left behind by other industrialised nations. Our Tibetan ancestors achieved realisation and were highly learned; if past generations of Tibetans had turned their attention towards mundane achievements, Tibet would be as advanced as any nation in the world. However, on the contrary, real happiness does not result from material progress, it needs to be found within our hearts. Realising this, Tibetans have focused on practising the holy Buddhist teachings.

Tibetan Buddhism and culture is the cherished treasure passed down from generation to generation of Tibetan people, and it is the wealth of everyone in the world. Accordingly, there is no need for Tibetans from the Buddhist Land of Snows to be embarrassed in front of people who have nothing but material riches.

The maturing power of the holy Buddhist teachings is nectar of the mind for all beings who can grasp the concept that we all have at some time been each other's father or mother, brother or sister, dear to all creatures living in the harsh circumstances which surround us. The Buddhist teachings are the quintessential instructions for becoming more and more happy, now and in the future. The complete profound nectar of the Buddhist teachings is currently in the possession of those from the Land of Snows.

Safeguarding the teachings for this whole age is the personal responsibility, not only of Buddhists, but of all those who have faith in true compassion and wisdom. The fragrant perfume of this holy root should be wafted to the eight directions constantly and, at the same time, the Buddhist teachings should be reviewed regularly to make sure they remain pure and unsullied. This is the most important task which Buddhists of all nationalities must be sure to do; that is why I am repeating this crucial point.

If we begin to differentiate between the enormous crowds which comprise the whole human race dwelling under the sky above us, we see they are made up of individual people. If each individual behaved well, knew right from wrong, and thought kindly of others, then the entire population would become peaceful and relaxed. In the same way, what is known as the united spiritual community of holders of the Buddhist teachings, is also made up of groups of individuals; so, if each student of Buddhism, and each individual member of the spiritual community had in their mind stream the wealth of the complete realisation of the three trainings of our tradition, then the unsullied teachings of the Buddha would remain untainted and pure.

A long time ago in a distant land, there lived a fully-ordained monk, a hermit, who spent his time in meditation, and who depended on begging for sustenance. He had few needs, was content with what he had, and he was learned and wise in the Buddha's teachings. At that time, there lived nearby a householder, a lay follower of the Buddha, who had great faith in the teachings; he maintained the five ethical disciplines, and he made a promise to become the hermit's patron and provide for him so long as he lived. This patron prepared all kinds of food and took it to the hermit, so that he would not be disturbed in his practice or suffer from heat or cold on the way to fetch his provisions.

At the same time, in the same area, another faithful householder had a son who took vows of ordination from the hermit monk and practised as a novice, living with his teacher. It happened that one day the hermit's patron was so busy and distracted by everything he had to do that he forget all about the food. So the hermit sent his novice to fetch the provisions. The hermit told him to go to the town, to maintain proper conduct according to the Buddha's teachings, and not become attached to anything.

The novice monk went to the patron's house, but he was not at home. However, the patron's strikingly beautiful sixteen year old daughter was there, and she called to the novice to come inside. The young girl thought to herself, " Novices are supposed to be celibate... Now, what alluring tricks can I use to rouse his desire and seduce him...?" The novice monk was very circumspect in his conduct and did not respond to her at all. At last, still hoping to tempt him, the girl prostrated to the monk. "Take everything -" she begged, "- take all the myriad kinds of jewels, all the gold and silver in this house. It's a treasury as vast as the Buddha of Fortune has! I'll become your maid servant, I'll serve and worship you. You must fulfil my wish!"

The novice thought to himself: "What negative things have I done to be faced with a situation like this? I'll willingly give up my body and life, but I will not violate the vows of moral discipline which I have taken with the Buddhas of the three times. Desire torments this girl and because of this she has no modesty or shame... If I run away, she'll come after me. If she catches me, she'll claim that we're lovers and, if the people of the village see us together, they'll despise me. It would certainly be better if I end my life in this house - here and now."

So he said to the girl, "Close the door firmly, there's something I have to do. It won't take a moment, then you and I can be together." The girl closed the door and went away. In the meantime the novice monk went into the next room, removed his robes, knelt on the floor and put the palms of his hands together to pray. "I'm not abandoning the moral discipline of the Buddha, his teaching, the spiritual community, teachers, or masters. In order to maintain moral discipline, I'm going to abandon my body. Wherever I am born, may I be ordained as a monk of the Buddhist tradition. By maintaining pure conduct, may my defilements be exhausted, and may I attain enlightenment!" He finished this prayer and, without a moment's hesitation, pulled out a knife, slit his own throat, and passed away.

Aghast at what had happened, the girl was overcome with remorse. When her father, the lay follower of the Buddha, came home she explained truthfully everything that had occurred. He in turn told the king of that region and everyone was amazed; praising the novice's moral discipline, they made offerings to his remains. They sent word to the hermit and, when the master arrived, he taught the Buddhist teachings, and the entire family of the lay follower of the Buddha took vows of ordination. They aroused the unexcelled mind of enlightenment, and the whole kingdom rejoiced.

SIX

PEACEFUL AND COOL INNER NECTAR

What is known as 'nectar' is a kind of medicine which alleviates illness and prevents death. It exists through the merit of the gods in the heavenly realms and represents a supreme substance that brings a life free from death. Because of these corresponding effects, the term is also used to refer to the holy Buddhist teachings.

All external sufferings can be relieved by external objects. If the physical body's relationship between the four outer elements is out of balance, the elements will be disturbed, resulting in illness, which medical treatment and drugs have the power to cure. Sufferings of hunger, thirst, heat and cold can be remedied by the provision of food and drink, clothes and shelter.

However, the root of these sufferings comes from the inner mind. It is the disease of afflictive emotions disturbing the mind stream. The method used to correct and relieve this disease is to rely on the greatest medicine of all, the holy Buddhist teachings. There is no other cure apart from this, because the holy Buddhist teachings can free us from the disease of afflictive emotions, and have the power of achieving the level of ultimate happiness. Because of this, the teachings are known as the mind's 'inner nectar'.

What are the causes and conditions of our suffering? The cause, why we and all beings circle in the three realms of cyclic existence, is the 'ignorance of same identity'. The condition is our non-recognition of awareness which results in mistaken conceptualisation of the world. As a result of this we become controlled by our experiences, which are really nothing more than hallucinations, and which are all bound together in the noose of the three sufferings. This is like being held captive in a dark prison, or being exhausted by suffering from the feverish illness of the afflictive emotions. The holy Buddhist teachings are the profound way to escape from this prison. They are pacifying and cooling, a soothing cure for our inner fever, just as the medicine camphor is highly effective in relieving our outward feverishness.

The afflictive emotions of desire, anger, delusion, pride, jealousy and so on are like poison, and are the source of our unhappiness and discomfort. We can see how unwise it is to come under their influence. There is a valid argument which concludes all freedom is happiness and all subjugation is suffering. In my opinion this does not just apply to relationships between people. We can understand when we become dominated by negative emotions all kinds of suffering is created, not just in the short term, but in our future lives as well.

For example, when someone loses control and comes under the influence of desire, they steal others' money and possessions, corruptly squander government or public funds, accept bribes and so on, until the law catches up with them and they face prosecution. Or, through strong attachment, desire goads a person to commit unethical sexual acts or abuse. Through the power of this and other immoral actions, not only do we bring physical and mental suffering upon ourselves and others, but there are many who literally lose their heads or limbs as a result. If we allow our moral discipline to become lax, our physical bodies will suffer, our vitality will fade, and our physical integrity will be disturbed, causing us to suffer from illness which will eventually destroy our lives.

In the same way, if we lose control under the influence of anger, we blurt out criticism without stopping to think, and yell in fury, subjecting others to all sorts vilification, which causes meaningless quarrels and fights, violence, theft and even murder. In the end, this behaviour causes disaster for ourselves and others, and becomes the cause of great regret. Anger inflames and agitates our minds, and this turmoil is the cause of many illnesses, such as debility and depression. Even while we are congratulating ourselves on defeating those we consider our enemies, our actions have just the same effect on us, as if we stabbed our own living body with a sharp knife. The benefit of taking medicine for one year is destroyed by one day of anger.

Losing control under the influence of delusion, we become confused, no longer certain that we should undertake positive actions and abandon negative actions. Like an animal, we only know how to eat, sleep and defecate, and our life is completely wasted. We destroy all the good things of our life, now and in the future. Delusion brings on the development of all suffering; it is the beginning of disaster.

If we lose control and are possessed by pride, we are sarcastic and disrespectful to others. Except for our own bodies, eventually everyone and everything else becomes an enemy. We beckon forth all kinds of suffering, having many enemies and few friends. If, from our point of view, our vastly superior ego is slightly damaged, we experience all the more suffering from our wounded pride. We create the cause of this suffering ourselves, and we never enjoy a moment's pleasure.

If we come under the influence of jealousy, overtly or in our hearts, we are consumed by negative, abusive thoughts of scorn and envy towards others. If we put others down, it is natural they will put us down. If we criticise others, of course they will criticise us in return. When we consider the reflection in a mirror, if our face looks filthy it is not a fault of the mirror, it merely confirms it is our own fault. A jealous person is never satisfied and has no happy times. Jealousy causes suffering of body and mind, and the illness of an unhappy envious mind cannot be cured by medicine or any number of possessions.

If we come under the power of miserliness, there is never a time when we are convinced we have anything at all. Even if we became the sole owner of a whole mountain of gold, we still would not believe it was enough. As misers we always covet and desire more, even if we possess more clothes and food than we could possibly wear or eat. We are exhausted by the suffering of accumulating, protecting and worrying about losing our wealth; our human life passes, and after death we continue to exist as a tormented spirit. At the time of death we must go naked, empty-handed, without wealth or the Buddhist teachings. There is not a moment's perception of happiness in this life. We cannot be carefree during the day nor relaxed at night, and we experience suffering in body and mind.

Since beginingless time our mind has been stained by negative imprints of habits which are hard to break without continuous effort. When strong afflictive emotions arise, we should be on immediate guard and therefore able to resist their influence. It is important to think about situations in the distant past and repercussions in the long-term future, and use whatever methods we can to defeat the enemy of our afflictive emotions. If we are able to do this, it will prove to be the sole remedy for all our problems; medicine which can both cure and prevent our sickness. This great holy medicine that we use to guard our cherished and protected body is more efficacious than any other medicine, even if we searched every hospital worldwide, and consulted the world's most eminent specialists.

To summarise: afflictive emotions are mistaken feelings and are, unfortunately, deceptive. Not only do they cause suffering in our future lives, but afflictive emotions also attract all undesirable things in this life. Even if you do not believe in future lives, you are someone who believes in this life and wishes to take care of your body. To do so, you need to abandon afflictive emotions or at least resist succumbing to the influence of strong afflictive emotions.

Because we have been negatively habituated over a long period, first we need to develop strong determination without becoming discouraged by difficulties, and go to war with negative emotions. Up to now afflictive emotions have vanquished many people. If you do not have persistent confidence, you will also be vanquished.

The tradition of Tibetan medicine recognises afflictive emotions as the cause of disease. Desire causes disorders of the wind humour. Anger causes bile humour disorders, and delusion brings about disorders of the phlegm humour. The three poisons of afflictive emotions are the root of all the different types of disease and cause imbalance of the three humours, wind, bile and phlegm.

The wind humour is located at waist level and pervades the lower body. The bile humour is located in the liver and gall bladder and pervades the middle body. The phlegm humour is located in the brain and pervades the upper body. When the levels of these humours increase or decrease they are transmitted through the skin, flesh, the body's channels, bones, the five vital organs, the six hollow organs, and so on. There are four hundred and twenty-five divisions of disease, which can be summarised as either hot or cold. There are five kinds of wind: life-sustaining, ascending, descending, pervading, and fire-accompanying. Five kinds of bile: digestive and metabolic, colour-regulating, accomplishing, sight-giving and complexion-clearing. As for phlegm, there are also five types: supportive, decomposing, experiencing, satisfying and connective.

Bodily constituents are seven in total: nutritional essence, blood, flesh, fat, bone, marrow and regenerative fluid. Together with excreta, urine and menses, they comprise the twenty-five bodily constituents. When the taste, potency and activity of these remain in balance, body strength increases, the skin appears healthy and regeneration and growth occur. If this is not the case and the constituents are not in balance, they become destructive and we experience suffering and terrible pain, and eventually, if one of the nine deadly diseases develops, our life ends.

The cause of the nine deadly diseases is primarily the afflictive emotions. Whichever afflictive emotion is the strongest, it results in the development of the characteristic disease. Therefore the three root afflictive emotions are called the 'three poisons'.

Not only do afflictive emotions destroy the comfort and happiness of this life, but also they generate the unbearable suffering of the lower states of rebirth in the future. We know who is a good or bad student of the Buddhist teachings when we encounter the enemy of afflictive emotions. If you are able to prevent yourself succumbing to the influence of afflictive emotions, by using the many paths of skilful means to overcome them, or by actually turning afflictive emotions into the path, illness and the pain of suffering will be reduced and your body will become healthy. When we are healthy we feel happy. When we are happy we experience less sickness. When we are free of illness our life will be long. When we have little desire and know when we have enough, all our wishes are inherently fulfilled.

The aspiration to have a long life and accomplish all our wishes is the summit of human happiness. It follows that an individual with such aspirations will naturally adopt the behaviour of the most noble class of persons. Someone with this kind of noble conduct will refrain from doing anything which harms others. Because they can recognise that such people refrain from harmful actions, all living beings will like and trust them. It is said it is supremely virtuous if someone is liked by everyone, and abandoning negative actions is the greatest of merits.

When we refrain from negative actions and perform positive actions, our minds do not come under the influence of afflictive emotions; this destroys the enemy of afflictive emotions which have been co-emergent with mind since beginningless time. Alternatively, subduing our minds is what is known as the Buddha's teaching of 'mental discipline', and is itself the essence of Buddhist teaching.

Not allowing our minds to be disturbed by afflictive emotions and remaining calm is the most supreme inner medicine which produces physical and mental happiness. If there is a path, or means of generating extraordinary happiness of body and mind for the time being and ultimately, then we should follow that path, whoever taught it, regardless of whether or not it was the Buddha. Generating happiness benefits us both physically and mentally.

All living beings are busy running around, chasing happiness. Having found a path of happiness for myself, it is not sufficient that that only I am happy. Just think if my family members, relatives and friends could achieve happiness like this! In the same way, reasoning step by step, all living beings do not want suffering and they are all the same in wanting happiness. Like me, they long for happiness, but do not know how to bring about its cause. In ignorance, through the power of delusion, we are all the same, running around in confusion. How pitiful!

We think, "Wouldn't it be wonderful if everyone could find a path to happiness?" When this thought arises it echoes the Buddha's holy teachings, and so we naturally find ourselves on the path the Buddha taught. In this way, however we think about it, if we take as a starting point the assertion that all beings desire happiness, it is clear that there is no better path of skilful means to achieve happiness than the holy teachings of the Buddha.

Long ago, when the Buddha was on the earth, in a certain region of India there was a king who ruled his kingdom as a tyrant, caring nothing for the well-being of his people. The elephant that the king rode killed countless people, crushing them underfoot at every step. All the people of the kingdom became very unhappy and fearful. At that time, five hundred girls from the kingdom's highest caste became disillusioned with cyclic existence, abandoned their families and took nuns' vows.

Not long after they were ordained, they visited the fully-ordained nun named Utpalavarna. The girls told Utpalavarna, "When we were living at home we were distracted by the constant round of daily tasks. We've taken nuns' vows, but we can't free ourselves from the influence of the afflictive emotion of desire. Out of compassion for us, please give us a Buddhist teaching so we may learn how to become repulsed by desire."

So the five hundred nuns made their request, and Utpalavarna taught them as follows:

> "Desire is like fire, it burns the mind. Through the influence of this burning mind, one person can only harm another. The result of this is that we fall to the lower states of rebirth where there is never any escape. The house we live in there is like a prison.
>
> Learn from my story:

89

I was born into a high caste and was given as a wife to the son of a family of similar caste; we had a son. Later I became pregnant again and my husband and I set out with our little son to make the journey to my parent's house. Half way there I felt discomfort in my womb, so that evening we camped by a tree. At midnight I gave birth to another son. My husband slept in a different place. He was bitten by a poisonous snake and died. The next day, when I found his body, I collapsed and fainted. When I regained consciousness, anxious to reach my parents' house, I carried my elder son on my back and held my small baby in my arms and struggled along, crying, unable to find anyone to help me on my journey.

A little further on was a large river which we had to cross. I couldn't carry both boys across the river together, so I left my elder son on the near bank. I carried my little one across the river and went back for the elder one. My son saw his mother coming and jumped into the river. He was carried away by the current and drowned. When I turned back, I saw my baby had been eaten by a wolf and only a little blood was left behind. I fell to my knees in a faint.

After a long while, I regained consciousness and struggled on. In a place not far from my parent's house I met an old acquaintance and asked after them. The neighbour told me, "Your parents' house caught fire and they and the whole household burned to death." Hearing this news, I was overcome. The neighbour picked me up, took me home and was kind to me.

Later, I became the wife of someone of equal caste. Living with him, I again became pregnant with a sentient being. I carried my baby to term and, while my husband was out celebrating with his friends, I gave birth. All at once my husband returned drunk. I was unable to get up and there was no one to open the door so he got angry. He broke down the door, came in and beat me. I told him I had given birth but it was no use, and he killed my baby boy, cooked him in butter and forced me to eat him.

I was devastated. I left my husband and escaped to a distant place. On the way I met a young man sitting under a tree. He told me his wife had just died. He had buried her corpse in a grave and was mourning in misery. I spoke with him and later on became his wife. Not long after that he fell ill and died. According to the religion of that land, a wife must be buried alive with her husband's body, and so I was interred.

That evening a gang of grave robbers arrived, dug up the grave and discovered me. The gang leader forced me to become his wife. Not long after that, the king caught the grave robbers' leader and killed him, and once again I was buried alive with a corpse. After three days a wolf dug up the grave and so I escaped. I was utterly distraught and I realised that there is no meaning in cyclic existence. I decided I must turn to the Buddha for refuge, and journeyed to the place where he was staying.

The Buddha knew the time had come to train me and he came out to welcome me. I was naked and so embarrassed that I covered my breasts and crouched on the ground. The Buddha instructed his disciple Ananda to give me something to wear. I put on the clothes I was given, and prostrated at the Buddha's feet, praying to become ordained. The Buddha handed me over to his aunt, the nun Prajapati, and I became ordained. As soon as I heard the Buddhist teachings I practised them earnestly, with great diligence. I attained the result of a Foe Destroyer and realised everything knowable of the three times."

The nuns then asked Utpalavarna about the karmic cause of her terrible experiences. Utpalavarna taught the following:

"In a time gone by a there was an extremely rich householder who had two wives. The younger one gave birth to a son. The older one became jealous and stuck a needle into the soft spot of the child's cranium killing him. When the mother cried, "You killed my son!" the jealous wife went mad, vowing, "If I did kill your son, may my husband be killed by a poisonous snake in every one of my lifetimes. If I have sons, may they be carried away by water and eaten by wolves. May I be buried alive repeatedly, and may I eat my son's flesh. May the home of my parents catch fire and they burn to death!"

I was the jealous wife. In this body I experienced the fully ripened karmic result of killing the baby and swearing the false oath. The cause for the Buddha kindly coming to welcome me, and the cause which later enabled me to achieve realisation is as follows:

Once long ago I took rebirth as the wife of a householder, and when a solitary-realised Buddha came begging for sustenance, this householder's wife had great faith, and offered him provisions. The solitary-realised Buddha demonstrated all kinds of magical powers, and the householder's wife, as I was then, made a prayer of aspiration: "In the future may I too achieve enlightened qualities like this." In this way I achieved the result of the completely liberated mind of a Foe Destroyer."

After listening to Utpalavarna's teaching, the torture of desire was completely exhausted in the five hundred nuns; they meditated and actually achieved the result of Foe Destroyers.

The perfect Buddha is skilful and has great compassion; he taught the remedy for the eighty-four thousand afflictive emotions: the eighty-four thousand collections of spiritual teachings. The root of all these afflictive emotions is the three poisons. It is for this reason that the Buddha taught the eighty-four thousand collections of teachings are also rooted in the three or four compilations of teachings.

The subduing remedy for the afflictive emotion of desire is taught in the collection on moral discipline, in twenty-one thousand teachings. The subduing remedy for the afflictive emotion of anger is taught in the collection of Sutra teachings, in twenty-one thousand teachings. The subduing remedy for the afflictive emotion of delusion is taught in the collection on manifest knowledge, in twenty-one thousand teachings. The subduing remedy for all three poisons is taught in the collection on secret Tantra, in twenty-one thousand teachings.

The subject matter of these is the three trainings of discipline, concentration and discriminating knowledge. These three trainings contain all paths of Sutra and Tantra. What is known as the holy Buddhist teaching combines teaching and realisation. Teaching comprises the three collections of teaching, and realisation comprises the three trainings.

First we need to study the Buddha's teachings together with the commentaries that clarify them, written by his highly learned followers. We should always be looking for more materials and opportunities to study. Having done that, we should analyse and contemplate on what we have studied. Finally, we need to apply what we have concluded through contemplation in our meditation. This process may be compared to a flight of steps which we have to climb from the bottom up. Additionally, we need to take the vows of individual liberation. There are eight kinds of vows for individual liberation:

* One day vow
* Layman
* Laywoman
* Female candidate (for ordination)
* Male novice monk
* Female novice nun
* Fully ordained monk
* Fully ordained nun

If we keep these vows with the extraordinary mind of bodhichitta focusing on benefiting all sentient beings, the vows will become those of the Mahayana spiritual approach. We take the vows of individual liberation with the mind of disillusionment with regard to cyclic existence, and we study and learn the teachings of the Hinayana followers. Then we need to take the vows of bodhichitta in a ritual. There are two lineages of these vows. The Tradition of Vast Activity was transmitted from Lord Maitreya to Asanga, and the Tradition of the Profound View was transmitted from Lord Maitreya to Nagajuna. It is appropriate to take vows in either of these traditions.

After that, we should study the teachings of the Middle Way, which determine the absence of self of beings and phenomena. Then we need to receive empowerment into the unexcelled secret Tantric teachings and study the resultant secret Tantric teachings. We should take these teachings as our own path, and put them into practice by developing great diligence in order to make manifest the enlightened qualities of realisation, and to understand what it is we must abandon.

If we talk in terms of the stages of Sutra and Tantra, first we practice Sutra, then Tantra. What we refer to as Sutra or Tantra, or the greater or lesser spiritual approaches - Mahayana or Hinayana - should not be regarded as separate or different. For example, the ages of a child and an adult are not the same, and for this reason the amount of physical strength they posses is also different. If a child and adult have the same illness, they are prescribed different doses of medicine. The method of physical treatment varies, and so needs to be adjusted to suit the individual's own requirements.

In the same way, people's minds are different, so accordingly the Buddha taught various spiritual approaches. Moreover, we need to know that all these approaches are unmistaken paths to enlightenment for us. If we are not sure of this, and take whichever path we happen to encounter, we will be like a lost traveller and lose sight of our destination. How then will we recognise the signs which mark our progress towards enlightenment? Therefore it is crucial to find the right path.

At first, the most important thing a follower of the Mahayana must aim towards is for themselves and others to reach the level of enlightenment. The chief cause of realising enlightenment is the arousal of bodhichitta, the fusion of wisdom and compassion; this is known as the 'precious mind of enlightenment', because all the omniscient enlightened wisdom of the Buddha comes from the root of compassion. Bodhichitta is the cause as well as the method which leads to achieving the perfect goal of enlightenment.

This mind of bodhichitta develops when we perceive that suffering is the nature of cyclic existence. The knowledge that there is not one being in samsara who at some time has not been our mother or father, and that when they were our parents they were as kind to us as our parents of this life, also helps us to generate bodhichitta. If we were to achieve liberation for ourselves alone and leave these beings behind, that would be a shameful and ignoble thing to do. With the thought of repaying their kindness, we should meditate on the love that wants them to be happy, and the compassion that desires them to be liberated from suffering.

If we do not develop in our mind stream pure bodhichitta, whichever amazing path we meditate on will be nothing more than a lion puffed up with pride, or a picture traced in the dark with a moving flame, a mere reflection; such a path will not become an authentic path.

If we want to enter the door of the holy Buddhist teachings, we need to develop in our minds renunciation, bodhichitta and the pure view. We need to accumulate the two collections of merit and wisdom, take the three trainings as the foundation, make the promise of the four immeasurables, and engage continuously in the practice of the ten positive actions and the six transcendent perfections. By doing this we will actually achieve liberation in this present body, attain the level of unexcelled perfect buddhahood, finally prostrate farewell to the filthy mire of cyclic existence, and attain eternal supreme blissful peace.

94

SEVEN

APPROACHING THE DOOR OF ETERNAL BLISS

Throughout beginingless cyclic existence until now, we have been distracted by the unachievable overload of mundane activity; everything we do is like last night's dream, a continuous flow of mere illusions, which can never be grasped or completed.

If you ask yourself the question: "Who am I?" The name given to you by your parents, or others, is not you. Your body is a collection of atoms, comprised of flesh, blood and bone, a mere vessel, like a clay pot. If you dissect your body, you find nothing that can be called 'me'. At this moment, your mind is also something illusory. Your mind resides in a human body, and accordingly has human perceptions, quite different from the mind you would have possessed if you were a dog in a previous life. In a future life, if you take rebirth as a snake, again your mind will not be the same. For this reason there is nothing certain that can be called 'me'. Neither is there any way to label 'me' the continuum of the basis where tendencies are imprinted. In our search for mind, we are unable to find anything possessing attributes, shape or colour, for example.

Since this is the case, through the influence of delusion, the object of our grasping at self, which we name 'me', does not go beyond the confines of body, speech and mind. Our body is like a servant. Our speech is like messenger. Mind is like a king; so if mind is able to enter an unmistaken path without delusion, then naturally body and speech will follow.

From this we can deduce that this self-grasping enemy holding on to an 'I' initiates the beginning of delusion and the experience of suffering. Turning our multifarious mind to contemplation of the Buddhist teachings, gradually the basis of delusions, holding the notion of a self, will subside. In order to do this, how are we first to enter the great door of the Buddhist teachings?

The teachings consist of a path which leads to cessation. The Truth of Cessation is the truth of passing beyond suffering. The Truth of the Path is a path which can be followed to pass beyond suffering. In order to achieve the realisation of the teachings, first we need to initiate the cause in order to attain the result. The holy Buddhist teachings need to be taught by a learned spiritual mentor. The first door of interdependent connection, which we must open, is that of paying respect and honour to the holy teachings and their teacher.

When it comes to studying the teachings, we should not study with the wish for material benefit or to gain worldly protection. We should do so by embracing the Three Supreme Methods. What are the Three Supreme Methods?

The first is the method of taking hold of the root of virtue by arousing the excellent beginning of the mind of enlightenment, or bodhichitta. This is generating the motivation to separate all sentient beings from the cause and result of suffering and establish them in perfect enlightenment, which is free from the two extremes. To do this, the thought of teaching and studying the holy Buddhist teachings is like a hook, the virtuous root is like a bundle of grass which we grasp firmly with the hook.

Second, in order to prevent the virtuous root from being destroyed by adverse conditions, we practise the Second Supreme Method, the excellent main part, without conceptualisation. We need to realise the view of the ground, the path and the result: the *ground* of the Great Middle Way, the *path* of the Great Seal (Mahamudra), and the *result* of the Great Perfection (Dzogchen). However, a new practitioner may start by formulating a concept approximating this view. To do this we need to develop the certainty that everything we see is apparent but without any self-nature, like an illusion, a dream, a mirage, or the reflection of the moon in water. When we are listening, meditating and practising the holy teachings we should focus our body, speech and mind all together.

Thirdly, in order for the root of virtue to increase more and more, we practise the Third Supreme Method, the excellent conclusion of dedication. Having completed a positive action, it is important for us to dedicate the merit quickly for the sake of others so they may attain perfect enlightenment; otherwise, once we have experienced the happy result, the merit will become exhausted. Merit accumulated over a great aeon will be destroyed in a moment's anger. Dedication prevents the merit from being destroyed by, for example, regretting the meritorious action, or showing off about being virtuous, and dedication also prevents the merit from being exhausted.

For this reason we need to have the mind that realises emptiness and sees the three-fold set, which consists of oneself, the practice and the action of practising, as inherently non-existent. Uniting this mind with the compassion and love of bodhichitta, we recite prayers of dedication and aspiration. When this is recognised as the correct view, the three-fold set is completely pure, and so this dedication is known as the 'dedication free from poison'.

Until we have realised emptiness, we may practise the approximate equivalent of this dedication by combining all the root virtues which we have accumulated in the three times, and all the undefiled virtue of the Buddhas and their spiritual children, together with the defiled virtue of sentient beings, into one. Then, for the sake of all beings, in order that they may attain the level of perfect buddhahood, we dedicate with our mind using the same method the Buddhas and their spiritual children used, in the manner of their utterly pure three-fold set. These Three Supreme Methods are cherished as vitally important by those of us who have embarked on the Mahayana spiritual approach and are striving for liberation.

The vast *motivation* of bodhichitta is to bring supreme benefit to all beings and has two purposes or aspects: wishing for *all* beings to *attain* buddhahood. It is with this motivation we arouse the supreme mind of bodhichitta.

The vast *means* of secret Tantric motivation is practised when we are receiving and studying Buddhist teachings on the secret Tantric approach of indestructible reality. We visualise the place, time, teacher, gathering and teaching as the excellent Five Perfections. It is said: "If we see the Lama as an ordinary person, accomplishments do not come from a dog"; so of all the Five Perfections, the most important is to see the teacher as enlightened. This is because the mind of the teacher is vast enlightened wisdom, the dharmakaya. The display of this enlightened wisdom is the form body of the Buddha, the rupakaya, and these two in inseparable unison are the vajrakaya.

This source of refuge has the nature of the three vajras: vajra body, vajra speech and vajra mind, and has all of the following nine attributes:

> Apparent and yet empty indestructible vajra body.
> Audible and yet empty indestructible vajra speech.
> Fully recollective and realised indestructible vajra mind.

Whether we realise it or not, we all have the essence of enlightenment. Therefore we possess the capability of realising enlightenment, and are able to attain the result. For this reason we visualise the whole assembly of students attending teachings as heroes and dakinis. This is the perfect gathering.

It is impossible for a teacher and an assembly who have achieved twofold purity to gather in a place which is not pure. Therefore, we should visualise the place as the supreme pure realm of Akanishtha, gorgeously arrayed, or another such pure realm. The perfect teaching is that of luminous Great Perfection, the highest of all teachings. The perfect time is the ever-revolving wheel of eternity. We need to understand through contemplation that everything in existence is pure primordially, and meditate with total focus.

Together with this motivation, we should practise right conduct. Right conduct includes three things we should abandon. The first of these is the three incorrect ways of listening to teachings, known as the Three Defects of the Pot:

> 1. If we do not listen attentively, we are like a pot turned upside-down. If water is poured onto an upside-down pot, no water goes inside. In the same way, if our ears are closed we will not hear anything that is taught, so we need to focus our sense of hearing and listen.

> 2. If we do not remember what we have been taught, we are like a pot with a hole in the base. However much water we pour in, none remains inside. If we are like this we will not understand the words or the meaning of the teachings, so we need to remember in our hearts both words and meaning.

> 3. If we mix the teachings with afflictive emotions, it is like putting good food into a pot containing poison; however much food we put in, it will all become poisonous. In this way when we receive teachings they do not remedy our afflictive emotions, but bolster them by making us feel proud, for example, so we need to avoid mixing up our negative emotions with the teachings and remember them correctly.

The Six Stains that we need to abandon are pride, lack of trust or faith, lack of effort, outward distraction, focusing inward and weariness.

We should also abandon the Five Wrong Ways of Remembering:

1. Remembering the words but not the meaning.
2. Remembering the meaning but not the words.
3. Remembering without understanding.
4. Remembering wrongly.
5. Remembering in the wrong order.

The Four Metaphors describe the reason why we should practise right conduct:

Think of yourself as sick.
The Buddhist teachings are medicine.
The teacher is a skilful doctor.
Diligent practice is the way to recovery.

Also, when we listen to the teachings we should practise the Six Transcendent Perfections. In this way, teaching or listening to the teachings has inconceivable benefit. The Buddha taught that if an animal so much as hears the sound of a conch shell summoning people to Dharma teachings, that animal will be liberated from rebirth in the lower states of existence. If this is true for an animal, if we have a share of the teachings and listen to them, contemplate their meaning and practise them in the correct way, then needless to say we possess the most supreme good fortune and have found the best thing that can ever be found.

A student of the Buddhist teachings cannot just simply call themselves a practitioner. We cannot go around saying, "I have faith in the Buddhist teachings". Just having other people accept the name and think we are Buddhists is no use at all in overcoming our obscurations, developing wisdom, or achieving the result.

To engage in genuine practice of the Buddhist teachings, at the highest level, with the wisdom that has realised selflessness, we need to root out and destroy self-grasping. We need to master the ultimate wisdom of the union of the Two Truths, which is the essence of emptiness and compassion, the result of which is the attainment of the two enlightened bodies. In order to do this it is necessary for us to complete the causal accumulations of merit and wisdom; and first it is important for us to develop faith and confidence in the teachings. For example, if we plant a burnt seed it cannot sprout a green shoot. In this way, someone without faith cannot give birth to the shoot of bodhichitta, or manifest the virtuous qualities of the teachings.

The Buddha taught:

"Through faith, realise the ultimate."

There are three kinds of faith:

* Faith based on awe
* Longing faith
* Faith based on conviction

FAITH BASED ON AWE

Faith based on awe involves having delight in our heart regarding the teacher and the Three Jewels, and wanting to engage with them. We have deep confidence in the enlightened qualities of those above us, without the stain of hypocrisy, and are delighted and clear about it. Faith based on awe is an undeniable feeling, like the sheer delight a young child experiences when meeting its mother.

LONGING FAITH

When we understand that, by casting aside cyclic existence and going beyond suffering, ultimate bliss can be attained, we feel an eager longing to practise the teachings. We understand the united and inseparable supreme quality of the perfection of relative perceptions and the perfection of ultimate wisdom, and so we practise in the correct manner, without becoming confused about what to take up and what to abandon. We should practise single-mindedly, like an entrepreneur totally focussed on acquiring wealth.

FAITH BASED ON CONVICTION

To know that the words and meaning of the Buddha's teachings and logic are unmistaken, and to have no doubt about the meaning of the teachings of the ground, path and result is known as faith based on conviction. Faith based on conviction drives our practice. For example, convinced that in autumn the harvest will yield good crops, we work very hard preparing the soil and planting seeds in the spring.

The first, second and third kinds of faith demonstrate a progressively greater understanding of the Buddhist teachings.

The benefits of having genuine faith are as follows:

* Faith is fertile soil in which the positive seed of the shoot of bodhichitta grows.
* Faith is like a sailing ship by means of which we may cross the perilous ocean of samsara.
* Faith is like a good bodyguard who will protect us from the enemy of afflictive emotions.
* Faith is like a good horse which will convey us to the land of liberation.
* Faith is like a wish-fulfilling jewel providing everything we desire.
* Faith is like a hero who will conquer the army of negativities.

Even if we have other positive qualities, without faith we are like an attractive person without any eyes. At first, generating faith is the basis for developing understanding of the holy Buddhist teachings. In this way, within a relatively short time, faith aids us in attaining the Buddha's wisdom.

In the beginning, faith engages us with a spiritual mentor who shows us the way, and from whom we learn. In the middle, faith searches out the holy teachings to study and, through contemplation and meditation, determines their meaning. In the end, faith accomplishes the holy, purified and accomplished result of enlightened wisdom.

So, because students need to be established on the path to liberation, just as we need to rely on an experienced captain when setting out on a sea voyage, our task is to find an unmistaken guide, and to actualise the ultimate level of realisation. Therefore we rely on the teacher with faith and trust.

With the eyes of faith, we look upon the three supports: images, scriptures and stupas. At the beginning, from prostrating, circumambulating, gathering the accumulations and purifying obscurations, up to eventual meditation on the advanced path, we must not, with foolish or ignorant faith, stray in any old direction that others recommend.

Beginning with our own desire to know, through the door of our own understanding, developed through investigation and examination, we will finally gain faith based on firm conviction.

Finding a protector is of the greatest significance and immense importance, one hundred times more advantageous than finding the legendary wish-fulfilling jewel. It is difficult to find the undeceiving, the supreme, but if we do so it will be very meaningful, and all this life's aims will be accomplished without hindrance.

All the causes and results of cyclic existence and enlightenment beyond suffering are contained within the Buddha's teaching on the Four Noble Truths:

> Suffering, its source, its cessation,
> and the path leading to the cessation of suffering.

It is said: "If we don't consume poison, sickness won't occur." In the same way, if the causal afflictive emotions and karma do not arise, then the resultant suffering of the three realms of cyclic existence will not come about. Through actualising the causal truth of the path, the resultant inexorable wisdom of enlightenment beyond suffering will manifest.

There are many ways of approaching the door of eternal bliss. Because they experience the suffering of the three miserable realms of existence, and their minds desire liberation from this suffering, people with modest spiritual aspirations abandon the ten negative actions and practise the ten positive actions. These people concentrate on the mundane path of meditation, and attain the level of the higher realms, the realms of gods and humans, thus escaping for the time being the miserable states of existence. This is one approach.

People with average spiritual aspirations understand the suffering of the six types of beings in cyclic existence. Knowing this, they practise moral conduct, controlling their minds and focusing on the determination to be free. They train in the mundane path of concentration meditation. Also, by removing the obscurations of afflictive emotions, such practitioners remove the obscuration which prevents realisation of the non-existence of personal identity, and part of the obscuration concerning the nature of reality. Because of this they realise, to a certain degree, the non-existence of phenomena and, as a result, they actualise the level of a Foe Destroyer. This approach just manages to attain liberation.

Great-hearted people, or those of great intellect, reject both extremes, neither suffering in cyclic existence nor individually residing in Nirvanic peace beyond suffering. Knowing how to remove the obscurations of karma, afflictive emotions and cognition, including habitual tendencies, such practitioners gain the result of the truth of the path, ultimate truth, the wisdom of the realisation of the two types of selflessness, and attain the enlightened dharmakaya. This is the unmistaken path.

The cause from which the suffering of cyclic existence is generated, and the enemy which destroys the seed of liberation, is all-pervasive karma and afflictive emotions, the root of which is misconstruing an existent self. The actual remedy is the transcendent wisdom which realises the non-existence of self. If we practise this, it is as if we kill off the illusionist, and so all the conjured illusions of cyclic existence are naturally destroyed.

Even more supreme than the approach of the Sutras is the peak of all spiritual approaches, Dzogchen Great Perfection, unembellished Ati, which nurtures the nature of primordial purity, without reinforcing our conceptualisation with thought. From the expanse of basic freedom wisdom, the obscurations of karma, afflictive emotions and cognition, including habitual tendencies, are overcome and the practitioner actually attains in this body the enlightened dharmakaya. This is the most supreme approach.

These four approaches work at different speeds. The long path is like crawling. The short path is like walking. The quick path is like driving, and the very fast path is like flying.

EIGHT

CONJUROR OF TRANSIENT ILLUSIONS

The sense organs of the eyes, ears, nose, tongue, body and mind which we possess perceive forms, sounds, smells, tastes, feelings, and so on. These are all transient phenomena and subject to disintegration. All forms of this human world are produced by the mighty elements and are therefore transient; even the elements themselves have the nature of growth, increase and disintegration. The great earth itself is merely a collection of atoms in essence. High cliffs with their towering peaks appear firm and solid. Great oceans, lakes and pools, rich in natural resources, all these will reach a time of disintegration. In the same way, the sun and moon, the planets of our solar system, and all the stars in the universe without exception will disintegrate.

How do we know that everything will disintegrate? The reason we are able to predict this disintegration is because originally all things formed. There is not one thing which, having formed does not disintegrate, or having been born does not die. Not only does something first come into existence and eventually cease to exist, but an object does not remain, even from one moment to the next, without undergoing change. Our own body undergoes great change from the time we are babies to when we are old. It is not as if one day we suddenly find ourselves old; many moments of time connect to create a gradual change. Not only have a few moments of our lives passed by while I have been saying these words, but also we have all taken another step towards the door of the City of the Dead.

Our bodies of flesh and blood cannot bear even the slightest feeling of heat or cold. If we merely prick our skin, a wound appears. Put our bodies under the slightest pressure and they break. Under traction, our joints come apart. Even if we do not do anything, the elements which comprise our bodies eventually become our inner enemies, and we die. The point when one breath is released and another cannot be taken separates life and death. Not only are the bodies of wandering beings fragile, but in the time it takes to click our fingers even rocks, mountains, and our whole environment, as we considered just now, move closer to disintegration.

Every form we see with our eyes, whether small or large, is impermanent. At the same time, the body of the conceived object which we label 'I', is impermanent. All the sounds we hear, sense objects of the ears, are the same as echoes. In fact, there is not one single phenomenon, whether it is sight, smell, taste, or physical sensation that is solid, stable, or firm. Not only that, but there is not one moment of consciousness of a subject which is authentic. For this reason, all the suffering and pleasure of our human lives is like last night's dream; when we awake there is nothing. Everything consists of deceptive phenomena.

Let us consider that we are travelling companions making for the same destination. We have ended up completely lost and the road ahead leads straight into the lair of a ferocious wild animal. If we imagine a death like that, lying in wait for us, do we dare continue to waste our time in reckless sloth?

Now, to demonstrate impermanence, I would like to give an example I have experienced physically myself. When I was a child I was slim, with large sparkling eyes and high symmetrical cheekbones. I grew up to have great physical strength, and in height I was neither too tall nor too short. My face was round and rosy, with two even rows of pearl-white teeth. My eyes smiled as brightly as the beautiful Morning Star. I became impressively handsome and whoever saw me wished they looked like me. Suddenly, totally unexpectedly, all this was destroyed.

In the year of 1982, in the last month of autumn, I had undertaken to travel to India for the benefit of the teachings of Dzogchen Monastery. On the way, I suddenly encountered negative conditions, and in a moment this particular physical form was changed utterly. It became disgusting and frightful, saddening to hear of and terrifying to behold, a shattered human body. The body that my loving mother cherished and protected more than her own life, and which, in their humility, the local and monastic community only occasionally permitted themselves to see, was damaged irrevocably for life.

On the rocky foothills of the white snow-mountain which pierces the azure sky, a smoke offering was made, and the smoke curled skywards like a turquoise dragon. Strings of multicoloured prayer flags, with the sky-blue of my elemental association as the chief colour, were hung on the mountain top's narrow peak, accompanied by victorious shouts and three clockwise circumambulations. As countless sheets of paper wind horses in the five colours were thrown into the sky, a white cloud blown from the east veered onto a southerly path, at the end of which a small vulture soared, flapping its wings. As I watched, I remembered my feelings of joy and sadness at the scenes of past events. I made a vow in my heart, with indestructible and unwavering determination, to complete the work of a brave hero.

Calling to the Victorious One, together with his Enlightened Children, to bear witness to me, whole-heartedly I took the vows of precious bodhichitta. I called upon the Buddhas of the ten directions, of the four times, the forces of positive deities, the auspicious deities and protectoresses for help. And then, in a small Beijing Jeep, together with a driver and several travelling companions, I departed, and we traversed winding trails, steep precipitous abysses and bridges over great rivers at top speed.

On the second day of this journey, in the twilight of dawn, as we were bouncing over the uneven roads, we came upon a black-faced girl by the side of the road carrying an empty water bucket on her back. According to Tibetan custom, if travellers pass an empty vessel it is considered to be an inauspicious sign. I did not take this as very important but, as is the Tibetan way, recited prayers to my personal yidam deity to reverse the negative situation, and visualised my yidam as I did so. While I was doing this, we began the ascent of a massive, high mountain. As we climbed the grey winding road, the mountain peaks of my homeland became hidden far behind in white clouds.

As we reached this unfamiliar region, the westerly wind drove in black clouds which obscured the light of the newly-risen sun, so we could no longer see the track. The wind whipped up the dust, and several mini-tornadoes, columns twisting between earth and sky, began to race around. At the same time we had just driven down a narrow mountain trail and were zooming forward like an arrow along the side of a terrifying ravine when suddenly, as if right on cue, looming out of the darkness with a horrible and terrifying roar, came a huge, fearsome, grim messenger of the Lord of Death, a freight truck bearing the insignia of the People's Liberation Army of China. Without hesitation and at high speed, it smashed into our small vehicle with a furious impact.

Our small jeep was crushed into a ball, injuring and pulverising us almost beyond recovery. At that moment I perceived a tremendous screech of metal grinding against metal, felt all the blood in my body rush into my torso, and an intense, unbearable, piercing pain in my head. Then I fell into unconsciousness.

Immediately, I went through the fearsome dissolutions of the death process stages, my outer breathing ceased, and the luminosity of the basic nature arose. At the demarcation point between life and death, when conceptual mind separates from wisdom, I was just about to take a step away from life but, due to the graciousness of the deities and my Lama, and on account of the truth of my pure sincere intention, and the karmic power of my previous strong prayers of aspiration, the process of dissolution reversed. From the state of full attainment through the three stages of appearance, increase and attainment, as if from an oblivious state of sleep, I gradually began to take in a new breath. Gradually the gross visual subjects of this life appeared to my senses and I began a new life in this world. I began this, a new chapter in the historical record of many lives and deaths of one human existence.

Of all the people in the jeep, I was by far the most badly injured. Because of the cuts and swelling that covered my face, I could only open my right eye, and all I could see was redness. Warm blood poured like water from the cuts in my face and body onto the freezing ground and cold stones. The glass windscreen in front of me had shattered into innumerable sharp blades which had slashed my body and clothes into rags. My left thigh bone had splintered into pieces, and I was unable to stand. The cheekbone on the left side of my face, including my eye socket, was damaged, so I could not open my eye or see. For several weeks everything I could glimpse from this eye appeared like drifting smoke or cloudy water, and blood flowed from it for some while.

During this time I wrote a poem with my warm blood and kept it, so that in the future I would be reminded of that time when the teacher of momentary impermanence had spoken directly to me; but because I was familiar with the spiritual advice of my Lama, and holy and enlightening Buddhist teachings, I did not feel unhappy. I practised the excellent bodhichitta training of giving all my virtuous karma and pleasure to others and taking upon myself the suffering of others. I practised experiencing in my body the suffering of the limitless sentient beings in cyclic existence in general, and, in particular, those of all mother-like beings in the lower realms, exchanging and purifying their suffering with the minor suffering that I endured. I meditated for them all to attain the seed of liberation in their mind streams and thus be quickly transferred to the blissful pure realm of Dewachen. Concentrating like this, giving happiness and taking suffering, was extremely beneficial.

Especially, with regard to the murderous truck driver, he was like any sentient being in desiring happiness and not wanting suffering. He had not been hurt, but still I prayed that he would not experience the undesirable fully-ripened result of his actions in this or future lives. I prayed that all the mind streams of those with whom I had either negative or positive karmic connections, including the truck driver, might be softened by the mind of bodhichitta. I hoped from the bottom of my heart that he, and all the different beings karmically connected with me, would not face fines or punishment under the law of the country.

I experienced the sensations of invasive surgical treatment slicing, cutting and stabbing my body, once again feeling as if I was dying. This continued for a long time, after which I was left with only half my body functioning as well as it once did.

Having recovered to a reasonable degree, and without returning back along the blood-stained road by which I had passed, I re-focussed on my previous goal of going to India and, enduring a thousand sufferings, once again set off on the long journey.

The moment before the crash I had a healthy, strong, vital physique like a god. A moment later it was as if a great tree had been felled; my clothes were bloody and torn and I was groaning and writhing in pain in the dirt by the side of the road, as if I had become a filthy demon.

In this world there have been many strong, wealthy, attractive people, who never gave death a thought but, suddenly encountering obstacles, had their life breath snatched away, as if something suddenly fell from the sky and extinguished them. Not only is my story one such an example, but I also wanted to mention the experience of returning from the point between life and death.

Due to the power of the positive karma accumulated in the past, we have now attained a precious human body, complete with all the freedoms and advantages. Numerous analogies and examples demonstrate that this is very difficult to find. Thrown together by karma, sometimes happy and sometimes unhappy, if we were able to experience life forever with our family, friends, partners and children, things would be all right. However, if one day we become separated from our loved ones, we will be very unhappy. Having concerns about sickness and death, we should think right now about what will happen one day to this body which we cherish so dearly.

The time from when I was a baby, first born to my parents and then growing up, has passed. Now youth has passed and I am at the stage of becoming old. In this way, with each passing day, the time of my human life is decreasing, and accordingly my body gets older and deteriorates as the elements that comprise it age. The four elements come into conflict and we become sick. Even using the word 'death' brings us to fear and fainting, but it is certain that we will have to pass down that terrifying path.

Of all the legendary kings and queens, all with great power and influence, who have come to this world, not one has ever found any other exit, only the vast path of death. Also, all the masters who have achieved control over their subtle physical energies and minds, have demonstrated the manner of passing beyond suffering. If this is the case, what permanence or durability do our bubble-like bodies possess?

If we just have the vague awareness that one day we are going to die, we assume that day is a long time off. Not to examine whether or not that very day has arrived today, is extremely dangerous. We have no certainty as to the length of our lives; therefore, not only is the time of our death unpredictable, but the cause of death is also uncertain. We think, "I won't die tomorrow", so we plan for next year. However, how can we be confident that we will not die tonight, and by next month we will not have taken the form of a disgusting animal? But, like an animal being led into a slaughterhouse, we have no other option except to stand there, waiting in line.

The Buddha Sakyamuni taught the following in the 'Sutra of Advice to the King':

"Great King, imagine that in each of the four directions there are four towering mountains, solid and stable. If they were to collapse, all trees, plants and living creatures would be completely crushed to dust. It would not be easy to make a rapid escape, prevent their fall with force, win their favour with wealth, or avert disaster with mantras or holy substances. In the same way, all beings are subject to what are known as the 'four great fears': sickness, degeneration, ageing and death. There is no easy way to make a quick escape from them, overcome them with strength, bribe them with riches, or avert them with concoctions or medicine."

The passing of our lives is brief as lightning in the night sky, or the cascade of water in a waterfall. Considering carefully we have not much time to stay, we should seize the essence of the freedoms and advantages and be diligent. We should follow the example of someone whose hair has caught fire and act swiftly!

Among all the holy Buddhist teachings, the first one to practise is the impermanence of life. All-knowing Jigme Lingpa teaches various ways to meditate on this in the quintessential instructions of his collection of writings, 'Dzogchen Heart Essence of the Great Expanse'. This is how you should meditate:

You suddenly find yourself in vast, barren and terrifying desert. There is not one person in sight, nor a single bird in the sky. A vicious wind whips with a hollow howl. You are alone in this place. As you feel sad and depressed, from out of nowhere a white man and a black woman appear next to you. They tell you that in the place known as the Illusory City of the Six Senses there is something called a multi-coloured wish-fulfilling jewel. They say, "In order to find it we must sail across an ocean... Will you come with us?" You decide to go, and follow them to the shore. The ocean is so vast it is as if the sky has fallen to the ground. It is unimaginably wide. Fierce waves surge up to the sky. The ocean is filled with many terrifying and malevolent sea monsters, enough to strike panic into the bravest heart, and other creatures which kill instantly anything they chance to meet. A monster comes close to the shore and you immediately think of escape but, yearning with desire to find the jewel, you board the boat with the two people and sail off.

When you reach the centre of the ocean, a sudden, vicious and overwhelming storm whips up in front of you. Terrified, the two people heave on the oars, but both oars break at the same moment. With each huge wave the boat is lifted up until it almost seems to touch the sky, and then is sucked down to the depths of the ocean. There is no way of escape, no friend to beg for help, nothing to hold onto. Abruptly, at this moment you reach the terrifying juncture called death, the moment between the exhalation of one breath and inhalation of the next.

You had a previous awareness of death, but you never thought it would come so quickly, and you have no confidence in the Buddhist teachings. Today you are going to be separated from your children and possessions, your family and relations. None of these is any use. In the depths of terror and despair you cry out, "What can I do?" screaming hopelessly.

At that moment, in the sky in front of you, your gracious Lama in the form of Orgyen Padmasambhava appears and approaches you, saying, "Hey! You seem to think the suffering nature of cyclic existence is just like a wish-fulfilling jewel. What a fool you are! You haven't remembered a single teaching on death. The cause of your current perceptions comes from your ignorance which clings to yourself as a real entity. The two deceptive people, the man and woman, are respectively co-emergent and conceptual ignorance. The great ocean is boundless cyclic existence. The boat is the illusory conditioned aggregates of your body, fragile as a bubble. The breaking of the two oars which guided the boat was the connected sequence of human life, night following day, coming to an end. This cannot be extended any further.

Child of the family, it is not possible for you to just die. All the white and black karma that you have accumulated is unmistaken, straight as a plumb line, and certainly will befall you. What's to do?"

You feel even more suffering and terror and, not knowing what else to do, you pray from the bottom of your heart to your Lama. At this point a single beam of light radiates from the heart centre of your Lama and touches your heart centre. At this moment the boat capsizes and your body and mind separate. You attain enlightenment in inseparable union with the Great One from Oddiyana in the Trikaya Palace of Lotus Light, and you pray that you have in your mind stream the fortune to be able to lead all sentient beings suffering from terror from these same causes straight to enlightenment.

Following this, allow all conceptual thinking of the three times to be unsupported, let all thoughts go free. Merely observe individual thoughts, whether flowing or concentrating, with mindfulness.

Also, the Great One from Oddiyana taught us to meditate like this:

You find yourself facing north on the edge of a dark unfamiliar ravine, not knowing how you reached that place. Alone, you cannot see anyone moving about, or hear any human sounds. All you can hear is the splashing rush of a fierce waterfall, the wind buffeting noisily around and howling through dry tufts of grass. The sun is gradually setting behind the western mountains. A high cliff looms above you and ravens caw. Finding yourself in this desolate place you exclaim, "I'm all alone – where are my friends? I'm wandering, lost in this empty ravine with nowhere to go... Where is my home, my parents, my children and wealth? Will I ever find my way home?"

Not knowing which direction to take, you wander aimlessly along a narrow path into the ravine. Before long some boulders below you collapse, the path crumbles beneath your feet, and you fall helplessly down into the deep ravine. Somehow you manage to grasp a clump of grass growing in the middle of the rock face. You hang on tightly, quivering with fear. Looking down, you cannot see the depth of the chasm. You can only see the sky above. The cliff face is vast and smooth as a mirror, and the wind howls around you.

As you hang there, from a crack in the cliff to the right of the clump of grass a white mouse appears. It bites off a blade of grass at the root and pulls it away. From a crack to the left of the clump appears a black mouse which also bites off a blade of grass and drags it away. As the mice return, one after the other, the clump of grass gets smaller and smaller. You cannot find a way to stop the mice. You tremble, terrified of dying. You think to yourself, "Oh no! Now the time has come for me to die. There is no way of escape. In the past I never gave death a thought, so I have no Buddhist teachings to guide me. How terrifying it is to die! I had no idea that I would die today, but suddenly the time of my death has come. Now I'll be separated from my children, possessions, friends and family, I'll never see them again. I must leave behind the wealth I've accumulated. I must go to a frightening and unfamiliar place, somewhere utterly unknown, and I'm terrified..."

As you cry out in despair, trying to think of some way to escape, in the sky in front of you your root Lama himself appears, seated on a lotus. He is holding a ritual hand drum and bell, wearing the six bone ornaments and dancing as he speaks. "All composite phenomena are impermanent, swiftly changing and disintegrating. This life is like a waterfall cascading down a mountainside. All beings who do not realise they will die soon are extremely foolish. There is not a single way to avert death; show devotion to your Lama."

As you hear this you think to yourself, "Oh no! Before my death came I intended to begin practising the Buddhist teachings, now I profoundly regret not doing it earlier. Now it is up to my Lama and the Three Precious Jewels to know if it is right for me to die, or not. Wouldn't it be all right if I could escape from this great ravine, all-knowing Lama?" The moment you feel this great devotion in your heart, a beam of light shines forth from your Lama's heart and touches you, just as the clump of grass breaks. The light lifts you high into the sky and you arrive in the pure realm of Dewachen. Visualise in this way:

In the pure realm, limitless light emanates from your heart and brings all beings of the three realms, without leaving a single one behind, to the pure realm of Dewachen. You should meditate with intense compassion for all beings. So Padmasambhava taught.

Thinking like this about the various ways in which death may come, it is not right merely to read the words, or just take it for granted that at some time everyone is going to die. Until you come to feel the real urgency of your current situation, you need to keep practising. This is the quintessence of practising the holy Buddhist teachings so, until you have gained the result of meditating on impermanence and death, you will not be able to progress in any other meditations or practice. Therefore, first it is very important to work hard at realising this.

NINE

ESSENCE-LESS DECEPTIVE PHENOMENA

For each of us, from this morning to this evening, from the beginning of this year to the end, from the time we were born to the time we die, the goal of all our efforts has been our own happiness. To this end, we have accumulated food, clothing, possessions and wealth in order to live comfortably enjoying them. In this way we strive to ensure we will live out the whole of our human lives in comfort; however, there is no end to these preparations. Our lives are spent in preparation. If we were to die suddenly, without having accomplished our goal, our lives would be wasted in the struggle. Who can know the extent of our terrible regret as we die? If lifespan could be bought with money, our first purchase would be a guarantee of infinite lifespan. On this basis we would then have the time and necessity for striving to accumulate enough possessions and wealth to live for such a long time. However, we do not know the length of our lives and therefore, if we take a long lifespan for granted, we deceive ourselves. Deceiving oneself is even worse than being deceived by others.

Our desire to be comfortable and happy is based on maintaining our physical bodies, but all this never-ending, difficult and miserable work in which we are so busily occupied, is actually done without any consideration for our physical welfare. Not only that, but neglecting our bodies is detrimental to our health and well-being. Protecting our bodies means protecting our lives. Protecting our lives depends on our life force, and the best and most crucial cause and condition for maintaining our life force throughout a long life is a happy and comfortable state of mind.

However, we have not a minute to spare during the day and we cannot relax at night. We suffer from not being able to get what we want, and from losing what we do have. We suffer from associating with people we do not like and from being separated from our loved ones. Those in lowly positions suffer from powerlessness, and those in high positions suffer from losing their status. Those in middling positions suffer from being overtaken by their peers. Families suffer from quarrels. Engaging with these and many other kinds of suffering is no different from whittling away at our own life force.

In the time that has passed since the earth was first formed to the present day, the number of people who have left their footprints on earth can only be reckoned by an all-knowing Buddha. Of those countless people there are sure to have been great numbers of learned scholars, people of status and power, riches and wealth, and the brave and courageous, far exceeding ourselves. Like us, all those people spent their lives accomplishing worldly activities. However, on the final day of their lives, every single one of them left their children, families and friends, and their own bodies, and travelled down the vast path of death. In the same way, in the past our ancestors engaged with the illusion of samsara, tense and anxious during the day and unable to relax at night, striving to achieve something useful in this life. They died before completing all they had to do. Now we are no different from them. We will inevitably travel down the same vast future path.

When we die, whether we experience happiness or suffering, positive or negative circumstances, fortune or disaster, depends entirely on the karma we have accumulated. It is certain that karma alone will dictate our future. At the moment, while we are alive, all the things we try to achieve by our strenuous efforts, whether in business, or other work, overcoming our rivals, protecting those close to us, building up financial profit, influence, or fame, all encourage us to become greedy and aggressive, but we cannot depend on any of these achievements.

Accumulating wealth through various means only serves to gratify the desires of our enemies and also thieves, if they can get their hands on it. We eat food in the hope that it will be delicious, but it ruins our health and becomes the cause of death. We hope that someone will benefit us so we befriend them, but they become our enemy. We harm someone thinking they are our enemy, but in the end they become our friend, and so on. The phenomena of cyclic existence cannot be relied upon. Like last night's dream, these things are deceptive.

As we grasp frantically at this futility, time passes with constant feelings of desire and anger, happiness and sadness, weariness, annoyance and fear. These afflictions which deceive us are our own fault. All these mundane appearances are like magical illusions and are deceptive by nature. We take the inherently untrue as permanent and reliable. How regrettable! Aren't we stupid!

Now, we must conquer the demon of self-grasping from its root. To make sure that working solely towards the heart of the Buddhist teachings is not a mistaken pursuit, we need to examine and analyse with great care. It is not sufficient to have just a vague understanding. Seeing that everything compounded is the cause of suffering, we need to meditate over and over again in order to approach that crucial point of understanding. The way to meditate on this is taught in the 'Heart Essence' scriptures of the Dzogchen Tradition:

Imagine you find yourself wandering in an unknown, distant and hostile place, with no idea which way to go. At that moment, eight strange young men appear and say to you, "We've come from the dark land of the Ground of All. In a region many months and years travel from here is a Land of Jewels where there are jewels more valuable than you can imagine. We're going to find them, regardless of the hardships involved."

You don't disagree with their plan; you come round to their way of thinking, and set out on the journey with them.

Sometimes you travel buffeted by gales, sometimes along narrow trails threatened by fierce wild animals, sometimes the boat in which you sail is tossed about by currents in great rivers. You suffer from hunger. The length of your human life is spent travelling on and on, night and day, in utter exhaustion. Your life is almost at an end. Your hair and beard have become white by the time you finally accomplish your desire and reach the Land of Jewels. There you find myriads of jewels, beyond anything you imagined. Overjoyed, you return to your homeland.

Three days' journey from home, in a place called the Plain of Four Gatherings, you meet seven evil bandit brothers who steal your hard-won jewels. They strip you of your clothes and bind your arms and legs. Wielding spears tipped with arrow heads, swords and other weapons, they yell fiercely, "You pathetic wretch! If you have a Lama, now is the time to pray. If you have a personal yidam deity, beseech his compassion. If you have a dakini or protector, call for their assistance. If you have none of those, meditate on the great enemy called death. You've reached the crossroads between this life and the next."

Hearing this, your heart begins race. "Aggh! I've spent the whole of my life, and endured so many difficulties, and it's all been for nothing. Not only that, but my precious life is about to end. Meeting such murderers in this deserted place, there's no one to beg for help, no refuge or protector. All my efforts have been wasted. I need more time to complete my life, but suddenly here is death!"

As you cry out, in the sky in front of you appears the form of the Great One from Oddiyana, making the four mudras, emanating and reabsorbing rays of light. Having driven away the wild bandits, he says, "Hey, poor creature! The activities of cyclic existence are like lethal poison, but you long for them as if they were thousand-flavoured nectar. The eight strange men, your travelling companions, were the vehicle of the eight modes of consciousness which deceives the wisdom of awareness. The jewels of the Land of Jewels were the happiness and comfort of this life, which cannot be permanent, like a dream.

You took suffering upon yourself, enduring the hardships of the journey, which forms the basis of your self-deception. Your hair and beard changed colour because you took suffering to be happiness, and your life was exhausted in this illusory state. The bandits who intended to kill you in the Plain of the Four Gatherings were the harmful effects of the four hundred and twenty-four diseases; and so, powerless, your life was about to be destroyed by the Lord of Death. Hey, you poor thing! However much you do, grasping at craving, it all turns out like this in the end."

Hearing this, you feel even more regretful about what you have done, and you realise that all the activities of this life are solely the nature of suffering. You pray one-pointedly to the Great One from Oddiyana and, as this experience increases, a ray of light like a hook emanates from the master's heart and touches your heart. At this moment you are instantly reborn in the Palace of Lotus Light. Meditate you become the holy leader of sentient beings. Allow your consciousness to rest in its natural state. So it is taught.

Meditating like this over and over again, we realise that all the activities we engage in for the sake of this life are solely the cause of suffering, and we should continue meditating until we have developed a heart-felt feeling of revulsion toward them. In order to cut the entanglement of attachment we feel for the objects of this life, the way to meditate on the suffering of cyclic existence was taught by the Great One from Oddiyana:

First, go alone to a mournful place like a cemetery. If this is not possible, go to some ruined place where people used to live, or a dry barren place, somewhere which inspires fear, or close by sick people or beggars, and so on. Alternatively, go to a place which used to be happy and comfortable but is now decrepit. But if you cannot manage any of this, go alone to a deserted location.

Sit on a comfortable seat in a relaxed position with your right leg on the ground and your left leg pulled in. Rest your right elbow on your right knee, and rest your right cheek in your right palm. Your left hand rests on your left knee. Sitting in this Posture of Sorrow, you will come to feel sad. Then think of the suffering of cyclic existence and say out loud: "Alas, cyclic existence is suffering. Enlightenment is happiness."

Think: "The suffering of cyclic existence is terrifying, like entering a pit of burning ashes. The suffering of the three lower realms of existence is unbearable and without end. There is not one single opportunity for happiness, so I can't stay here. With the utmost urgency, I must find some means of escape."

Meditate like this: "This cyclic existence is a great pit of fire, intensely hot, deep, vast and high, in which all sentient beings, including myself, are crying out." Again, with anguish cry this out loud: "From beginningless cyclic existence until now I've been burning! I am terrified!"

As you cry out, your gracious root Lama appears, wearing the six bone ornaments, and holding in his hand a hook of light. Meditate that he says to you the following words: "Hey, there is no comfort in cyclic existence, it's like living in a pit of fire. Now there is a single opportunity to escape. The suffering of the three lower realms is limitless, and with no opportunity for happiness, so now it is time for you to escape from this pit of fire."

As you hear the sound of his words think to yourself: "I've been in this fire pit of cyclic existence for such a long time. Now, listening to my Lama's words, I can escape from this fire pit and, what's more, all these sentient beings can be liberated without exception." You think this and arouse intense bodhichitta, at which instant the hook of light in your Lama's hand touches your heart and whisks you off to the Pure Realm of Great Bliss. Instantly, you yourself are holding a hook of light, and all sentient beings in the fire pit are gradually pulled out and arrive in the pure realm; no one is left behind. Meditate like this.

Also, Guru Rinpoche taught that we should think in detail about the suffering of cyclic existence, night and day, fixedly without distraction. Meditate like this until sadness has developed.

From renouncing cyclic existence, resolve on the need to practise the holy Buddhist teachings, and experience of non-attachment to this life will grow. If we do not renounce cyclic existence, meditation becomes meaningless, so practice of the Buddhist teachings will not be pure. In this case there will not come a time when we are liberated from the suffering of cyclic existence.

TEN

PRISON OF THE THREE SUFFERINGS

What is known as 'feeling' can be divided into three categories: pleasurable feelings, suffering and neutral feelings. At this stage we are going to talk about suffering, of which there are also three divisions. All the pleasure that we experience is ultimately not real happiness but is subsumed within one of the three types of suffering.

As it is taught:

> "There is no happiness in cyclic existence.
> In a cesspit there are no good smells."

This is explained in the following way: happiness and suffering are opposites, therefore all feelings that are not happiness, including neutral ones, are subsumed into the category of suffering. We beings in cyclic existence have never experienced supreme undefiled happiness, so we do not know what it is like. We see suffering as happiness. Greater than the pleasure of scratching an itch is the pleasure of not itching. However, we have assumed these fleshly bodies because we have created negative karmic causes, so we assume unhappiness is happiness. For example, when a pig is wallowing in filth it enjoys itself. In the same way, we have not experienced true pleasure so we take suffering to be happiness.

> "The physical pleasure of being healthy
> is not thought of except when sick.
> The happiness of human life,
> is not recalled except when dying."

In the same way as, in the legend of King Gesar of Ling, Gyatsha, having taken the body of a hawk, sings this verse to his younger brother, we have seen it is more pleasurable to become a human than take rebirth as an animal. And compared to the heavenly realms, the difference in enjoyment is as great again as that between the experience of animals and humans. It is considered that, of all the realms of cyclic existence, the heavenly realms are the most happy; however, in the same way as in the previous examples, compared to a pure realm, the heavenly realms are full of suffering. Beyond comparison, the bliss of the mind which is experienced in concentration meditation far transcends the feeling of pleasure we ordinary beings get from food, clothes and possessions. For this reason, we need to strive for a method to escape the prison of the three realms of cyclic existence, and it is high time for us to pursue the state of liberation and eternal bliss.

What are known as the 'three higher realms of cyclic existence' are the realms of gods, demigods and humans, and below the three lower rebirths of hell, tormented spirits and animals. In all these six there is never any true happiness. The experience of the six realms is solely the nature of suffering.

The World-honoured Buddha taught:

> "Cyclic existence never affords even
> a pin point of happiness."

By attaining the physical basis for life as a god or human being, it seems as if we have some chance of happiness; however in truth there is never any happiness. If we take the example of our human body, we experience the general sufferings of birth, ageing, sickness and death. Particular suffering includes the suffering of needing to keep and maintain whatever we possess. If we lack anything, then there is the suffering of striving to obtain it. There is also the suffering of meeting hated enemies, and of separation from our loved ones.

In addition there are the three sufferings: manifest suffering, the suffering of change and all-pervasive suffering. Manifest suffering occurs for example when, in addition to our father dying our mother also passes away. We experience the suffering of change when in the morning we are happy but in the afternoon we become miserable. The general state of the three realms of cyclic existence is without pleasure, because of the all-pervasive suffering of conditioned existence. Because of this, we never pass beyond the confines of the three sufferings.

We sometimes seem to have the experience of happiness, but in actual fact it is not happiness at all, and moreover the suffering of the three negative rebirths is even more difficult to bear. It is absolutely intolerable. However, because of the power of karma, there is no other place to go. How terrifying! With hearts full of sorrow we should develop uncontrived compassion for the beings of cyclic existence. A student of the Buddhist path cannot maintain the casual attitude that it is enough to have an intellectual grasp of compassion. We need truly to take into our hearts the sufferings of each of the six kinds of beings and meditate until we develop an unshakeable compassionate mind.

In order to develop the mind of compassion, the scriptures of the 'Heart Essence' teach we should meditate in the following way.

Go to a remote place or meditate at night and think like this:

You find yourself wandering in the foothills of a great snow mountain. The ground is completely frozen. Suddenly the wind whips up a terrible blizzard and this snowstorm darkens the sky. You fear you are freezing and long for a way to warm yourself. In a split second, as in a nightmare, you are born in a hot hell. Beneath your feet, the whole ground is red-hot burning iron. Everything is incarcerated in red-hot iron. Everywhere, above and below, is filled entirely with flames, burning fiercely without respite.

This is the Reviving Hell, and here beings experience suffering throughout the 1,620,000,000,000 human years of their lives. These limitless beings are like ourselves and, because of the karmic power of hatred, they attack each other with cunning and terrible weapons and hack each other into tiny pieces. Experiencing unbearable pain, they sometimes lose consciousness, and when they feel they have died, a voice from the vault of the sky proclaims, "Revive!" which causes them to recover their senses, and so they experience extreme intolerable suffering without respite.

The beings of the Black Line Hell have a lifespan of 12,960,000,000,000 human years. The terrifying Guardians of Hell draw eight black lines on their bodies and dismember them with a sharp saw. Completely unable to bear the pain, they shriek violently and can think of nothing but escape.

In the Crushing Hell the lives of beings are 103,680,000,000,000 human years. They are trapped between mountains shaped like elephants, lions, goats and rams which squash them like a blister, so blood spurts from every pore in their bodies. They long to escape from this unbearable pain and suffering.

In the Hell of Howling, beings live for 829,440,000,000,000 human years. Arriving inside an iron house, the door is welded shut. Fire burns from all directions and their bodies are burnt into small fragments. Knowing there is no escape, they howl and howl, at which time this hell becomes what is known as the Hell of Great Howling, where beings have a lifespan of 6,635,520,000,000,000 human years. Here beings are thrown into another iron house contained within the first. They know that even if they escape from the inner house they cannot escape from the outer one and their suffering is redoubled; they are in extreme torment.

Beings in the Hell of Heat live for 53,084,160,000,000,000 human years. There, blazing iron stakes are thrust up the backside straight through to the crown of the head. Flames blaze from all the sense doors: the eyes, ears, nose and mouth. Sometimes, the whole body is cooked in molten iron and these beings experience the suffering of their flesh separating from their bones.

Again, in the Hell of Intense Heat, beings have a lifespan of an intermediate aeon, an incalculable number of human years. Here three-pronged blazing stakes are thrust up and out of the crown of their heads and right and left shoulders, and their bodies are rolled up in sheets of blazing metal like bolts of cloth. Beings are cooked naked in molten iron, their flesh and skin separating. They become gray like a skeleton. Having been born in this hell, the suffering beings experience is a hundred times greater than the previous hell. It is unbearable, they scream violently and long to escape.

The period of time it takes for a planet to form, exist, be destroyed and remain in emptiness is called 'four short aeons', which is equal to one intermediate aeon. This is the lifespan of a being in the Hell of Ultimate Torment. In every cardinal and intermediate direction, white-hot fire burns without respite. Bodies burn, at one with the fire. Screams resound but there are no bodies to be seen. Beings experience unbearable suffering and wail and shriek terribly. Meditate on this.

Having meditated on the hell realms, Orgyen Daychen Gyalpo, one of the twelve manifestations of Guru Rinpoche, suddenly appears in the sky in front of you and says:

> "Hey, unfortunate sentient being! You've accumulated terrible negative karmic causes. Motivated by hatred, you became very angry with those to whom you owe special respect, your parents, Bodhisattvas, Buddhas and so on. The result of this is to experience suffering akin to that in the hell realms. Now, admit all your negative karmic actions with great regret. Meditate on great

compassion for all beings who, like you, are also in hell. In that way, by generating the courage to take upon yourself the suffering of others, you will escape from this place."

Long ago, our teacher Sakyamuni had the name Pakshida and took rebirth in a hell realm where he toiled drawing a heavy cart. His companion, Kamarupa, was too weak to pull the cart and the guardians of hell grew angry. They hit Kamarupa on the head with iron hammers. Pakshida developed boundless compassion for his companion and said to the guardians, "Tie his cart harness round my neck." Out of kindness he chose to exchange his comfort for the suffering of his companion, but the hell guardian responded, "What do you think you're doing? Sentient beings must undergo their own individual karma". They hit Pakshida over the head with an iron hammer, killing him instantly, and he was reborn in the Heaven of the Thirty-three. Thus he escaped the suffering of hell.

You hear Orgyen Daychen Gyalpo's words, together with the legend of Sakyamuni Buddha. You think to yourself: "If there is a way for sentient beings like me to escape from this suffering, then I could bear it, even if I had to go on suffering here myself." As soon as you generate this resolve, from the heart of the Great One from Oddiyana a white ray of light like a hook shines out and touches you, and you attain enlightenment, inseparable from him. You become empowered to achieve spontaneously the two benefits of self and others. Just as from Guru Rinpoche's heart, a beam of light shines forth from your own heart for all sentient beings in hell, and the hell realms are emptied. The teachings tell us to meditate in this way.

Again:

You are completely exhausted, in a terrifying burning desert. As you stagger along, the thought of a cool breeze comes to mind; because of this, immediately the entire ground is covered with snow and ice, and howling blizzards surround you. In all directions loom snow- mountains which pierce the sky. Like your body, the bodies of sentient beings born in the Cold Hell of Blisters are covered with erupting blisters, and their skin and flesh cracks from the cold. With even more suffering than that, and with lifespans even longer than the hot hells, are the Cold Hell of Open Blisters, the Cold Hell of Whimpering, the Cold Hell of Howling, the Cold Hell of Chattering Teeth, the Cold Hell of Splitting Like an

Utpala, the Cold Hell of Splitting Like a Lotus, and the Cold Hell of Splitting Greatly like a Lotus, all filled with suffering from intense cold.

Around both the Eight Hot Hells and the Eight Cold Hells are Neighbouring Hells, where there are all kinds of treacherous combinations of earth, water, fire and wind, and boundless ephemeral suffering is experienced. Meditate on all of these.

Because we are greatly attached to our possessions, wealth, food and clothes in this life, we are unable to make offerings to sacred objects, worthy recipients of offerings, nor do we give to those in need of charity. What is the use of having wealth unless we use it to benefit others? Under the influence of miserliness we will be reborn as hungry ghosts.

Meditate on this:

Those hungry ghosts with external obscurations see a pleasant river in the distance and, weak with exhaustion, drag themselves towards it, but when they arrive at the bank they find armed men on guard forbidding them to quench their thirst. Alternatively, their object of desire, in this case the river water, has changed to become disgusting pus and blood, and so on. Similarly, those hungry ghosts with internal obscurations suffer from being unable to find food or drink for months and years, and then, even if they do find a morsel of food or a drop of water, their mouths are the size of the eye of a needle and they suffer from being unable to consume anything.

Later, even if they are able to pass a little food or drink into their mouths, their throats are the size of a horse's hair and they suffer from being unable to swallow anything. Even if they do manage to swallow something, their stomachs are the size of the King of Mountains and can never be filled. Their arms and legs are merely the size of a blade of grass, so they also suffer from being unable to move themselves around. Additionally, there are what are called hungry ghosts with obscurations of food and drink. As soon as they consume something, it burns them internally. Some are so hungry they eat their own flesh. During the cold of winter, even sunshine feels cool and, in the summer heat, even the moon feels hot. This they experience and suffer. Meditate on experiencing this suffering yourself and also on others suffering in these ways.

As for animals, there are two kinds: those that live in groups and those that live separately. They suffer from being eaten by one another, and experience suffering of exhaustion from being used and exploited. Meditate on this.

Even in the higher realms there is no happiness. When the time comes for those born as gods to die, in the last seven days of their long heavenly lives, signs of death appear. As they possess clairvoyance, the gods suffer from knowing of their imminent descent down to the unfortunate states of being.

Humans suffer from the general sufferings of birth, ageing, sickness and death, as well as the suffering of the three sufferings, the extent of which are beyond imagination, and include the death of one's mother closely followed by the death of one's father.

The demi-gods are constantly tormented by anger and jealousy, and thus experience killing and maiming by weapons on the battlefield, and so on.

Bring to mind all the suffering and lifespans of the six types of beings, one by one in separate practice sessions. From this, experience these sufferings in meditation and when, as before, you cry out fiercely, in the space in front of you appears your root Lama as the Great One from Oddiyana, Guru Rinpoche:

> "Hey, poor samsaric being! From the cause of the five poisons of afflictive emotions you behave without any consideration, wrapped up in self-cherishing. Because of this, you've done all kinds of non-virtuous actions, the fully-ripened result of which is your experience of all these manifold sufferings. Therefore, abandon the cause of these, and come to understand that your suffering is the karma you yourself created. From this meditate with happiness that, through your experiences of suffering, your bad karma is being exhausted."

Additionally, think powerful thoughts of compassion for others' suffering, by which you should meditate on the extraordinary mind of bodhichitta, and thus rely on the antidote of taking upon yourself all their suffering.

"There is a method to escape from this!" Thus Guru Rinpoche speaks and, just as you attain this confirmation, you think to yourself: "Just like me, all six types of suffering migratory sentient beings are so pitiful. May I experience their karmic share of suffering and be able to endure suffering one hundred thousand times greater than this. May all sentient beings be freed from suffering!"

The moment you arouse this aspiration your negative karma is exhausted, and all the terrifying appearances vanish, deceptive, just like phantoms in a dream. You attain enlightenment inseparable from the Great One from Oddiyana. You emanate rays of light to all sentient beings of the lower realms and, without leaving one behind, bring them all to the level of the four kinds of awareness holder. Thinking this, cut the thread of conceptual thought and let mindful consciousness relax freely.

When we contemplate the extent of suffering we should not be detached from the experience like someone observing from a distance. We should think how it would be in actuality, if we ourselves were really born in such a place, and experience the suffering. When we think in this way, we feel a clear sense of misery; this is disillusionment with samsara. When the thought of desiring to escape from this suffering grows, this is renunciation, from which compassion is aroused for all the six types of sentient beings who have been our parents. Harmful negative actions are abandoned and we strive solely to do positive virtuous actions, like making offerings to the Precious Jewels.

In order to meditate on the difficulties of finding the freedoms and advantages, the Great One from Oddiyana taught the following:

Go to a place where there are many kinds of insects, ants, or animals and sit cross-legged. Place your hands in your lap in the gesture of meditation and meditate like this:

This world is wide and vast like the sky. There are limitless wandering beings of the six kinds experiencing suffering. The sky, the air and the ground are all as if alive with movement. Meditate on this. In the middle of all this, on the top of a high mountain, you alone have gained a human body. The mountain is steep and you are starting to lose your footing. You think to yourself: "Among all these suffering sentient beings, I alone have attained a human body. This has come about through the power of virtue. Having attained a human body like this and letting it go meaninglessly to waste by falling off this mountain would be a great shame. Just now I have attained a human form like this, which is hard to attain, but in no time I am sure to fall over this precipice. What shall I do?"

Thinking about this terrifying prospect, you cry out in despair, at which time your root Lama appears in the sky above you with the gesture of bestowing protection and says to you, "Hey! The human body complete with the freedoms and advantages is hard to find. This is the only time you have attained it. You may have achieved it, but it is not permanent. You'll quickly fall down to the bad states of existence. Think about how soon this will happen. If you do not accomplish the great objective of this physical basis at this time, in the future it will be difficult to find a human body like this. With this human body as the basis, swiftly attain buddhahood!"

The moment you hear this teaching you cry out, "Alas, among countless beings like me, I alone have attained a human body, which is so hard to attain. So this time I will liberate myself from samsaric suffering, and I will liberate all beings without exception!" Think like this.

Immediately, on arousing this aspiration, the essence of a ray of light from the heart of your Lama touches you; at which moment you arrive in the blissful pure realm. From your own heart limitless light emanates, and all sentient beings without exception are brought to the realm of bliss. Think like this, and meditate with intense compassion for sentient beings. So Guru Rinpoche taught.

In this way we need to meditate on the difficulty of finding the freedoms and advantages until we renounce cyclic existence. If we develop continuous effortless and naturally-arising compassion, together with diligence in practising the teachings, spiritual experiences will develop and our minds will change. Therefore we should practise earnestly. One sentient being, by meditating on the path, attains buddhahood. And again the difference is a change in their mind stream.

At the moment we are a mass of problems under the power of delusion. When we sleep we are confused by all sorts of suffering in our dreams. When we wake, these sufferings naturally disappear. In the same way, if our current confused perceptions dissolve, we will attain pure vision and enlightened wisdom. At this point we will possess all enlightened qualities. Therefore, in order to fulfil all the needs and wishes of sentient beings and lead them to enlightenment, we should avoid losing this great opportunity, which combines minimum hardship with the potential to achieve great results, and strive using all our means.

ELEVEN

THE TORCH OF EVER-BLISSFUL LIBERATION

The suffering of the three unfortunate states of existence is beyond endurance. In the same way, beings in the three higher realms also experience inconceivable suffering. However, if we think "No problem, the Buddha will protect us from all general and specific suffering." this is not the case. Individual sentient beings must experience individually their own karmic perceptions. For this reason, even if one thousand Buddhas appeared for the sake of one sentient being, they would have little capacity to help. This is not because the Buddha has no compassion or blessing, but because there is no way of mitigating individual sentient beings' karmic vision. For example, when we are sleeping there is no way for anyone to control our dreams. For the same reason, if sentient beings were not dependent on their karma, and it was possible for the Buddhas to lead us out of samsara, then one compassionate Buddha, with light rays of compassion, would without doubt have emptied this conditioned existence of beings many aeons ago.

However, if we ask, "Then are Buddhas completely unable to benefit sentient beings with their blessings?" this is also not the case. Buddhas first generate the great enlightened mind of bodhichitta and, from that point on, all their activities are solely directed at benefiting sentient beings.

However, as Buddha Sakyamuni taught:

> "Negative actions accumulated by migratory sentient beings cannot be washed away by water. Neither can the suffering of migratory beings be dispelled by the hand of the Buddha. Also, the mental realisation of the Buddha himself cannot be transferred and given unequivocally."

The holy Buddhist teachings are medicine. They are like nectar which dispels the five poisons. Through receiving and realising these teachings, beings become liberated. We may think: "Now the Buddha is no longer alive, who can I study with to receive the nectar-like holy teachings?" Among migratory beings, including gods and demons, lords of all beings including Brahma, powerful political figures, the kings and ministers of this world, and so on, not a single one is able to teach this nectar-like path. A path like this is taught only by Lamas, spiritual guides, so for this reason we need to train with spiritual masters and spiritual friends.

Additionally, in order to practise the Dharma in the proper way, it is not enough just to read the scriptures. Butter is made from milk. With butter, lamps can be filled and lit, and light is produced. In the same way we need to extract the essence of Buddhist practice, and we do this by following the personal instructions of our Lama.

The Buddha Sakyamuni taught in the 'Summarising Sutra':

> "Train continuously under learned gurus.
> Why? Because from them comes enlightened wisdom.
> In the same way those who are sick take medicine to become well,
> Train under the spiritual master without straying."

We need to find a qualified Lama through examination of his or her qualities. Unless we do this it is unwise to trust someone merely because they are named 'Lama', or just because they wear red or yellow Buddhist robes. Among this kind of people there are also those who bring the Buddha's teachings into disrepute.

The Buddha taught:

> "My teachings will be destroyed by someone like myself."

In this case, what kind of spiritual teacher do we need? Generally speaking, we need a teacher who has trained his or her mind stream perfectly in the Three Higher Trainings: 1. Training in the highest moral practice. 2. Training in the highest meditation. 3. Training in the highest wisdom. We need a teacher who has studied extensively, and knows the wisdom of the scriptures; one who has great loving compassion for feeble wandering beings, and enthusiastic diligence in working for the benefit of others.

On top of that, a preceptor and master of the outer path of individual liberation needs to have the twenty-one sets of five qualities, and to have taken full ordination for at least ten consecutive years. We need a teacher with pure moral discipline, who has steadfast, learned and righteous qualities.

Spiritual masters of the inner Bodhisattva path should possess qualities of serenity and gentleness, and love all beings as a mother loves her only child. They should be a great unacquainted friend to all beings, and have a mind stream full of love and compassion.

In general, masters of the esoteric secret mantra should have received the empowerments and maintain the sacred commitments. They should possess the qualities of the Ten Attributes and the Eight Natures, and so on.

More specifically, a teacher of the Great Perfection should be accomplished and a holder of the lineage. They should hold the treasury of teachings of the Hearing Lineage which brings liberation through hearing. They need to excel in accomplishing the Two Benefits as practised by former masters of the lineage. Always diligent in practice, a master's attainments are amassed like clouds. In control of their own perceptions, they overwhelm the perceptions of others with their splendour. Regarding beings with loving compassion, they guide them on the path to liberation. Because they have discovered the mind of the Victorious Ones, they are the embodiment of the Three Precious Jewels.

In particular, masters of the esoteric secret mantra should have received the empowerments of the tradition of the Great Perfection, have pure sacred commitments, and have matured their mind stream. They should possess complete understanding, experience and realisation of the Four Landmark Visions of the path of Trekcho of primordial purity, and of spontaneously accomplished Togal practice. They also need to have the blessings of the lineage.

If we are to use only one method of examination to determine the authenticity of a master, then we should examine whether or not they have bodhichitta in their mind stream. If they have bodhichitta, all their connections with beings, positive and negative, are meaningful and there is no mistake.

If we differentiate between masters, there is the Outer Lama who is expert in elucidating theoretical misconceptions, the Inner Lama who graciously teaches the instructions of secret mantra, and the Secret Lama, the root master who introduces the unborn nature of mind. Another classification includes the Lama of the Natural Basis, the Lama of Pure Natural Mind, and the Perceptible Symbolic Lama.

In the same way, the student who trains with a Lama must also possess all the right characteristics: great faith and diligence, great intelligence, little reifying attachment, great respect, conduct that accords with secret mantra, sacred commitments, and he or she should also work hard at practice.

It is taught that if such a master and such a student team up, this is like a bird with two wings, easily able to fly into the sky; and to that extent the attainment of enlightenment will be without difficulty.

Be wary of placing your trust in whoever you meet! You should only train with a Lama after you have first examined them. It is said: "Not to examine a Lama is like jumping off a cliff. Not to examine a student is like drinking poison." The Lama is like a guide on the path to liberation. If you meet up with a bad guide who takes you down a wrong path, it will not only be detrimental in this life but forever more. For this reason, examination and analysis of a teacher is extremely important.

After having examined and entrusted your spiritual training to a Lama, whatever they do, generate the certainty of seeing their actions as positive. It is never appropriate to perceive anything the Lama may do as erroneous. Even if you see them doing some small action which appears to you to be impure, it is like the filaments which appear before the eyes of someone who has eaten datura, or when someone suffering from jaundice sees a white conch shell as yellow. From beginningless time, due to the power of familiarisation, things have appeared to us as impure; so we need to be aware it is not the Lama but our own perceptions which are impure.

The Bhikshu Sunaksatra always saw Buddha Sakyamuni as mistaken. Araya Asanga, while he was practising Lord Maitreya, had not completely purified his obscurations and, instead of seeing the Buddha, saw a bitch whose hindquarters were full of maggots. We need to remember these examples.

The Buddha Body of Ultimate Truth, the dharmakaya, is internal luminosity, the youthful vase body. This primordial protector is seen by the wisdom of perfect renunciation and realisation. Until we gain the perceptions of a Buddha, these visions are not within the sphere of our mundane experience.

The Body of Perfect Enjoyment, the sambhogakaya, is seen by extraordinary beings, tenth level Bodhisattvas, and no others. We lack positive karma to meet the Emanation Body of the Buddha, the nirmanakaya. It is not that we have been abandoned by the three Buddha bodies but, in the same way as the sun does not shine on a north-facing cave, it is our fault that in our present situation we are not fitting vessels to meet with these beings.

However, in many Sutras and Tantras the Buddha taught, for beings of this degenerate strife-torn age, the Buddhas will appear as emanations in the form of spiritual masters to benefit ordinary beings. For this reason, our Lama also is truly not an ordinary being. From our personal point of view, our Lama guides us in the teachings in person, and is therefore even kinder than the Buddhas.

Even if we met the Buddha in person, he would not do anything more than guide us on the path to omniscience. Thinking about this with confident faith motivates us to train with our Lama. The way to do this is by paying respect and practising the three ways to please the master: by means of material things, service and practice with the doors of our body, speech and mind.

With the door of our body, it is important when walking not to go on the Lama's right side. We should not step on the shadow of the Lama's body or head, trample on a strand of the Lama's hair, or on his or her pillow or seat. Students should not accept the Lama rising for or prostrating to them. Having received even just three words of profound instructions from a teacher, a student should not take a seat higher than them. These and other actions are to be avoided with the door of our body.

With the door of our speech, we should not speak badly of the Lama, make fun of or belittle them. With the door of our mind, we should not have even the slightest thought of rivalry or malice. A student should not do anything of importance, even if it is Dharma-related, without first getting the Lama's approval. If the Lama gives instructions to do something, regardless of whether it may appear good or bad, a student should do it according to instructions. By doing this the student can then receive the profound teachings.

By keeping in mind the aspirational thought of the need to equalise the wisdom mind of the Lama, first the student establishes the Lama's blessings and reverses their clinging attitude towards cyclic existence. Secondly, the expanse of wisdom is opened. Thirdly, innate understanding arises and uncertainty towards ultimate awareness wisdom comes to sincere resolution. When the student arrives at this stage, of the three ways to please the master, the student should do so solely by the offering of practice.

Teaching and studying the holy Buddhist teachings is not like learning ordinary educational subjects, skills or crafts, where we are free to pick and choose what we study. Buddhist teachings are not given to whoever is most important, nor are they sold for riches or goods. Qualified masters and students explain and study the teachings in order to liberate all sentient beings from the suffering of samsaric existence, and to ensure the precious teachings of the Conqueror remain in this world and not become degenerate.

Entering the door of the holy Dharma is not just a means for living through the short period of human life in this single lifetime. Our motivation should be to alleviate the suffering of ourselves and others for lifetime upon lifetime. Therefore, studying the Dharma is hundreds and thousands of times more incomparably beneficial than education in any discipline which will only be of benefit in this life.

Currently in this world the teachings of Buddha Sakyamuni are still flourishing, so the sun of the holy Dharma has not yet set. To cross by boat to the other side of a river, we need to depend on a skilled boatman, and a blind person needs a sighted guide. In the same way, finding an excellent teacher to show us the path to enlightenment is most crucial in this extremely important task.

To find a genuine spiritual guide, first we need to examine them and, following that, train with them. To begin training first and only then examine the teacher is the wrong way of going about it, and so is inappropriate.

Now the Buddha is not here in person, however the spiritual master is an emanation of the Buddha and his representative. The Buddha himself said as he was passing away:

> "Do not be distressed, Ananda, do not grieve!
> In future times, I will manifest
> As spiritual masters to bring benefit
> To you and all others."

This means, in order to train beings of this degenerate age whose afflictive emotions need to be tamed, the Buddha himself will purposefully take human rebirth in the form of spiritual masters.

What difference is there between an ordinary person and a Lama? Of course Lamas are flesh and blood, just like us. A Lama still needs to eat food, wear clothes, and similarly their experiences of heat and cold, hunger and thirst, comfort and discomfort are all the same as ours. They also share our difficulties of birth, old age, sickness and death. If we think like this, we appreciate why, in order for people to be able to relate to him, even the Buddha appeared in the form of a human being to tame wandering beings. In the same way, of course Lamas also appear to our human perceptions in human form.

We value gold, diamonds and other precious things. Because of this, in the Tantras of the secret mantra all assemblies of deities arise, and appear to beings whose afflictive emotions need to be tamed, embellished with valuable ornaments, and the temples of the pure realms are formed from precious jewels, and so on.

In this modern time, the immaculate teaching of the Conqueror, complete with both traditions of Sutra and Tantra, is only wide-spread in Tibet. Accordingly, not only is Tibet the home and wellspring of Buddhism, but it is also a precious land where holy spiritual masters are born. Among all the worldwide philosophical and spiritual traditions, none surpasses the learning of the Tibetan tradition of Buddhism in definitive understanding of the crucially important question of future lives.

This understanding is not reached merely by following the words of one scripture. Building on the foundation of the lineage transmission of empowerments, oral transmissions, instructions and secret guidance, the practitioner of Tibetan Buddhism follows the master's exposition of the holy teachings, taking them up one by one and putting them into practice. This matures their own and others' mind streams, and through the door of liberation the practitioner aims to achieve the ultimate result.

In this way the spiritual master attains the blessings of the lineage and the realisation experience of practice, and becomes a representative of the Buddha, a fount of Buddhist teachings, and the head of the spiritual community.

Because they are difficult to find, the extant Buddhist teachings are the most radiant and luminous of jewels. Nowadays, on the peak of the world surrounded by snow-mountains, their continuity has never entirely disappeared; it still remains. All beings with wisdom and intelligence understand the Buddhist teachings are incomparably more precious than any other object of value.

Whatever the valuable object, it is only natural that a seemingly-identical fake will appear. For this reason we understand the need firstly to examine and only then train with a true master. When outer appearances are the same, we must be careful because it is easy to make mistakes. Therefore it is important to use all the recommended methods of examination and investigation when finding a master.

Tibetan Buddhism, famed worldwide as a precious ornament, can be classified into many different subdivisions which follow the lines of transmission of the earlier and later secret mantra teachings and the founders of the various traditions.

From the time when the three, the Abbot Shantirakshita, Master Padmasambhava and Dharma King Trisong Deutsen, came together in Tibet, they founded the Ancient Nyingma Tradition, and propagated the original teachings of what became known as Tibetan Buddhism. Divided between the Tantric Section and the Sadhana Section are the three transmissions: The Long Transmission of the Canonical Tradition, the Short Transmission of the Revealed Treasures, and the Profound Transmission of Pure Vision. From these are further divided the Mental Class, the Spatial Class and the Esoteric Instruction Class, the transmission of which is divided between the Explanation Lineage and the Hearing Lineage, and each has its followers.

From the lineage which originated from Glorious Jowo Je Atisha to the Seven Masters Possessing the divine Dharma, the holders of the Jowo Kadampa Tradition were the three masters Ker, Ngog, Drom, and others, with all the different transmissions. More recently, the Unequalled Great Tsongkapa Lord Lozang Dragpa once more gloriously clarified the teachings and founded the New Kadampa, or Riwo Virtuous Gelugpa Tradition.

From the Powerful Lord Yogi Sri Dharmapala, transmission of the Path and Result practice passed to the Great Sakya Kunga Nyingpo, Jamgon Sakya Pandita, and so on, as holders of the Tradition of Glorious Sakyapa.

The teachings of the Kagyu School were transmitted by Marpa of Lhodrak Chokyi Lodro (Marpa Lotsawa) to Jetsun Milarepa, Dakpo Chandra Prabha Kumara (Gampopa), and so on. Within this school the teachings are classified into divisions known as the Four Great Kagyu Traditions and the Eight Lesser Kagyu Schools.

The teachings of the Shangpa Kagyu School were transmitted by the learned and accomplished Khyungpo Yogi. Transmitted by Padampa Sangye and Machik Labdron, the Shije Tradition was thus brought to Tibet. Khyejo Lotsawa and others transmitted the Jordruk Lineage. The learned and accomplished Orgyenpa transmitted the Threefold Vajra Approach and Accomplishment Lineage.

These are the Eight Great Chariots of the Practice Lineage, all with their followers, the teachings of which still continue uncorrupted in Tibet to this day. Each one of these long-standing traditions maintains the traditions of both Sutra and Tantra.

In a summer garden full of multicoloured flowers whose perfumes fill the air, a bee chooses the nectar it prefers to drink. In this way, according to our individual fortune and karmic propensity, we choose to practise the holy Buddhist teachings which suit us best; so to suggest one of the traditions is superior and the others inferior is a naive and mistaken way of thinking. Each of the traditions is an authentic path, a method for becoming enlightened, and a medicine to relieve suffering.

Just like smelted, cut and beaten gold, the quintessential consolidation of the immaculate teachings of the One Gone to Bliss was collected by many successive generations of Tibetans, and is a true treasure of world heritage. This is the source of future teachings, and a precious inheritance for future generations of beings. The teachings are the accomplished, profound and excellent realisation, the endowment of the immortal, accomplished awareness holders. They are the essence of the transition-less eternal holy path, ultimate essence of the treasury of teachings of individual transmission, the way taken by many learned and righteous accomplished ones, and the swift path to move on in the body of rainbow light.

The unmistaken source of these individual lineages is the holy Lama who has attained the signs of accomplishment of their specific path and is possessed of authentic characteristics. To whichever Lama you are connected by your karmic destiny, they are the Lord of the Mandala and

Protector of the World. All those who desire liberation, raise the holy feet of the Lama to the crown of your head, take them as the jewel of your heart, for they will never mislead you!

TWELVE

TREASURE TROVE OF WISH-FULFILLING GEMS

"At first, skilfully examine the Lama.
Then, skilfully train with the Lama.
Finally, skilfully emulate the Lama's realisation and action."

Take this summary as the foundation of practice.

We need to train with a spiritual master and receive the nectar of the holy Buddhist teachings, those profound and extensive instructions which are a supreme panacea to cure the hundred diseases of the afflictive emotions. However, it is not enough just to receive the teachings. It is not enough to keep medicine in a cupboard; a sick person must actually take medicine. In the same way, if we do not abandon distractions and focus one-pointedly on meditation, only ever receiving and hearing teachings, then we are not going to grasp the supreme meaning.

Profound wisdom has been present in our mind streams from the very beginning. In order to awaken it, we need to access in our own mind stream that which is at the very core of our root master's sacred mind.

What is meant by saying a student relies on a master? It means a student needs to train with their master. We should understand that training with a master does not entail simply taking for ourselves what we want from the master, as if the Lama is a musk deer and the teachings are musk. With faith and devotion, the student needs to attain in their mind stream the state of mind and conduct of the Lama, exactly and however this may be; in the same way as, for example, a clay tsa tsa replicates the form of the tsa tsa mould, exactly as it is. Similarly, we need to attain the certainty of the Lama's mind essence.

Having found a spiritual master who has holy wisdom, we should train with them. When studying with them we should never be distracted, even if we encounter hundreds of difficulties, or even threats to our own bodies or lives. In the same manner that the Ever-weeping Bodhisattva Sadaparudita trained with the Buddha Dharmodgata, train with the

Lama without weariness, so as to receive, through faith and steadfastness, into our own mind streams all the enlightened wisdom that resides in the holy mind stream of the Lama, as if filling a vase to the brim. Unless we do this, just making our outer appearances resemble the master is of no benefit at all.

Other than the Lama, there is not one person, nothing that is a more exalted basis to which to go for refuge, or gather the accumulations. Moreover, when the Lama is bestowing empowerments or giving teachings, he or she is the true identity of the Three Precious Jewels, the Three Roots and all the Buddhas of all directions combined. The Lama's blessing and compassion is completely indivisible from that of all the Buddhas. It has been taught by many holy masters serving one mouthful of good food to the Lama during a period when he or she is giving teachings or empowerments is more meritorious than hundreds or thousands of offerings made at other times.

When we meditate on the deities endowed with defining characteristics of the Development Stage, these deities appear with their manifest aspects; however we need to meditate knowing their essence is our root guru, so blessings can be received. The entrance of the extraordinary wisdom of realisation of the Perfection Stage into our mind streams depends entirely on our devotion and the blessings of the Lama. It is for this reason that every Sutra and Tantra teaches the Lama is the actual Buddha.

The wisdom mind of the Lama is inseparable from that of all the Buddhas, however to the perceptions of those of us humans whose afflictive emotions need to be tamed, Lamas appear cunningly in human form. When the Lama is actually with us, whatever they say should be put into action, and so on, in order that we please the Lama with service of all three: body, speech and mind. And we should strive to merge our minds inseparably with the enlightened mind of the Lama, because if we only become certain of the Lama's enlightened qualities at a later stage, i.e. after death, it will be a little late.

"At first, skilfully examine the Lama." This tells us we should examine the Lama before we receive empowerments or teachings. As I have already mentioned, if we first receive profound empowerments and teachings and only afterwards examine the Lama, we have the proper order mixed up. Having begun training with a Lama and having finished receiving empowerments and teachings, we should see with devotion whatever the

Lama does as good. If we develop wrong views regarding the Lama, this will be the cause of our own ruin. We should practise pure vision, thinking only of the Lama's enlightened qualities.

All the blessings of the Buddhas and the Lama should be drawn to us by faith and devotion in our hearts; this is the result of gathering the accumulations and purifying the obscurations, therefore it is crucial that we are kind to ourselves in this respect by following this instruction. So, when we find a potential teacher, we examine and analyse them, but it is not enough just to have found a genuine guide. We can only attain results by having first put into practice the teachings of which actions to adopt and which to abandon. In this way we practise according to instruction.

For this reason, those of us who wish to attain enlightenment quickly need to gather the two accumulations of merit and wisdom. The way to do this is by basing our mind stream on both great compassion and the essence of emptiness, immaculate wisdom. Using only the method of great compassion, we cannot be liberated from cyclic existence. Meditating on emptiness devoid of compassion is also not an authentic path. Only by practising the path of the union of emptiness and compassion can we avoid residing in the extremes of samsaric existence or nirvanic peace and attain the level of buddhahood.

In order to suit the mental capacity of beings wishing to learn, the Buddha taught the Dharma of the great, medium and modest spiritual approaches, with both provisional and definitive meaning. The teachings which we want to follow are those of truly definitive meaning, the swift path for attaining enlightenment in the shortest possible time. However, it is not as if the Lama can throw us skyward like a stone and enable us to attain liberation. Each individual needs to gather the accumulations and purify obscurations, thus progressing with certainty along the levels of the path. It is also vital to maintain the vows of Individual Liberation, bodhichitta and Tantra, as well as the Bodhisattva precepts and sacred Tantric commitments which the Lama has taught.

First we need to enter into the refuge of the Three Precious Jewels, enter the door of the Buddhist teachings and, at the same time, take the vows of a lay person accepting the Three Jewels. This involves maintaining accordingly the fundamental principles of rejection, acceptance, and their associated aspects.

Progressing by stages, the vows for lay practitioners are as follows.

The Temporary Vows of the Eight One-Day Precepts of the Outer Vows of Individual Liberation are:

1. Not killing.
2. Not taking what is not offered.
3. Not engaging in sexual misconduct due to desire.
4. Not lying.
5. Not drinking intoxicating liquor.
6. Not eating food at the wrong time.
7. Not using malas etc. while dancing and so on.
8. Not using a high or grand seat or bed.

The precepts observed by male and female lay devotees include:

1. Practicing one of the above precepts.
2. Observing several of the precepts.
3. The 'complete' layperson vows.
4. The 'pure conduct' layperson vows.

Following these are the Four Root Precepts of the Novice:

1. Not engaging in sexual conduct.
2. Not taking what was not given.
3. Not killing.
4. Not telling lies.

And the Six Branch Precepts:

5. Not drinking intoxicating liquor.
6. Not dancing, and so on.
7. Not wearing malas and so on with attachment.
8. Not taking high, grandiose seats.
9. Not eating food at the wrong time.
10. Not accepting gold or silver.

In addition, there are the two hundred and fifty-three monastic precepts of a fully-ordained monk, and so on. We should maintain whichever of these vows we take in the appropriate manner, exactly as directed.

Taking the inner Bodhisattva vows includes:

1. The aspiration and application precepts.
2. The discipline of refraining from wrongdoing which subsumes the Two Truths.
3. The discipline of accumulating virtue.
4. The discipline of acting for the benefit of sentient beings.

Once these vows are taken they should all be maintained steadfastly.

In addition, there are the vows associated with the three Tantra sections: Kriya Tantra, Upa Tantra and Yoga Tantra of the outer Tantras of Buddha Sakyamuni. Finally, there are the vows of the inner Tantras of skilful means, the three yogas: Mahayoga, Anuyoga and Atiyoga.

It is particularly important, by maintaining the root and branch precept stages of the Great Perfection, we should practise diligently, without weariness. By these means, those who become deeply nauseated by the worldly activities of this life, leave for the kingdom of accomplished knowledge holders of the lineage, following the path of those who have passed into the rainbow body of light.

It is beneficial to practise in a sacred place which has the power to bless ordinary beings. The most excellent and supreme of sacred places is the peak of the world, a land of snow-mountains, complete with the enlightening qualities of seclusion.

> Peaks of mountains pristine with white snow
> reach up to the blue expanse of sky.
> Beneath this clarity shine turquoise lakes,
> offerings of pristine water
> arrayed amongst rocky crags.
>
> Plants blossoming with many-coloured flowers
> adorn these jagged mountain sides
> surrounding naturally perfect cave houses.
> White clouds scatter dewdrops of rain,
> the youthful sun casts rays of warming light,
> into solitary secluded forest depths.
>
> In grassy meadows, rich with myriad healing herbs,
> on hill tops robed in mist,

peaceful birds and animals romp and play.
Rain falling from clouds brings satisfaction to the heart.
The eastern path, whence sun and moon rise, is vast.
Cool winds blow gently from the south.

Three summer months, the cuckoo's melodious song
resounds.
Three autumn months, plants and herbs ripen, setting fruit
and seed.
Three winter months, river water hides behind white ice.
Three months of spring, flower-filled meadows flourish on
the plains.

In nature's kingdom samadhi naturally arises, distractions and bustle are
rare. There are no cries of misery or suffering. Through the inner bliss of
concentration the heart is naturally and deeply satisfied.

Meet and form a bond with a holy spiritual friend; a congenial
companion who has taken sacred commitments, is free of the five
poisons, stable of mind, easy-going, diligent in practice and loving
towards you. Then train your mind in the common, uncommon and
special preliminaries. Through learning the history and origins of the
teachings of the lineage, develop conviction in the extraordinary
teachings.

Following this, mature your mind stream by receiving empowerments.
Then receive the teachings of the stages of the main practice and the oral
instructions, by which your mind stream will be matured and liberated.
Conduct the stages of practical training in accordance with traditional
practices, as well as integrating them with your own experience. From
time to time, undertake the stages of training to remove obstacles and
enhance practice. Ask questions of the spiritual master and senior
Dharma brothers and sisters. Correlate these answers and apply yourself
earnestly to the heart of practice.

One day, meditation and post meditation, day and night, become united
in no meditation. Time passes in the luminous wheel, and you become
united with the realisation and action of the regent of the Victorious
Ones of the three times, the holy Lama. On this ground of comfort the
continuity of heart's bliss is unbroken. Great benefit for self and others is
accomplished spontaneously, now and forever more!

THIRTEEN

HOW THINGS APPEAR: DEPENDENT ARISING CAUSATION

When we see ourselves in a mirror, our expressions of happiness, sadness, contentment and suffering, and so on, are clear. Not only that, but we can see marks, blemishes, wrinkled skin and tangled hair, all exactly as we have them. What appears in the mirror arises on the surface of the glass, but what is actually there is a part of our own bodies and exists nowhere else.

In the same way, in our lives we experience suffering created by enemies, suffering of being separated from loved ones, suffering of meeting with what is undesirable, and so on. But our experiences of all sorts of suffering do not come about from something outside ourselves; some external, causeless, condition-less disaster, imposed upon us as if we ourselves were never at fault. These things happen because we have a karmically-produced physical body, perpetuating aggregates subject to degeneration. Fire has the nature of heat, and water has the nature of liquid. In the same way, because the constituents of our physical bodies are manifest because of the truth of suffering, they have the nature of suffering. This is the true nature of material things.

From what cause does suffering arise? It comes about from the all-pervasive origin of karma and afflictive emotions. The ultimate root of this comes from co-emergent ignorant grasping at a self.

The first link in the Twelve Links of Interdependent Connection is ignorance; the ground of samsaric confusion, or the very nature of delusion. The opposite of ignorance is awareness. If we realise the wisdom of awareness, we will no longer be confused. Therefore, if we had not come under the influence of ignorance, there would be no initial confusion. If, while confusion is rampant we gain this wisdom, the continuum of confusion becomes cut.

If, when we are dreaming, we can recognise that we are dreaming and wake up, then in this way we free ourselves from the confusion of the dream. So, by this analogy, we can understand the real root of the suffering we experience is ignorance. From ignorance develop habitual tendencies, consciousness, name and form, the activity fields, contact, feeling, craving, grasping, existence and birth, continuing on to old age and death; and once again we complete the cycle. In this way, the wheel of cyclic existence comes into being, and the continuum of suffering is not cut. So, in confusion we experience the suffering thrown at us by previous karmic actions and afflictive emotions, while at the same time we are also creating the causes for future suffering, the results of which we continue to experience.

In this way, from beginingless time until now, we have experienced tremendous suffering. The tears we have cried are deeper than the four oceans, and the bones from our dead bodies would form a pile higher than the king of mountains. However, we continue to create the causes for more suffering. This is because we are under the control of delusion.

If the cause is sowing a barley seed, then the result is growth of a barley sprout, and if the cause is sowing a wheat seed, then the result is growth of a wheat sprout. If causes are created based on wrong views, hatred and so on, then the result will be suffering. If causes are created by practising the ten virtuous actions and so on, then the result of the bliss of gods and humans will be attained. If the cause is based on practising the path of the three degrees of enlightenment (the path of an Arhat, a Pratyekabuddha and a Buddha), the result will be to attain the level of the three degrees of enlightenment, and so on. This defines the concept of dependent arising: 'based on one thing, another is produced'.

These causes and conditions cannot be established as truly existing, able to be fixed, or to have an unchanging or permanent nature, therefore they are impermanent and empty in nature. Because of this, it is demonstrated the essence of dependent connection is emptiness.

If a cause does not involve wrong views, hatred and so on, the effect will not bring about suffering. For this reason, the Buddha taught all the knowable phenomena of the three: cyclic existence, nirvana, and the path, come about from causes. Anyone who does not wish to experience suffering should put a stop to the causes of suffering. For example, drinking poison will bring about sickness but, if we can stop the cause of drinking poison, then the resultant sickness will not occur. On the contrary, if we stop the resultant sickness but at the same time do not prevent the cause and still drink poison, then once again the resultant sickness will develop in a never-ending loop.

The principle is if we abandon negative causes, resulting happiness will be brought about.

The Blessed One taught:

> "Do no evil whatsoever.
> Practice virtue perfectly,
> And tame your mind completely.
> This is the teaching of the Buddha."

Here the paths of the three types of individuals, modest, middling and great, are completely and unmistakably summarised in this one stanza. This stanza teaches the entire framework of the teachings in a summary of the process of abandoning harming others from the very root, and taming our own minds.

These teachings on karma tell us from our present body we can know where we were born in the past and, by looking at our karmic actions, where we will be born in the future.

We ordinary beings living in cyclic existence are completely ignorant of which actions we should adopt and which actions we should abandon; therefore, although we desire happiness, we destroy its causes as if they were enemies. We do not desire suffering, however we grasp eagerly at its causes and rush to experience them.

The following are examples of how this works: The visual faculty is attracted to form, so a moth dies in the flame of a butter lamp. The faculty of hearing is attracted to sound, so a wild deer, lured by the sound of a flute, is killed by a hunter. The taste faculty is attracted to taste, so a bee drinking nectar gets stuck in a flower and dies. The touch faculty is attracted to sensation, so an elephant dies in a pool.

Sense pleasures are like this: We see some tempting food; it looks good and tastes delicious but, when we have eaten it, we become aware the food has been laced with fast-acting and deadly poison. Under the influence of attraction to sense pleasures, the sufferings of cyclic existence are generated.

Hidden dormant afflictions have been tainting our mind streams since beginingless time. The analogy is of water with salt dissolved in it. In the same way an old health problem can resurface if we eat the wrong food or use our bodies in an awkward way, our afflictions become manifest. We become attracted to and yearn for the five desirable objects of our sense faculties, we grasp eagerly at the negative causes of rebirth in the three lower realms, and we specifically achieve the resultant suffering, in just the same way as if we ate poisoned food.

In this case, all of us who want to be happy need to practise the cause of happiness: positive actions or virtue, and be certain to abandon negative actions. When an expert physician is treating an illness, first they need to identify the disease and then prescribe medicine which will treat the problem. In this way, we need to recognise the roots of suffering are negative actions, non-virtues.

Negative actions can be summarised into ten groups:
1) Killing, 2) taking what is not given and 3) engaging in sexual misconduct through desire - these are the three physical non-virtues. 4) Lying, 5) divisive talk, 6) harsh words and 7) gossiping, are the four verbal non-virtues. 8) Covetousness, 9) malice and 10) wrong views, are the three mental non-virtues. The opposites of the Ten Negative Actions or Non-virtues are the Ten Positive Actions or Virtues.

The causes of these actions bring about karmic results which propel us into future experiences. There are three kinds of result: 1) the fully ripened result, 2) the result which resembles the cause, and 3) the dominant result, all three of which ripen for both positive and negative actions.

The fully ripened result of killing is to be born in hell and the lower realms. The result which resembles the cause is to attain briefly a higher birth, but to have a short life. The dominant result is consuming food, drink or medicine has little beneficial effect.

Similarly, the fully ripened result of taking what is not given is to be born in the lower realms. The result which resembles the cause is to be poor. The dominant result is for one's harvest to fail or be destroyed by frost and hail, in other words loss of wealth or possessions.

The fully ripened result of engaging in sexual misconduct is to be born in the lower realms. The result which resembles the cause is for one's partner to be unfaithful. The dominant result is to be born in a filthy and frightening place, as well as many other unthinkable results.

Correspondingly, the fully ripened result of protecting life is to be born in the higher realms. The result which resembles the cause is a long life. The dominant result is to be free of illness and have a healthy constitution.

Abandon taking what is not given, and rebirth will be in the higher realms. The result which resembles the cause is to have great wealth. The dominant result is to enjoy excellent prosperity.

The fully ripened result of abandoning sexual misconduct is to be born in the higher realms. The result which resembles the cause is to have a loving partner. The dominant result is to be born in a comfortable and pleasant place.

None of these kinds of results will be encountered if the karma has not been created, but what has been accumulated can never be lost. Karmic results do not ripen upon others, but ripen exclusively on those who have accumulated them. The developed fully mature consequence of a particular karma only ripens on a physical body possessed of a mind stream, and this happens in three ways: 1) As karma experienced in this lifetime as perceptible phenomena, 2) as karma experienced in the next rebirth, and 3) as karma experienced in subsequent lives after the next rebirth.

Accumulated karma does not mould, rot, or dry up, and therefore can never be lost. Either the result is experienced and then the karma is exhausted, or the karma is mitigated by confession complete with the Four Powers, in the same way as snow melts in the sunshine. In addition, if bodhichitta is aroused in the mind stream then negative karma is naturally purified, in the same way as the sun dispels darkness.

Whichever positive or negative action is strongest, then that result will be experienced first. The result of weaker actions will be experienced later. If actions are of equal strength, then, at the point of death, whichever positive or negative state of mind is closest will determine which kind of karmic result is experienced fully, as a good or bad rebirth.

Through examination we need to recognise which non-virtuous traits are predominant in our mind streams. Think: "I have accumulated innumerable non-virtues like this in the past. But not just in this life, the amount I have accumulated in many previous lives is incalculable. I was not possessed of attentive mindfulness and so did not recognise I was accumulating unimaginable negative karma; now I am filled with terrible regret! From this point on, I will give up all gross and subtle misdeeds which are defined by the ten non-virtues, and cultivate their antidotes. I will practise the opposites of the non-virtues, the ten virtues, with the same urgency as a dancing girl beats out the flames burning her skirt." We need to meditate on this until we are fired with enthusiasm.

At this time think: "If I died now, there would be nowhere for me to go, no alternative but to experience the suffering of the lower realms." Only when we feel this terror do we finally see the hidden threat of karma. However, it is not enough merely to experience fear and hopelessness. Through the door of the complete Four Powers we need to confess our faults without wavering, vow to refrain from doing such things in future, regret what has been done, and practise the Bodhisattva conduct.

> "Misdeeds have no good qualities,
> But confession purifies them,
> And this is a quality of misdeeds."

Lord Nagajuna taught:

> "Whoever was heedless before
> Later becomes heedful,
> As did (the former murderer) Angulimala."

Pray: "From this time onwards I regret all the negative actions I have done. I resolve never to do such things again in the future. I will practise, seeing all worldly activities in just the same way as a person suffering from jaundice regards oily food, until I grow sick at heart with nausea."

FOURTEEN

THE WESTERLY BLISSFUL PURE REALM

At this point, in order to help beginners entering the path of the Dharma to overcome discouragement and generate enthusiasm for the result of practice, the Blessed Buddha, King of the Sakyas, praised the Blissful Pure Realm of Sukhavati in many Sutras and Tantras, and taught four causes for being reborn there.

THE FOUR CAUSES are:

1. Bring to mind again and again the array of Sukhavati and Lord Amitabha.
2. Constantly accumulate a great many virtuous deeds using many different methods.
3. Generate the bodhichitta of supreme enlightenment.
4. Dedicate these roots of merit in order for them to become the cause of rebirth in Sukhavati, and make prayers of aspiration.

THE FIRST CAUSE, the way to bring to mind the pure realm of Sukhavati is as follows: It is taught that Sukhavati is located to the west of our universe, beyond countless other Buddha realms, in a world system in the upper heavens. There the entire ground is formed from seven types of naturally-occurring precious substances, which feel soft underfoot and spring back after each footstep. Merely walking on the precious ground generates great feelings of comfort and bliss. The ground is as smooth as the palm of a child's hand, vast and spacious, limitless beyond vision, bright and radiant.

Trees formed of many different precious substances flourish in myriad colours. The trees' branches are adorned with blessed beautiful and precious ornaments. Three times during the day and three times during the night, wind blows through the trees, and a delightful rain of blossoms showers the ground to a depth which equals the height of seven people of average stature. The previous blossoms are blown away by the wind, and the ground is delightful and beautiful.

In the trees perch many decorative species of beautiful emanated birds, who sing from the limitless treasure trove of their throats, surpassing all mundane instruments. Their songs are melodious to the ear and in harmony with the heart, proclaiming far and wide the sound of the profound and vast Dharma.

Many trees of the gods grow here, including the Tamala tree, Agaru, and Snake-heart Sandalwood. Meadowlands formed from precious materials shine blue-green like turquoise. Rivers and streams flow smoothly, without any silt, and their banks are covered with gold sand. These waters have the eight excellent qualities: 1) coolness, 2) sweetness, 3) lightness, 4) softness and 5) clearness. They are: 6) free from impurities, and drinking them 7) soothes the stomach, and 8) benefits the throat. Here and there are bathing pools edged with red pearls, and golden steps lead down to the water. One has only to think how warm or cool the nectar-like waters of the pools and rivers could be, and that is the temperature they become. The size and temperature of the rivers and pools becomes exactly how each individual desires them.

Completely filling the lakes, pools, ponds and forest parks are the beautiful, fragrant flowers of the gods, including water lilies and blue and white lotuses. The lotus flowers are completely filled with light and light rays. On the tips of all the light rays, in a most spectacular display, are numberless emanated Buddhas working for the benefit of beings. In this land not even the names of the hell and lower realms, or the eight unfree states are heard. Not even the names of desire and the six afflictions, the five poisons, diseases caused by disorders of the four elements, enemies, conflicts, malevolent forces, and so on, have ever been heard.

In this the Blissful Pure Realm of Sukhavati all feeling is solely of the nature of bliss, never tainted with any suffering. There is no difference between day and night; it is always day time. There are no women who are not enlightened, and no birth from the womb. All the beings here are born miraculously from lotus flowers; they are golden in colour and adorned with the thirty-two excellent marks and eighty excellent signs of great beings.

Beings here have miraculous pure perception, and other sublime perceptions of the Five Eyes, which include eyes with clear insight and physical eyes. In a mere instant, beings in this pure realm can travel miraculously to billions upon billions of other pure realms. With their clear insight they can see all these realms, and they can also hear all sounds made by these realms' beings, and know their minds. They have the sacred compassionate mind, which wishes benefit, bliss, and so on, for others. They have ocean-like wisdom with perfect recall and eloquence, and so on. The retinue of Lord Amitabha is beautiful, with these and other limitless enlightened qualities.

Also, there are hundreds of thousands of mansions, all formed from precious materials, inconceivable celestial palaces, throne-loungers made of valuable substances, lavished with layer upon layer of quilts and coverlets, and woven fabrics of the gods; all of this appears when summoned just by thinking. Everything one desires appears as soon as it is brought to mind; jewellery, clothing and whatever fulfils any of the five desirable qualities of the senses, without anyone claiming ownership. Everything one could want in the way of offering substances and ritual articles appears just by thought.

Everyone dwelling in this pure realm discusses the unexcelled Dharma, for they are all Bodhisattvas. For each being there are many emanated goddesses who make multifarious offerings. In the melodious songs of all kinds of birds, the wind whispering through the trees, the flowing rivers, and so on, is heard the sound of the Three Precious Jewels, the Ten Bodhisattva Levels, and the Transcendent Perfections; but when one enters complete meditative absorption these sounds do not arise.

In the centre of the pure realm is the Tree of Enlightenment called All-Illuminating Precious Lotus, which is five thousand miles high. The boughs and branches cover a distance of two and a half thousand miles and the leaves, flowers and fruit flourish continuously. The whole tree is completely covered, adorned with all kinds of jewelled ornaments and dangling threads of gold. There are long necklaces, jewelled tassels and decorative strings of crystals, red and blue pearls and so on, and latticework and pendants of myriad jewels, draped with festoons of small bells.

If one sees this Tree of Enlightenment, hears the sound of wind wafting through its branches, smells the fragrance of its flowers, tastes the flavour of the fruit, is touched by its light, or has any of these experiences, one is freed from illness and, having seen and contemplated this tree, one will not be distracted until enlightenment is attained.

In front of the tree is the towering throne of its Lord made of precious materials, ornamented by jewels, and raised up by eight peacocks. On the throne, seated on sun and moon cushions is the Bhagavan, the Tathagata, the Arhat, the utterly perfect Buddha, protector Amitabha, flawless and absolutely pure. His body is red, like a great mountain of coral bathed in the light of ten million suns. He has one face and two hands, and is resting in meditative equipoise. In his hands he holds an alms bowl filled with wisdom nectar. He is wearing the three Dharma robes. His legs are in the full lotus position. He is adorned with the thirty-two excellent marks and eighty excellent signs. He shines with light and light rays which pervade numberless pure realms. All who are touched by this light feel physically blissful and mentally full of joy. He emanates unlimited rays of light which bestow supreme bliss.

On his right is seated the very embodiment of the compassion of all the Victorious Ones, the noble lord Avalokiteshvara. His body is white in colour, like a great snow-mountain bathed in the light of ten million suns, in the attire of the sambhogakaya, ornamented with various silks and jewels. He is in the standing posture, his right hand in the gesture of giving protection. His left hand forms the gesture symbolising the Three Precious Jewels, holding the stem of a white lotus flower at the centre of his chest, the petals level with his heart.

On the left is the very embodiment of the power and strength of all the Victorious Ones, Son of the Victorious Ones, He Who Has Attained Great Power, Vajrapani, like a mountain of lapis lazuli with the attire of the sambhogakaya. He is in the standing posture, right hand in the gesture of giving protection and his left hand holding the stamen of a blue lotus, symbolising the sign of indestructible power.

From the bodies of the two Bodhisattvas, lights and rays emanate. The three main figures are luminous like the sun and moon among stars, and huge like the king of mountains surrounded by small hills. The overwhelming presence of their excellent marks and signs is radiant and the eloquent sounds of their Dharma teachings are perfectly distinct. Completely surrounding the serenity of the essential enlightened wisdom mind of the Buddhas is the boundless retinue of Bodhisattva monks wearing the three Dharma robes.

Hold this complete visualisation in mind. In this way, the members of the assembled gathering face us and all beings, their faces aglow with delight, gazing with smiling eyes. They hold us in mind with their compassion. Think of them with yearning; they are the great guides who lead us. At whatever time, whether walking, sitting, sleeping or eating, do not forget them. It is taught this is the main practice which will cause us to be reborn in the Blissful Pure Realm of Sukhavati.

THE SECOND CAUSE of rebirth in Sukhavati is, in general, through striving to generate many boundless roots of virtue through the three doors and, in particular, to gather the accumulations, we need to practise the Seven Branches.

The First Branch is prostration: With physical devotion, put your palms together at the level of your heart and make prostrations. With devotion of speech, recite prayers. With reverence of heart, have faith and devotion. Prostrate facing a westerly direction.

The Second Branch is offering: Make real and imaginary offerings of incense, water, lamps, food, and so on. Offer whatever you have without miserliness, offer with pure intention. Mentally emanate everything which is desirable in the realms of gods and humans, everything which is good and of great value. Emanate inexhaustibly, offering everything.

The Third Branch is confession: By way of the four remedial powers, confess all negative actions and downfalls accumulated by you yourself and all other sentient beings since beginingless time. Confess with the three doors, body, speech and mind, combined together as one.

The Fourth Branch is rejoicing: Rejoice with joy at all the virtue which has been accumulated in the three times by all ordinary people and noble beings.

The Fifth Branch is requesting: Pray the Conquerors, together with their infinite spiritual heirs residing in the pure realms of the ten directions, continuously turn the wheel of profound and vast Dharma without ceasing.

The Sixth Branch is beseeching: Pray, and make prayers of aspiration for the Buddhas, Bodhisattvas, and holders of the teachings, all spiritual masters, wherever they are, not to pass into nirvana but live for a long time.

THE THIRD CAUSE for rebirth in the Blissful Realm is to cultivate the attitude of supreme bodhichitta. In order to bring all sentient beings to eternal bliss, the level of buddhahood, we should cultivate the attitude of supreme bodhichitta, which incorporates aspiration and engagement. These practices should be undertaken appropriately.

THE FOURTH CAUSE to be reborn in Sukhavati, and the Seventh Branch, is dedication. Dedicate all roots of virtue to the cause of being born in the Blissful Realm, dedicating in just the same way as Noble Manjushri, without any conceptualisation. Pray: "May I cut all the entanglements of fixated attachment of this life for myself and all sentient beings, and then, having died and moved on, take miraculous birth sitting in the full lotus position in the heart of a lotus flower in the Blissful Realm."

Make these prayers of aspiration with the thought as soon as you are reborn your body will be perfectly complete, adorned with the excellent marks and signs. You will behold the face of the Buddha and have good fortune to listen to the Buddhist teachings. You will attain miraculous powers and so, whatever offering substances you desire, all will appear in the palm of your hand, just by thinking without any effort. By emanation you will be able to travel to other pure realms and cultivate the ocean-like conduct of a Bodhisattva.

Pray: "One day, may my enlightenment be prophesied; the time, place and my name when I will be thus gone to nirvana. At that time, may all those who have been my mothers since beginingless time, all suffering sentient beings, as boundless as the sky, may they too be liberated from the ocean of suffering. May I be able to lead them to the island of liberation and complete enlightenment!"

Together with this and other prayers of aspiration, practise the four causes of being born in the Blissful Realm. Then, having died and passed on, you will take rebirth in the pure realm of Sukhavati, just as the Buddha taught, not just once, but many times in the Sutras and Tantras. The Three Precious Jewels are never misleading, therefore we should practise diligently!

FIFTEEN

INFALLIBLE AND PERMANENT SUPREME REFUGE

The foundation of all Buddhist paths, great and small, the entrance way to the sacred Dharma, and the basis for all vows is the one crucial action of going for refuge to the Three Precious Jewels. The reason we need to go for refuge is because of our fear and dread of samsaric suffering. Other than the Three Precious Jewels, there is nothing which can give us refuge from the suffering of samsara; therefore we should go for refuge to the Three Precious Jewels.

Go for refuge with fear, faith in the Three Jewels, and with the thought of great compassion for all beings. What should we fear? The object of our fear is the endemic, boundless suffering of cyclic existence, the root of which is birth and death. The causes of suffering are defiled actions and afflictions, which we should regard as our enemies. If we meditate solely on emptiness without compassion, we will not experience boundless enlightened qualities; for this reason we should consider the one-sided peace of nirvana as a hidden crevasse. For the time being, all improper conceptual thought patterns opposed to the path leading to enlightenment should be regarded as poison.

We are afraid of conflict, accidents and sickness so, in order to protect us from these fears, we go for refuge to the Three Precious Jewels. We need to be certain of this from the very beginning. Due to the power of the supreme basis, just reciting the words of the refuge prayer without knowing any of the reasons for doing so, will become the eventual cause for attaining liberation one day. However, although this is true, it is not an authentic way to go for refuge which will develop the knowledge and wisdom of the path, so we need to understand the true reasons for going for refuge.

Going for refuge is like opening the entrance to the sacred Buddhist teachings. The door of refuge is opened by faith. Faith is classified into three categories. As I already mentioned, when we see representations of Buddha body, speech and mind, and the Lama or spiritual master, or hear the exemplary life stories of holy masters, we feel a sense of awe and our faith grows. This is faith based on awe.

Through learning the enlightened qualities of the Three Precious Jewels, we develop the earnest desire to accomplish those qualities in our own mind streams and in the mind streams of others. This is longing faith. Because only the refuge of Three Precious Jewels and no other can protect us from the suffering of samsara, we take refuge with the infallible Three Precious Jewels forever, and this is faith based on conviction. In this way, through the door of extraordinary faith and devotion, we must first go for refuge with heartfelt conviction, affirming, "You know best!" We do not turn to anyone or anything else.

The Buddha taught in the Sutras:

> "Those without faith
> Do not practise virtue,
> In the same way as a burnt seed
> Does not sprout a green shoot."

The Three Precious Jewels have inconceivable compassion and blessing; however, allowing these blessings to enter into our mind streams depends solely on faith and devotion.

The essence of going for refuge is undertaking a commitment: we promise to take the fully enlightened Buddha, complete with the three qualities of wisdom, compassion and spiritual power, as our teacher. We vow to follow this teacher and no others. This is causal refuge. We promise to take this teacher as embodying the goal which we ourselves will ultimately accomplish, and vow to strive for this goal and no others. This is resultant refuge.

Accordingly, we promise to take the sacred Buddha Dharma, which includes teachings and realisation, and the members of the sublime spiritual community, the Sangha, as the path and our companions, and not to rely on any other paths or companions. This vow is the causal refuge. We promise to take these two as the goals we will ultimately accomplish in our own mind streams. Having ourselves assimilated the sacred Dharma of realisation, the corresponding cause is to turn the wheel of the Dharma of scriptural teaching for others and lead them into the gathering of sublime beings, so the continuity of the heritage of the Three Precious Jewels is not broken. This vow is the resultant refuge.

INFALLIBLE AND PERMANENT SUPREME REFUGE

Three subdivisions of going for refuge are as follows:

The way beings of modest capacity go for refuge is through renunciation, knowing the difficult-to-find human body with the freedoms does not last very long, in fear of the lower realms, and in order to accomplish rebirth in a higher realm.

Wherever we are born in samsara we are bound by the causes of suffering, so if we go for refuge in order to enter into personal peace and happiness, this is the way of beings of middling capacity.

Going for refuge with the motivation of great compassion and supreme bodhichitta in order to enlighten all sentient beings is the way beings of great capacity go for refuge.

The ways to go for refuge are as follows:

The tradition of the common lesser spiritual approach, Hinayana, considers the Buddha as the teacher, his teachings as the path, and the spiritual community as companions on the path of practice. Hinayana practitioners go for refuge to the Buddha manifesting realisation, together with the Dharma which resides in the mind stream of the sublime beings.

In the general tradition of the extraordinary inner and outer secret mantra, going for refuge is done by offering body, speech and mind to the Lama, relying on the personal yidam deity and taking the dakini as a friend.

Particularly in the tradition of the Great Perfection, the subtle channels are taken as the basis for the emanation body, the nirmanakaya, subtle wind is purified as the sambhogakaya, and subtle drops are perfected as the dharmakaya. This method is going for refuge in the swift path. We meditate on the gross causal channels, winds and drops, taking ourselves as the being of sacred commitment. The subtle wisdom channels, winds and drops are meditated on as the wisdom being. In dependence upon these objects of refuge, purity becomes manifest and enlightenment is attained.

The vajra refuge of the natural state is that which resides in the enlightened mind stream

159

of the objects of refuge, wisdom comprised of the twofold knowledge; or, in other words, that which is the indivisibility of the three: empty essence, luminous nature and all-pervasive compassion. The way to accomplish this in our own mind stream is by going for refuge, therefore we need to familiarise ourselves with the appropriate intention and practice, and then go for refuge.

The way to visualise the accumulation field for taking refuge is as follows:

Unlike the place you find yourself in at the moment, where the earth, stones, hills, houses, and so on, are all impure, the pure realm is limitless in size, formed of myriad precious substances, and naturally beautifully-arrayed. The precious ground is as smooth as a mirror and in the centre, a little way directly in front of you, is the trunk of the five-branched wish-granting tree, which bears luxuriant leaves, blossoming flowers and countless clusters of ripe fruit. To the east, south, west and north, the sky above is latticed by leaves and branches, which are decorated with beautiful ornaments and bells of myriad jewels.

Of this tree, the central branch is slightly higher than the rest, and here, on a precious throne supported by eight great lions, on a stack of lotus, sun and moon cushions is seated the quintessence of all the Buddhas of past, present and future, the incomparable treasure of compassion, the Lake-Born Vajra of Uddiyana, Padmasambhava, inseparable from your glorious root guru. His complexion is white, tinged with red, and he is sitting in the full lotus position. In his right hand he holds a golden vajra in the threatening gesture. His left hand rests in his lap, holding a skull-cup filled with the wisdom nectar of immortality and a coral vase ornamented at its rim by a sprig of the wish-granting tree.

On his body he wears, from inner to outer garments, a white secret vajra robe, a blue mantric robe, a red monastic robe and a maroon brocade cloak, one on top of the other. On his head he wears the lotus crown which liberates on sight, which is made of five kinds of silk and topped by a vajra and a beautiful vulture's feather. Embraced in his lap, symbolising the union of unchanging great bliss and emptiness possessing all the supreme aspects, is his consort, the Dakini Yeshe Tsogyal. She is white in complexion and holds a curved knife and skull-cup.

Above Padmasambhava's head are the Great Perfection lineage masters: Dharmakaya Samantabhadra, Samboghakaya Vajrasattva, Nirmanakaya

Garap Dorje, Master Manjushrimitra, Guru Shri Singha, Scholar Jnanasutra, Great Pandita Vimalamitra, Orgyen Padmasambhava, Dharmaraja Trisong Detsen, Great Translator Vairotsana, and Dakini Yeshe Tsogyal; these last three are known as the three heart-disciples: the king, the subject and the friend. Next, All-knowing Longchen Rabjam, Vidyadhara Jigme Lingpa, Jigme Gyalwe Nyugu, Migyur Namkhar Dorje, Great Khenpo Pema Banza, Orgyen Tenzin Norbu, Shenpen Choki Nunwa, and Jigme Yonten Gonpo, each complete with their own individual ornaments and attire. Visualise them sitting one above the other, the seat of the upper figure almost touching the head of the one below.

On the foremost branch of the tree is the Bhagavan Conqueror Sakyamuni, surrounded by the one thousand and two Buddhas of this fortunate aeon and the infinite victorious ones of all times and directions. On the right branch are the spiritual heirs of the victorious ones, Lords of the Three Families: Bodhisattvas Avalokiteshvara, Manjushri and Vajrapani, who are chief among the Eight Main Bodhisattvas, surrounded by the Noble Sangha of Bodhisattvas.

On the left branch are the two supreme Shravakas, Shariputra and Maudgalaputra, surrounded by the Sangha of noble Shravakas and Pratyekabuddhas. On the hindmost branch, surrounded by a lattice of rainbows and lights, is the Precious Jewel of the sacred Dharma in the form of sacred texts, with the six million four hundred thousand stanzas of the Great Perfection Tantras on top.

On the surrounding leaves and branches beneath the four main branches of the wish-granting tree are the glorious Dharma protectors and guardians, manifested by wisdom or karma. All males face outwards to prevent outer obstructions getting in. All females face inwards to prevent accomplishments from leaking out.

The forms of all the assembled deities of the refuge field blaze with refulgent light. They confront you and all beings with joyful faces and gaze with smiling eyes. Their minds are the nature of wisdom, compassion and spiritual power, and they think of you with loving-kindness. Consider with their speech and Brahma-like voices, they relieve the suffering of the lower realms.

Consider your father of this lifetime is on your right side, on the left your mother. In front of you is your hated enemy with all those who have harmed you or put obstacles in your way. Behind you are those to whom you owe karmic debts. A vast crowd of all the six types of sentient beings in human form, gathered like infinite particles of dust, covers the whole of the vast surrounding area.

With a voice full of devotion, begin reciting the verses of going for refuge, and as you do so the whole crowd joins in the recitation in resounding tones. With physical devotion, join your palms together. With devotion of the heart, think with fierce longing: "From this moment until they reach the heart of enlightenment, all mother-like sentient beings have no hope or refuge other than you. You, assembled deities of the Three Root Precious Jewels, think of us!"

Recite the refuge prayer of our 'Heart Essence' tradition regularly. When you are accumulating a number of refuge recitations, do your recitations in sessions of practice. At the very least you certainly need to accumulate one hundred thousand recitations of the refuge prayer.

When it is time to end a practice session, once again feel tremendous faith and devotion. The assembled deities of the refuge field emit limitless light rays from their bodies. The moment these light rays touch your body, and those of all other sentient beings, everyone suddenly dissolves into the assembled deities. The members of the refuge field also gradually merge from the outside towards the centre, and dissolve inseparably into your Lama and the Great One of Oddiyana. Your Lama then melts into light and disappears within this light. Rest for a moment in non-conceptual meditative equipoise. When you arise from meditation, dedicate the merit for the benefit of sentient beings. At all times, in a state of non-separation from mindful awareness, familiarise your mind with the assembled deities of the object of refuge.

When walking, meditate in the sky above your right shoulder the refuge field, as a focus for circumambulation. When sitting, as a support for prayer, meditate the refuge field is in the sky above the crown of your head. When sleeping, in order to recognise delusion within the delusion of dreams as luminosity, meditate the refuge field is in the centre of your heart. In this way, while doing any action, including walking, sitting, eating and sleeping, maintain a state inseparable from the vivid presence of the object of refuge divinities. Through this, with faith in the Three Precious Jewels based on conviction, focus your mind, heart and speech and exert yourself reciting the refuge prayer.

However, it is not enough to just go for refuge, we need to practise the points of training of going for refuge. The first of these are the three things to abandon:

1. Having gone for refuge to the Buddha, do not go for refuge to worldly gods.
2. Having gone for refuge to the Dharma, do not harm any sentient beings.
3. Having gone for refuge to the Sangha, do not get involved with teachers of non-Buddhist philosophy, or people of that kind.

Additionally, the three trainings to be accomplished are:

1. Having gone for refuge to the Buddha, consider representations of the form of the One Gone to Bliss as actual Buddhas and venerate them with prostrations and offerings.
2. Having gone for refuge to the Dharma, consider representations of the Precious Jewel of Dharma in the form of scriptures and letters as the actual Precious Jewel of Dharma, and make prostrations and offerings as before.
3. Having gone for refuge to the Sangha, consider representations of the Precious Jewel of the Sangha, ordained monks and nuns, as the actual Sangha and so venerate and respect them.

The three supplementary precepts are:

1. Make offerings to the Precious Jewels continuously.
2. Always recite the Refuge prayer.
3. Having been accepted by a spiritual master, engage in practising the Dharma and train in conduct which accords with the Dharma.

The benefits of going for refuge in this way, and maintaining the precepts of training, are limitless. Briefly, when we join the Buddhist family we come under the protective refuge of the Three Precious Jewels, whereby all illness, suffering and harm from humans and non-humans is pacified. Our previous karmic obscurations are purified. In all our successive lives we will not be separated from the presence of the Precious Ones, and ultimately we will attain the level of buddhahood. There are these and limitless other benefits.

There is a great difference between Buddhist practitioners who have taken the Three Precious Jewels as their source of refuge and accepted the four seals of the view that signify the Buddha's Teachings and those who do not follow a religion, or who follow non-Buddhist religions. There are differences both in terms of physical and mental comfort and happiness, and temporary and ultimate benefits and risks.

When Buddhists are travelling, we should not sit hunched over with our mouths shut, nor should we open the door of speech and let loose a store of all kinds of gossip, creating the causes for fights, quarrels, disagreement and mutual hostility. We should not think improper thoughts, or sprawl about with an undetermined state of mind, oblivious and miserable. We should travel cheerfully with our minds full of joy, chant and sing, recite mantras and prayers with faith and self-confident trust, and make prayers and aspirations to accomplish the purpose of our journey.

When it is time to do something, we should adhere to the law of cause and effect and use discrimination to decide what we should cultivate and what to avoid. Even if great success is not immediately achieved, we should not jump recklessly into the dangerous chasm of ignoring karmic law.

When eating, we should offer the first choice portion to the Precious Jewels, and incidentally complete the accumulation of merit. When sleeping, we should meditate in our hearts on the Lama, the essence of the union of the Precious Ones, so we are never separated from blessings.

As children, we should sharpen our intellects by reciting dharanis and mantras of wisdom and flourishing intelligence. Growing up, the conduct of Dharma should be cultivated, so the supremely noble path is found. As an adult, the law of cause and effect should never be violated, so both ourselves and others remain happy. When old, we are prepared for the future, so both physically and mentally we feel comfortable. Even if death comes now, a Buddhist already has familiarity with what lies in store, and so has no fear. When we die, the Dharma we have practised comes to welcome us and our positive actions follow behind us as support, and so we seize the entrance of the path to liberation.

The sacred Dharma moderates excess continuously, and protects us from problems associated with satiety. In times of misery, the Dharma is a comforting friend. There is no better hope than the Precious Ones, because whatever happens, we take our grief or joy onto the path; so if we gain a little we are not filled with pride and if we lose a little we are not disheartened.

On the other hand, if we do not accept causality then we do not understand we must bear responsibility for the fully-ripened result of any negative actions we commit. If we do not understand this, then we feel no concern if we profit at another's expense. In the same way, if two people with similar selfish vested interests meet, they use crafty schemes to find new ways of profiting from each other. Because they consider there are no future lives, they grasp solely at the appearances of this life. Fooled into exhausting themselves chasing ephemeral rewards, their lives end and they are left empty-handed on the brink of death.

In childhood people like this are not taught it is wrong to kill. They mix with bad companions in their youth. As adults, their selfish negative motivation brings ruin to themselves and others. In old age, with nothing to fill their time, they gamble, drink and smoke, committing endless non-virtuous actions in the wait for death. Finally, having entered into a seamless coffin... the kind of feelings they endure I will not speak of here.

At the moment, when we are thirsty we can swallow a refreshing drink. When we are hungry we eat whatever food we want. When it is cold we wear warm clothes, and on hot days we find means to stay cool. In the same way, when we are sick we take medicine, when we feel stiff we get a massage. Bedding and sofas, skyscraper apartments, vehicles to transport us around, and so on; we obtain all the things we need for this short human life.

In the same way, certain scientists, experts in their field, exert widespread influence. Kings and politicians have power to rule over whole countries. Some even possess weapons to destroy whole continents. However, apart from reserving a sealed coffin, such people have done nothing to prepare for death. How stupid!

At this time, while we are alive, while we have a home, family and friends, wealth and possessions, it is certainly better to recite the mani mantra even just once than to have a mountain of gold weighing many hundreds of thousands of ounces; for, when the time comes, we will go naked and empty-handed into the intermediate state of death.

Stricken with disease, our flesh and blood dries up. Our noses run and we dribble. Medicine and food cease to provide hope. Urine and vomit stain our bodies. Our mouths hang open and we clench our teeth. The movement of our breath ceases. At this time, of all our possessions and wealth, we cannot even take with us a single needle and thread. Moreover, this body's conglomerate of flesh and blood, that which we call 'I' and perceive as being ourselves, is also left behind and we must leave; we feel deeply unsatisfied because of our attachment. At this stage, our wealth and possessions, the objects of our attachment, are of no help, and through the influence of our attachment to them, they actually cause us harm.

All the possessions and wealth which you have accumulated through striving your entire life, gained through all manner of evil deeds and suffering, spiteful talk, underhanded methods, and so on, you yourself have no time to enjoy. All your possessions will be shared among others, at which time you will be filled with regret, but it will be useless. At the time of death nothing whatever, apart from the sacred Dharma, will be able to provide refuge. A single word of the holy teachings is more exalted than all the property that exists in the universe; but because, until you come to die you do not understand Dharma's true value, then you are confused and distraught.

The Precious Ones are your sacred protector, refuge and support, and provide continuous protection to everyone impartially.

When you give presents and bribes of money to those in positions of power, such people will provide you with help, but when your wealth runs out they regard you with disdain and at worst may have you thrown into jail as a criminal. When you are well off, all your friends and relatives throng around you in a crowd. If you become poor the opposite happens, friends shun you and you rarely have visitors. When you are young everyone is very attentive, but it is not like that when you are old. A few days after your death even mention of your name is avoided. People do not dare go into the house where you lived, thinking there might be a ghost.

While you live, pray to the Three Precious Jewels and the benefits will include protection from the Eight Fears. When you die there is reliable refuge; you will not need to experience the suffering of the lower realms. So in this way, during our current existence our minds are happy and our hearts joyful, and this brings physical well-being and therefore long life. If things go well, trust the compassion of the Precious Ones and the blessings of the Lama, and faith and devotion will flourish abundantly. If things go badly, understand negative karma accumulated in past lives is being exhausted, so difficult circumstances become our kind companions. At all times make prayers of aspiration:

> "Whatever happiness I have, may all sentient beings enjoy the same.
> Whatever sufferings I have, may they not befall any other sentient beings."

With the protection of the good heart, not only will we be happy in this and future lives, but everyone who comes into contact with a good-hearted person will also experience happiness. For example, within a household, whatever example is set by the behaviour and attitude of the adults, this is the way younger family members learn. If their elders teach a bad attitude and coarse behaviour, then the character of the youngsters will also be contaminated by these traits, and they will always be negative and aggressive. Such peoples' neighbours and companions will always be unhappy.

Similarly, if the president or king of a country is benevolent, then the laws and statutes of the country they administer will naturally be beneficial and conducive to the happiness of the whole population. Not only will everyone be contented and physically and mentally comfortable, but naturally others will want to engage and trade with that country. On the contrary, if someone has a violent nature then everyone will want to escape from them, and they will make all those around them miserable.

Buddhists meditate with the concept when we breathe in we take upon ourselves the suffering of all sentient beings and, when breathing out, we give all our happiness to every single sentient being. The meditator also makes aspiration prayers that whoever sees them, hears their voice, thinks of them, or touches them will be liberated, so that no one who has a connection with them will stray down a mistaken path. We all should practise this way of living.

SIXTEEN

THE PRECIOUSNESS OF WONDROUS MIND

Having turned away from a misleading path, upon the foundation of having gone for refuge to the infallible Three Precious Jewels, we should turn our backs on the modest path of practice and train in arousing the mind which aspires to supreme enlightenment.

First we need to train our minds in the Four Boundless Qualities by meditating on Compassion, Love, Joy and Equanimity.

1) BOUNDLESS EQUANIMITY

So compassion and the other three Boundless Qualities do not become partial or biased, first we need to meditate on Boundless Equanimity, using as an example a wise sage inviting guests to a banquet. When a sage invites guests to a feast, he makes no distinction between guests of high or low status, powerful or weak, good or bad, outstanding or mediocre. We should meditate until we manifest this same attitude.

Having been under the deluding influence of ignorance from beginningless time until now, we fall into bias and prejudice, and because of this we hate our enemies and are attached to those close to us, whereby we accumulate all manner of negative karma riddled with the three poisons. It is for this reason we are wandering in this vast and limitless prison of suffering.

If we analyse carefully, there is actually nothing that irrevocably determines someone as an enemy or rival. Our child in a previous life becomes an enemy in our present life. Through the power of karmic retribution, in many cases our current enemy becomes our child in our next life. Even in the space of this lifetime, someone who was once antagonistic towards us will later become our friend, and we cannot be certain someone who is now our friend will not become our opponent in the future.

Of all the sentient beings under the sun, there is not one who has not been our parent. Except for the fact that, after we have been parted by death we do not recognise each other, we still need to think deeply about the times we have been born as the child of these beings, and how they took care of us with the same love shown us by our mother in this present life. Therefore, first meditate on anyone for whom you harbour great resentment and hatred as having been your parent in previous lives, and meditate so your feelings towards them become neutral, neither positive nor negative.

Following this, think about those towards whom your feelings are neutral; countless numbers of beings who have all been your parents in past lives. Think of the kindness and concern they must have shown you. Meditate on them until you feel they are as dear to you as your parents in this lifetime. Finally, you need to meditate until you have the same loving feeling towards enemies, friends and all neutral wandering beings as you have towards your parents in this life.

2) BOUNDLESS COMPASSION

We need to meditate on boundless compassion using as an example a mother bird taking care of her chick. When a mother bird is rearing her chick, until it has succeeded in learning to fly, she keeps it warm under her wing and feeds it with her mouth. Like this, we should practise compassion towards all sentient beings both with our actions and speech, as well as with our minds.

Having trained our minds in boundless equanimity, we focus on all sentient beings of the three realms equally, as the object of great compassion. Every single one of these beings desires happiness. However, they destroy the cause of happiness as if it were an enemy and actually strive for the causes of suffering. That which they desire and what they actually do are contradictory. Think: "Wouldn't it be wonderful if all beings were able to become happy according to their own individual wishes!" Meditate until this wish for others to be happy becomes no different from your own desire for happiness.

In a state of mind which is never separate from this ceaseless compassion, we make sure, by means of gentle and agreeable conduct, the actions of our compassionate body bring no harm to others, but only benefit. With our actions of compassionate speech, we are not scornful, disrespectful, sarcastic, or anything like that, but speak truthfully and pleasantly. With our actions of compassionate mind, we do not harbour the desire to gain anything for ourselves from others or pretend to be someone we are not, but sincerely maintain a good heart, wishing to help everyone; we also make determined aspirations and promises to bring benefit to others.

3) BOUNDLESS LOVE

We train in feeling Boundless Love using as an example a disabled mother who lacks both her arms. This mother's child is carried away by a fast-flowing river. If the child of such a mother is swept away by a torrent of water, the love she feels for her child is so great that she would rather be swept away herself if that would save her child from drowning. However, having no arms, she has no way to save her child and does not know what to do. We need to meditate regularly on this benevolent Boundless Love.

The extraordinary cause of attaining the level of buddhahood is the precious supreme mind of enlightenment, or bodhichitta, the root of which is vast love. Because love comes about from its causes, if we want to develop bodhichitta in our mind stream, we need to accustom ourselves by concentrating our practice entirely on being loving. This in turn develops from beautiful compassion for all sentient beings, which grows from recognising that all beings have been our mothers, and remembering their kindness. Therefore, we think about how all sentient beings have at one time been our mothers and how extremely kind to us they were.

To do this, first of all, in a positive way, bring to mind the appearance and manner of speech of your mother in this lifetime. Think in the following way: "Now my body's fully grown and my mind is developed. I've met with the teachings of the Buddha and have been accepted by a spiritual master. These factors which enable me to practise Dharma have not come about because of my own power, but through my mother's kindness.

First, my kind mother carried me in her womb and I took all my nourishment from her body. When I was born, I was feeble and pretty disgusting. My neck couldn't support my head and my legs couldn't support my body. She gazed at me with eyes full of compassion, spoke to me in soft tones, and held me to her warm body. Thinking only of me, she forgot her hunger during the day and sleep during the night. She cared for me with such love that she'd rather die than see me sick. She fed me with whichever food was most nutritious and dressed me in whichever clothes were softest. At all times and in all situations she was concerned about me getting sick or dying. The negative karma she's accumulated for my sake alone makes it difficult for her to be liberated from the lower realms of existence.

If all my mothers from past lives hadn't died and were alive now, they would still always be thinking about me and doing things for my sake, confused with hope and fear, caught in a net of suffering. When they died, it's inevitable the negative karma they accumulated for my sake will have formed the cause, and conditions will have formed the connection, for them to have been reborn in hell. There, on a ground of burning metal and in forests of weapons, they experience suffering being killed, cut up and eaten by many vicious Guardians of Hell, wild animals, birds and dogs generated by their negative karma. Alternatively, if they haven't been reborn in the hot hells, then maybe they've taken rebirth in the cold hells, or as a hungry ghost or animal and so on. What to do?"

Think: "This is terrible. May this suffering together with its causes ripen upon me!" Remain meditating in this state for a long time. Having done that, think like this: "What's the benefit of meditating just by wishing? It's of no benefit because I don't have the capacity to help. Now, the one who does have the ability to protect against the suffering of samsara is the perfect Buddha." Therefore think: "I must attain the level of full realisation so I may be of benefit."

Like this, think in the same way about your grandparents, siblings, relatives, and so on, as well as all those towards whom you feel neutral. Finally, bring to mind the manner of previous rebirths of your hateful enemies and others towards whom you feel aversion. Then go through the same process of meditation for all sentient beings.

Alternatively, watch an animal about to be slaughtered by a butcher, or imagine the situation in your mind. Now suddenly, the butcher's sharp knife is held to the animal's neck and the continuum of its cherished life is severed. Meditate that this sentient being, seeing this world with its failing eyes for the last time, is not an animal but yourself. What can you do? You don't have wings to fly away. You don't have claws to burrow into the ground. You don't have the strength or energy to defend yourself. You can't find any place to escape to or hide. There is no one to protect or support you.

At this moment, not only do you lack the fortune to enable you to stay with your cherished father, kind mother, beloved children, lifelong companion or anyone else, but you are also going to be separated from the body you have treasured and protected. It is time to go to the place with no refuge or protector: the intermediate state after death. Thinking like this, take to heart the suffering feelings of terror and sorrow, and train your mind.

Having done that, meditate that the animal being led to slaughter is your kind mother in this life. Your loving mother who gave birth to you, brought you up with compassion until you were able to take care of yourself. She fed you with her sweet breast milk and thought of nothing else but you. Today your kind innocent mother is being led to slaughter. In a moment her vital breath will depart and the next moment her body will become a corpse and collapse to the ground, yet she still looks back at you with her sweet eyes... How unbearable! Take upon yourself all the suffering your old mother experiences, exactly as you feel she is suffering.

With unbearably fierce love, when you are almost in tears, think: "The creature experiencing the suffering of being led to slaughter is not my mother in this life, but has been my parent in a past life, and at that time cared for me with nothing but kindness, just like my parents in this life. Due to the influence of ignorance, they continue to create the causes of suffering and experience this and many similarly unbearable torments." Think of your suffering parents with tremendous love.

Following this, in stages, consider all those born in the hell realms, those born as hungry ghosts, and so on, eventually including all sentient beings under the sun. Meditate with unbearable love thinking: "Wouldn't it be wonderful if all beings were free from the causes and conditions of suffering!"

4) BOUNDLESS JOY

We should train in Boundless Joy using the example of a camel who, having lost her offspring, finds it again. The camel is a creature which is extremely loving towards its young, so when she finds her offspring after losing it, the camel becomes all the more happy. Similarly, we should never be without Boundless Joy, feeling happy ourselves if any sentient being is happy and comfortable.

Think about and meditate joyfully on any influence, power, wealth, learning and so on, possessed by anyone to whom you are close; your children, relatives and friends. When this feeling grows in your mind stream, turn your attention to a few people towards whom you have neutral feelings. Think of their long life, wide circle of friends, abundant possessions, and all the respect and honour others show them, without any feelings of competitiveness or jealously. Meditate on how wonderful it would be if they became even more prosperous and never were separated from happiness and comfort.

Doing this helps us to avoid developing the negative attitude which cannot tolerate the wealth and good fortune of others. This negative attitude inflames our own mind streams searing our positive mental qualities and antagonising us against all our enemies, particularly those of whom we feel jealous. Meditate again and again on feeling especially happy about all the fortunate aspects of your enemies' lives, everything they possess which brings them happiness, and finally rest in a state of meditative equipoise without any conceptual focus.

AROUSING BODHICHITTA

Having meditated on the Four Boundless Qualities, we turn to the main practice of arousing bodhichitta. What we call bodhichitta is the practice of attaining the level of perfect buddhahood solely for the sake of other sentient beings, without even the slightest selfish desire. If we subdivide bodhichitta in terms of its nature, there are two types: relative bodhichitta and absolute bodhichitta.

There are also two kinds of relative bodhichitta: aspirational bodhichitta and engaging bodhichitta. Aspirational bodhichitta is the development of the extraordinary mind which wishes to enlighten all sentient beings. Engaging bodhichitta is the actual engagement in practice of the Six Transcendent Perfections, including generosity and so on, in order to establish all sentient beings in perfect buddhahood.

Now, a beginner, through the power of training extensively in this kind of relative bodhichitta, will at some stage realise ultimate truth or, in other words, will see the true nature of all phenomena, ultimate wisdom. At this time absolute bodhichitta will grow in their mind stream.

It is appropriate to practise either of the two lineage traditions of developing bodhichitta. In the Profound View tradition of bodhichitta transmitted down from Araya Manjushri to Nagajuna, to begin with the bodhichitta vows are taken in a ritual where they are conferred by a master. In the same way, so the bodhichitta we have attained does not degenerate and increases more and more, we need to retake or reaffirm the vows over and over again at all times. The way to do this is by visualising in the sky in front of you the development of bodhichitta field of accumulation in the same way as it is visualised when going for refuge in chapter fifteen.

In the same way as the sky is boundless, the number of sentient beings is also limitless. Likewise, from beginning-less samsara there is not one of the limitless, endless numbers of sentient beings that has not been our parent. Similarly, when they were our parents they looked after us only with kindness, the same as our parents in this lifetime.

All these parents are in thrall to a great demon of ignorance and delusion. They do not know how to embark upon the path which leads to the causes of happiness, or abandon the path which does not. They are separated from a guide or spiritual friend. They have sunk into the waves of the vast ocean of endless samsaric suffering. They are without protector or defender. To abandon them and strive for ways to make only our own selves happy would be shameful and worthy of scorn.

Rather, we need to think: "I will train in the impressive actions and conduct of the Conquerors and Bodhisattvas of the past, for the sake of establishing all sentient beings at the level of perfect buddhahood." To do this we recite the arousing bodhichitta prayer of our 'Heart Essence' tradition and accumulate many recitations.

When the time comes to end our practice session, in just the same way as we concluded the Refuge visualisation, the assembled deities merge inseparably with our Lama and the Great One from Oddiyana, who then merges with us. We think vividly that absolute bodhichitta has developed in our mind stream and remain in a state of meditative equipoise without any conceptual focus for as long as possible. Finally, make prayers of dedication and aspiration.

We should never separate our minds from the precious mind of bodhichitta to which we have promised to commit ourselves in the presence of the Conqueror and the Bodhisattvas. It is not enough merely to take the vows of bodhichitta; we need to train in the practices of the Bodhisattvas.

There are differences in the practices of aspirational arousal of bodhichitta, depending on our courage. The three types of meditation are:

1. Equalising self with others.
2. Exchanging self with others.
3. Cherishing others more than ourselves.

The training in engaging bodhichitta is the practice of the Six Transcendent Perfections. Of these practices, the first one is:

1) MEDITATING ON THE BODHICHITTA OF EQUALISING SELF WITH OTHERS:

We and all other sentient beings are the same in that we desire happiness and we do not desire suffering; there is no difference between us. Make prayers of aspiration that both you yourself and others attain happiness together, and train your mind so you abandon the habit of harbouring feelings of attachment to yourself and aversion to others. In addition, strive in whatever way possible to do the same in your actual actions.

2) MEDITATING ON THE BODHICHITTA OF EXCHANGING SELF WITH OTHERS:

Visualise in front of you a wretched sentient being, tormented by suffering. When you breathe out, give all your happiness and merit to them in the form of white energy, in the same way as you would take off your jacket and put it on them. When you breathe in, take in all their negativities, obscurations and suffering in the form of black smoke. Meditate like this over and over again from the bottom of your heart. Start with one being and gradually build up to meditating on all sentient beings.

When you yourself happen to be sick, or experience some kind of suffering, think: "May the suffering of all samsaric beings tormented like me ripen on me, so they may all be freed from misery and have happiness!" And if you experience happiness, comfort or enjoyment you need to meditate by thinking: "May all sentient beings have joy like this!" This is the essence of the consummate meditation of all practitioners on the Mahayana path.

Giving rise to this determination in your mind, even just once, will purify many aeons of negativities and obscurations, and great increase of the two accumulations will be accomplished. We should also strive in actuality towards giving others our happiness and merit and taking all the suffering of others upon ourselves.

3) CHERISHING OTHERS MORE THAN OURSELVES:

Up to now, we have held the view as long as we ourselves were able to find ways of being happy and comfortable, it did not matter what happened to others. We need to reject this selfish and negative disposition. Think: "From now on, in this life or in future lives, whatever suffering I experience, if I'm sick or in pain, suffer adversity, or even fall to the lower realms, it's OK. Whatever happens I must find ways to bring happiness and comfort to all other sentient beings." Thinking like this, you should meditate from your heart and make prayers of aspiration. Also, strive directly in your actions to do whatever you can to this end.

ENGAGING BODHICHITTA: TRAINING IN THE SIX TRANSCENDENT PERFECTIONS.

These are the five transcendent means or methods of conduct for the accumulation of merit: 1) Generosity, 2) discipline, 3) patience, 4) diligence and 5) concentration, plus the wisdom accumulation of 6) wisdom, making six in all.

1) GENEROSITY
The first of these is Generosity. The practice of training in having a generous attitude involves giving our body, all our possessions, good fortune, power, life, merit and so on, plus our roots of virtue and all we have to all sentient beings, cutting through any entanglement in miserliness or thought of ownership.

This comprises three aspects: 1) The generosity of giving material things involves giving our possessions, valuables, food and clothes to others. 2) The generosity of Dharma involves connecting others' mind streams with virtue, by giving empowerments and teaching the Dharma, and so on. 3) The generosity of protection against fear involves protecting the lives of others, and so on.

Of these, in particular the generosity of giving material things is divided into three or more kinds of generosity which we need to practise in stages. 1) Generosity of giving small amounts of money and gifts. 2) Great generosity of giving horses, elephants, even one's child or wife, and so on. 3) Tremendous generosity of giving our head and limbs without thought for our bodies or lives.

First think like this: "However much wealth we have, it's never enough. Not only will none of the possessions I have now accompany me when I die, but if I'm avaricious and attached to them, they will be the cause for me to be reborn in the lower realms. Even now, I suffer from the stress of piling up possessions, hanging on to what I have, and fear of losing everything."

Thinking about the intrinsically deceptive and essence-less nature of things, offer them up to the Three Precious Jewels and hand them down to the poor and destitute, and thus familiarise yourself with putting your money and possessions to meaningful use. Finally, train in the transcendent perfection of generosity until you would also be willing to give your own head and limbs were it necessary.

2) DISCIPLINE

Discipline involves continuous mindful care, making sure to abandon what is negative, maintain what is positive, and protect the three vows which are: the Hinayana vows of individual liberation, the Bodhisattva vows of the Mahayana, and the secret mantra vows of the Vajrayana. These vows should be kept in accordance with all the specific circumstances for observance and abandonment.

There are three divisions of discipline: 1) Abandoning doing what is non-virtuous is the discipline of refraining from misdeeds. 2) Accumulating even small roots of virtue is the discipline of practising virtuous qualities. 3) Acting for the benefit of others through such means as being generous, having pleasant speech, meaningful conduct and being consistent, is the discipline of influencing others positively.

Through the doors of our body, speech and mind we must abandon from their root the ten non-virtuous actions which do not benefit others, and practise benefitting others fundamentally. Using techniques taught as an antidote, we can gradually abandon all intrinsically evil deeds, together with forbidden misdeeds (e.g. actions forbidden by the Buddha for renunciates but not lay practitioners, like eating after noon), and benefit sentient beings directly and indirectly, without pretending to do positive things while actually behaving negatively. The foundation of all positive qualities is to maintain discipline in which our mind is able to bear witness, so therefore we must certainly practise this, no matter what.

3) PATIENCE

Patience is the principle of forbearance and remaining undisturbed; this is divided into three types: 1) Patience when wronged involves not holding any resentment or thoughts of revenge. 2) Patience which bears hardship involves being able to endure difficulties and hardships for the sake of practising Dharma. 3) Patience to face the profound truth without fear involves being able to take on board profound teachings such as emptiness.

Those of us who are practising the holy Dharma and strive for liberation must not lose our temper. We must meditate on patience when others, out of anger, are rude or violent, no matter what they do to us. For the sake of practising Dharma we need to be tough-hearted and be prepared to cross blazing infernos and fields of razor-sharp blades. It is vitally important when we make an effort to practise that we develop strength of mind which is completely unwavering.

4) DILIGENCE
Diligence is a steady mind which delights in virtue and so engages in positive actions without slacking. There are three divisions: 1) Not being put off by adverse conditions is armour-like diligence. 2) Getting down to things without procrastination is diligence in action. 3) Not being satisfied with just doing a little practice or work for the Dharma is the diligence of never considering what we do is sufficient.

Heartfelt determination with no laziness or procrastination prevents our lives from running out while we keep putting off practice until tomorrow or the next day. By relying on a fervent stream of extended diligence to accomplish our lifelong objective, attaining the level of perfect buddhahood, we engage in continuous endeavour, delighting in virtue without any slackness. Diligence is essential for the accomplishment of liberation.

5) CONCENTRATION
Concentration involves rejecting distractions and bustle and choosing a secluded place to meditate in one-pointed samadhi. There are three types or levels of concentration: 1) When we engage in concentration meditation and temporary experiences such as bliss, clarity or no thought arise with a 'coating' of attachment, this is termed the 'Approach of a Child' concentration. 2) When we are free of attachment to experiences, however grasp at emptiness as a remedy, this is termed 'Revelation of the Ultimate Meaning' concentration. 3) Free from fixation on emptiness as a remedy and abiding in non-conceptual samadhi of reality, is the concentration of a Tathagata.

When first engaging in concentration meditation, follow the sevenfold body posture of Vairochana, the three gazes and three postures of Dzogchen practice, and so on. In this way no concepts whatsoever are formed; rest equably in a state not fixating on anything.

This concludes the five method and conduct aspects of the Transcendent Perfections.

6) TRANSCENDENT WISDOM

Wisdom has three aspects. 1) Listening to the words and meaning of the Dharma is wisdom through study. 2) Understanding through reflecting on the meaning of what has been learnt is wisdom of reflection. 3) Putting into practice the fruit of reflection, so realisation of the true nature of reality is born in mind, is the wisdom of meditation.

Learning, reflection and meditation must be done in this order. First we need to remove all doubts by careful study and reflection. Having done this, we meditate on the main practice. At the time of practice, untrue illusory sensory appearances, while not existing, appear to exist. Apparent unceasing phenomena fade within the mind which realises them as merely apparent. Settling into the state which realises the true face of the natural state, dharmata, open and bright like the sky, liberated from the net of conceptual elaboration of existence and non-existence, being and nonbeing, where meditation and post-meditation are indivisible, is true transcendent wisdom.

In this way, there is nothing which does not arise from the mind, from the appearance of form to our senses right up to all phenomena subsumed within total omniscience. The realisation of mind as inseparable clarity and emptiness is the view. Determining the view, we maintain it with unwavering attention. This is meditation. In this meditative state we gather without attachment the two illusory-like accumulations. This is the conduct.

If we train extensively like this in the three: view, meditation and conduct, depending on the extent of our familiarisation, we will recognise our dreams as dreams and also, while dreaming, no seemingly-existing hallucinations will appear. If we meditate continuously, integrating day and night, when we arrive at the crucial moment of death, we will unlikely be deluded. If we have indwelling confidence of non-confusion at the brink of death, then no delusion will arise in the intermediate state of reality, or the intermediate state of rebirth. Because non-confusion is liberation, it is the single most excellent method by which we may be liberated from this great ocean of samsaric suffering.

To know the fundamental root of all the eighty-four thousand teachings the Conqueror taught is summarised as emptiness, of which the essence is compassion, and to strive to develop this in our mind stream is, of all the essential points, indisputably the most crucial.

SEVENTEEN

THE PRISTINE UN-ECLIPSED MOON

What are termed 'afflictive emotions' are co-emergent with delusory appearances due to the effect of ignorance, or non-recognition of rigpa awareness. It is because of the influence of these afflictive emotions we experience all our various kinds of suffering. If afflictive emotions were to disappear, we would be freed from all suffering. Correspondingly, freedom from suffering is not just mere happiness, but supreme happiness.

This being the case, the aim of all those who desire happiness is the same, as is the fact they pursue happiness. However, the ways beings go about trying to create a happy state of mind are different. Some try to create the causes of happiness, while others try to create the results of happiness. This is the same as trying to totally prevent the causes of suffering, or alternatively finding ways to try and relieve the effects of suffering.

Buddha Sakyamuni recognised suffering as being like a disease, and he taught we must abandon the causal origin of this disease-like condition: our afflictive emotions. To help us understand this analogy, we consider the example of a sick person constantly tormented by an agonisingly painful disease, or someone who has a disease which is not yet causing pain but which will gradually prove fatal. Whatever the case, we need to recognise the disease from which we are suffering. Having understood it, we need to work to find a cure.

According to Tibetan medicine, whatever the nature of disease, whether the origin of pain lies in the wind, bile or phlegm humour, or a combination of all three, the root of disease will have developed from the three poisons, or afflictive emotions: ignorance, attachment and aversion. If the leaves of a poisonous plant are burnt but the roots are not destroyed, the poison still remains. In the same way, if we want to achieve happiness without suffering, first we must destroy the root of suffering: afflictive emotions. This is the supreme method of achieving happiness.

To cure the fever of the afflictive emotions we need to follow a path of practice which is like a calming and soothing medicine; this enables us to actualise the abandonment of the afflictive emotions and achieve resultant happiness. It is for this reason the first teaching Buddha Sakyamuni gave in this world was the Four Noble Truths, in the First Turning of the Wheel of Dharma.

Now, we are all travelling on a path which seeks lasting happiness but, having chosen between the swift and slower paths, we are following the swift path of the Mahayana. Moreover, we have also entered the door of the Vajrayana teachings. Of the nine levels in the Vajrayana, we have embarked upon the supreme spiritual approach, the Dzogchen teachings of the 'Heart Essence of the Great Expanse'. Now, without gathering the accumulations, purifying obscurations and drawing the blessings of the enlightened mind stream of the masters into our own mind stream, there is no other method of practice; so we need to train our minds in these essential practices of the path.

When a naturally attractive person bathes and, having cleansed themselves by washing thoroughly, puts on their best clothes and decorates themselves with various ornaments, they look beautiful. In just the same way, all sentient beings possess the seed of enlightenment, completely uncontrived, unsullied and unstained. What is more, the gross stains of the two adventitious obscurations of dualistic perception can be cleansed. Through means of purification, and adorned by the fine ornaments of the two accumulations, we may manifest extraordinary and distinctive supreme beauty. In this way, by the power of purifying the obscurations and completing the accumulations, we need to actualise the enlightened wisdom of a Buddha. The development of these unprecedented inner qualities is reliant on a change in our mind.

The chief obstacles, which prevent the arising of the experience and realisation of the profound fundamental nature of all things, are negative actions and obscurations accumulated since beginingless time, together with their habitual tendencies. In order to purify negative actions we need to use the remedy of all the four powers.

As is frequently repeated in the scriptures:

> "Generally speaking, there is nothing positive about negative actions; only this - they can be purified through confession."

But, merely repeating prayers of confession and purification of negativities parrot-fashion, however much we do it, will only mitigate our negative actions and downfalls to a very small extent. We will not be able to purify them completely. Of the many suitable methods taught to enable us to confess negative actions and downfalls, the meditation and recitation of Vajrasattva is extremely profound.

In order to make confession, it is essential we rely on all four of the remedial powers.

1) Having taken refuge in Vajrasattva, do not stray from the mind of enlightenment, aspirational and engaging bodhichitta. This is the power of support.

2) Acknowledge negative actions done in the past as being negative and, with a deep feeling of regret, confess them without concealing anything. This is the power of remorse for having done wrong.

3) Regret all your past wrongdoing and vow from now on you will not act negatively again, even at the cost of your life. This is the power of resolution.

4) In general, the remedy for previous negative actions is accomplishing positive actions. More specifically, there is nothing more profound than meditating on the bodhichitta mind of enlightenment and maintaining an ongoing experience of the unfabricated fundamental nature of things. Therefore, in a state unseparated from these two, visualising the deity and reciting the mantra is the power of applied antidote.

This is a summary of the four powers, and it is in this state of mind we meditate on and recite the mantra of Vajrasattva. I will now speak briefly on the method of visualisation.

1) THE POWER OF SUPPORT:

Resting in your unmodified ordinary form, visualise in the sky above the crown of your head, at the approximate distance of one forearm or an arrow's length, a white lotus flower with a thousand petals. Upon this is a full moon disc, the same size as the anther bed of the lotus, and perfectly complete in all aspects. In the centre of the moon disc, visualise a white syllable HUM radiant with luminous rays of light. Suddenly, the HUM changes into the essence of your root master, embodiment of all the Buddhas of the three times. In appearance he is the Sambhogakaya Teacher Vajrasattva, white in colour, like a snow-mountain bathed in the rays of a newly-arisen sun, or a pure crystal.

Vajrasattva has one face and two hands. At his heart, in his right hand he holds a five-pronged vajra of awareness and emptiness in the manner of bestowing. In his left hand, he holds against his hip a bell of appearance-emptiness. His two legs rest in the full lotus position. His body is ornamented with the thirteen adornments of the sambhogakaya. The five silken garments are: 1) silken crown, 2) white silken shawl, 3) silken scarves, 4) waist sash, and 5) a lower garment. The eight precious ornaments are: 1) a crown, 2) earrings, 3) a choker, 4) arm bands, 5) necklace, 6) long necklace, 7) bracelets and rings, and 8) anklets.

Embracing Vajrasattva in inseparable union is his consort, white and ornamented with precious jewels. The bodies of the male and female consorts appear without any self-nature. Think that, with the knowing aspect of their wisdom mind, they consider you and all sentient beings with tremendous loving kindness.

2) THE POWER OF REMORSE AT HAVING DONE WRONG:

> "Generally speaking, I myself and all sentient beings, from beginingless samsara until now, have accumulated inconceivably numerous negative actions of body, speech and mind. In particular, the ten negative actions, the five actions with immediate retribution, the five subsidiary actions with immediate retribution, the four serious faults, the eight perverse acts, all transgressions of the outer monastic discipline of individual liberation, the inner Bodhisattva precepts, and the secret Tantric sacred commitments of the awareness holders."

Specific wrong doing includes disobeying the instruction of your master, fighting with your vajra brothers and sisters, and so on. Honestly admit your entire catalogue of negative actions, everything you may have done wrong, with no hiding or concealment, and ask for forgiveness. Pray that, at this very moment, all negative actions and obscurations will be cleansed and purified, leaving no trace. Meditate like this and recite the prayer of confession, the Vajrasattva sadhana.

3) THE POWER OF RESOLUTION:

> "Up to now, under the influence of ignorance, I have accumulated much negative karma."

Promise with all your heart never again to do these kinds of negative action, even if it costs you your life.

4) THE POWER OF APPLIED ANTIDOTE:

Keeping in mind the pure symbolism of the visualisation, recite the prayer from: "Ah! I am in my ordinary form..." and so on. At this point, visualise in the heart centre of the non-dual Vajrasattva male and female consorts, upon a moon disc, a white HUM syllable the size of a flattened white mustard seed, drawn as if with a hair.

As you say the hundred syllable mantra, visualise each of the hundred syllables circling around the central HUM, one after the other, almost touching. Recite the hundred syllables in the manner of a prayer. This causes compassionate wisdom nectar to drip down from the syllables like water, in the same way as fire melts ice. Passing through the form of the male and female consorts, the nectar flows from the point of their union and touches the crown of your head, and the heads of all other sentient beings.

As if cleansing and rinsing out your whole being, all sickness appears as rotten blood and pus, all harmful spirits emerge in the form of creatures such as frogs, snakes, spiders, scorpions, fish, tadpoles, and so on; and, in the guise of oozing smoke and liquid charcoal, all negative actions and obscurations pour out from your two lower orifices, the soles of your feet, and all the pores of your skin.

A fissure splits the ground beneath you and below is Yamaraja, the karmic Lord of Death, surrounded by all the male and female beings to whom you owe karmic debts. They open their jaws and stretch out their hands and claws, into which the effluent falls, but now it is not putrefied blood and so on, but has changed its nature to become nectar, so all the beings become satisfied and content. Debts and karmic retribution and revenge are negated. The crack in the earth closes. Think as you recite the hundred syllable mantra that karma which might have led to an untimely death has now been redeemed.

Visualise in the centre of your body, now transparent inside and out, the central channel. Extending from this is the crown chakra of great bliss with thirty-two corolla-like channels turning downwards like the spokes of an umbrella. The sixteen corolla-like channels of the throat chakra of enjoyment turn upward. The eight corolla-like channels of the Dharmachakra at the heart centre turn downward. The sixty-four corolla-like channels of the emanation chakra of the navel face upward.

Once again, visualise nectar flowing from Vajrasattva's body, filling your body as before. From the crown chakra of great bliss to all the four chakra channels, your whole body fills up entirely with the flow of nectar, like a crystal vase with milk, purest white. Moreover, when your crown corolla-like channels fill up, you receive the vase empowerment, giving rise to the wisdom of joy. Consider your karmic obscurations are purified and you attain the nirmanakaya. Similarly, when your throat corolla-like channels fill, you receive the secret empowerment, giving rise to the wisdom of supreme joy. Consider obscurations of afflictive emotions are purified and you attain the sambhogakaya. When your heart centre corolla-like channels fill, you receive the wisdom-knowledge empowerment, giving rise to extraordinary joy. Consider conceptual obscurations are purified and you attain the dharmakaya. When your navel corolla-like channels fill, you receive the word empowerment, and innate wisdom arises in your mind stream. Consider obscurations of habitual tendencies are purified and you attain the Svabhavikakaya.

As soon as you recite the words of remorse, beginning: "O Protector, through my lack of knowledge..." etc. Vajrasattva, smiling with delight, grants your prayer saying: "Fortunate one, all your negative actions, obscurations, faults and downfalls are purified." He then melts into light and dissolves into you, on which basis, visualise yourself also as Vajrasattva. At your heart centre visualise a moon disc with a sky-blue HUM at its centre. To its east is a white OM, to the south a yellow VAJRA, to the west a red SA, to the north a green TVA. From these, five correspondingly-coloured rays of light shine forth, and from the tip of each radiate countless goddesses bearing myriad offering substances. They make offerings to the Conquerors and their enlightened children, the Bodhisattvas, delighting them so that they in turn emanate countless rays of light which dissolve into the syllables in your heart centre. Once again they radiate rays of light outwards to the six kinds of wandering sentient beings, which purify all their negativities, obscurations and latencies, and the entire outer universe becomes the pure realm of Manifest Joy. All the sentient beings living in the central region become Buddha Vajrasattva. All those in the east become Vajra Vajrasattva. All those in the south become Ratna Vajrasattva. All those in the west become Padma Vajrasattva. All beings in the north become Karma Vajrasattva. Consider that all are reciting OM VAJRA SATTVA HUM with a tremendous resounding harmony, and recite this heart mantra many times.

By means of this key visualisation of the secret mantra Vajrayana tradition, inconceivable accumulations of merit and wisdom are perfected through many easy methods, and additionally, we are able to accomplish benefit for great numbers of sentient beings. Vajrasattva is in nature the single embodiment of the hundreds of families of the Great Secret. Meditating on Vajrasattva's nature as being inseparable from your root master is the meditation practice of Guru Yoga; moreover it is the approach of the Jewel which Embodies Everything, which makes it extremely profound.

Finally, the outer pure realm dissolves into all the assembled deities. The five Buddha families of Vajrasattva dissolve into you. You dissolve into the OM at your heart centre. The five syllables at your heart centre dissolve into each other; OM dissolves into VAJRA, VAJRA into SA, SA into TVA, TVA into the shapkyu of HUM. The shapkyu dissolves into small ra, small ra into the ha, ha dissolves into its head, the head dissolves into the crescent moon, crescent moon into the bindu drop, bindu drop into its nada, which becomes thinner and disappears. Remain relaxed for a moment in a non-conceptual state of equipoise. Then, when a thought once more breaks through, again vividly visualise the universe and everyone in it as the pure realm of Vajrasattva, with assembled deities. With this dedicate and make prayers of aspiration.

EIGHTEEN

TREASURY OF IMMEASURABLE MERIT

All people born in this world share the same human identity; we also engage in the same kind of activities. However, some people hold positions of power and authority and are very wealthy, others are poor, starving and miserable. These situations come about through the interplay of various causes and conditions. If we have accumulated the causes of merit through being generous and so on previously, then in the future we will be born into a wealthy life and enjoy many possessions. If we have been miserly or stolen others' belongings, then this cause will result in poverty in the future.

Accordingly, completion of both accumulations of conceptual merit and non-conceptual wisdom, and simultaneous perfection of the qualities of abandonment and realisation, purified from both the obscurations of afflictive emotions and the obscurations concerning the nature of reality, is what is known as the attainment of the two Buddha Bodies: the dharmakaya and the rupakaya. Those who, for the time being, want to attain the higher realms of gods and humans, and ultimately achieve the transcendence of buddhahood and pacify suffering completely, must first gather the accumulations.

When we make offerings to pure beings, we do not do this because Buddhas and Bodhisattvas have any wish to acquire these desirable objects. However, because we ourselves are not free from attachment to objects of desire, we make offerings of such things in order to complete our accumulation of merit. If we make offerings to pure objects with pure aspiration, then we will complete the accumulation of merit.

When making these offerings to Buddhas and Bodhisattvas, if we offer our prize possessions to which we are greatly attached, but without fixating on their value, then through the power of our attachment, the merit we receive is correspondingly great. However, if it were the case that those with only meagre possessions, and those who own nothing of any value, have no means of making offerings, then all faithful rich people would be reborn in the higher realms and all poor people would go to the lower realms. But this is not the case. If our minds are pure, whether we make offerings of actual worth or mentally created offerings, Buddhas and Bodhisattvas are able to accept them, and in that way we can complete the accumulation of merit. By completing the causal accumulation of merit we attain the result: the supreme accumulation of wisdom.

It is taught:

> "As long as roots of virtue are not complete,
>   true emptiness will not be realised."

In a region of ancient India, a son more beautiful than any other in the world was born into the family of a householder. Both the baby's hands were clenched into fists. When his parents opened his fists, they found a gold coin in the palm of each hand. When those coins were taken out, more appeared. Each time they took a gold coin another always appeared, and they filled up their storeroom with gold. His parents named the boy Golden Jewel.

The boy grew up and, having became a monk, took full ordination. At this time, as he prostrated in front of each member of the spiritual community, wherever his hands touched the ground a gold coin appeared, and he used these coins as offerings to honour each member.

Through diligence, Golden Jewel attained the result of an Arhat. At this time Ananda asked the Buddha why Golden Jewel manifested gold coins. The Buddha taught nine thousand and one aeons ago, when the Buddha Kanakamuni came to this world, there was a poor man who made a living by collecting and selling wood every day. At one time, because he had strong faith, the poor man offered two gold coins which he had earned from selling wood to the Buddha and his retinue. Out of compassion, the Buddha accepted the offering. From this cause, for nine thousand and one aeons, gold coins spontaneously appeared in both the poor man's hands and he became limitlessly wealthy. So it is taught.

Again, in a time gone by, there was a miserly householder who sold anything he could acquire in exchange for gold and buried it in a pot. Over time he filled seven pots with gold and hid them underground; not long after this he died. Because of his attachment and yearning for the gold, he was reborn as a poisonous snake and he coiled himself around the pots, guarding them. Later the town fell into ruins and became deserted. The snake also died, but was once again reborn as a snake, jealously guarding the gold as before.

The miser took rebirth many times as a snake and tens of thousands of years passed. In his final rebirth as a snake he became unhappy and thought, "I've taken this same form again and again because of attachment to this gold. Now I'm going to make an offering to an extraordinary object in order to accumulate some merit." Thinking this, he slithered to the side of a wide road and hid in a clump of grass. A man passed by and in a human voice the snake called him over. The man was afraid and said, "I'm not going over there, you'll kill me." The snake replied, "If I wanted to kill you, I would, even if you didn't come over here... But I don't, so calm down!" Feeling braver, the man approached the snake, who asked him, "If I entrust you with a mission to perform a meritorious act, could you help?" The man promised he would do his best.

The snake led the man to where the pots of gold were hidden underground, chose one of the pots, and said, "Take this gold, offer it to monks and request Dharma teachings. Come and get me on the day the teachings are held." Just as the snake had instructed, the man offered the gold to the attendant of a community of monks, and explained exactly what had happened. On the day of the teachings, the man put the snake into a small basket and went to the monastery. At the time of the midday meal he placed the snake at the end of the row of monks. The snake watched with faith as the man made plentiful offerings of flowers and so on. When the monks had finished eating, they taught the Dharma to the snake. The snake was overjoyed and also offered the other six pots of gold to the monks. From this virtuous karma, the snake was reborn in the heaven of the thirty-three.

In this way, wealth amassed through miserly behaviour brings about suffering in this life; when we acquire it, when we guard it, and when we worry about losing it. Not only that, but subsequently, fixated attachment to money and possessions will cast us down into the lower realms and will impede transmigration to the higher realms and liberation.

But if we were to say: "If this is how it works, supposing I had no possessions, then would liberation be within my grasp?" that would not in fact be the case; for just as the rich are attached to gold and silver, the poor are equally attached to pots and pans. There is no difference whether we are bound by golden thread or coarse rope.

A worldly person who is not free from attachment gains ephemeral happiness from food, wealth and possessions. The rich wear themselves out acquiring property and are completely attached to it. There is no quick way to put a stop to this, so those with wealth need to understand how to gain maximum benefit from their money. When someone dies, it is not in their power to take with them their food, clothes, possessions or anything else belonging to this life. If their possessions are divided up after they die, their reaction may well cause them to take a worse rebirth than the snake in the above story; for not only will they feel covetous, but also certainly both overwhelming attachment and anger.

The infallible method for accumulating wealth in this life is by being generous. In the same way as, however much water we draw from it, a well constantly fills up again, if we are generous our wealth naturally increases. For example, if we make an offering to a pure object with a pure mind it is generally very meritorious. In particular, when we practise the secret mantra Vajrayana, there are certain skilful means of gathering the accumulations to which we should apply ourselves.

In general, if we desire the best for ourselves, first it is very important to gather the accumulations. If we do not complete the two accumulations of merit and wisdom, there is no way of attaining the twofold purity of buddhahood. This being the case, among all the paths of skilful means by which we may gather the accumulations, the most excellent is the offering of the mandala. In the practice tradition of Dzogchen there are two mandalas: the accomplishment mandala and the offering mandala.

The choice of material for the mandala base depends on whatever we can afford. The wealthy choose the most costly gold or silver, those with no money find a flat stone. As for material to use for the heaps of offerings, anything from the best turquoise and coral to wheat or barley grains is suitable. Whatever you use, it must be clean and pure, and the mandala base needs to be properly wiped.

First, arrange the five heaps of the accomplishment mandala. Meditate that the central heap is the Buddha Vairochana surrounded by the assembled deities of the Buddha family. Then, from the front, circle clockwise to place four heaps in the four directions. The front heap is Buddha Akshobhya surrounded by the host of deities of the Vajra family.

The left heap is Buddha Ratnasambhava surrounded by the host of deities of the Ratna family. The heap at the back is Buddha Amitabha surrounded by the host of deities of the Padma family. The right heap is Buddha Amoghasiddhi surrounded by the host of deities of the Karma family.

Alternatively, we can visualise the host of deities of the five branches of the accumulation field for taking refuge. Whichever it is, place the accomplishment mandala on a high shrine or altar. It is also appropriate to offer this to representations of Buddha body, speech and mind. And if you do not have an accomplishment mandala, it does not present problems if you visualise the field of merit in your mind.

THE METHOD TO OFFER THE OFFERING MANDALA:

Hold the base of the mandala with your left hand and wipe it with the inside of your right wrist. In accordance with the widely practised thirty-seven part mandala, when you are ready to put the heaps in place, as you recite: "OM VAJRA BHUMI..." sprinkle some fragrant water. Then, with your right finger and thumb, take the heap of flowers. Reciting the mantric syllables: "OM VAJRA REKHE..." and so on, circle the heap clockwise around the mandala base, finally placing it in the centre. If you have a fence of iron mountains, now is the time to place it on the base; if not, circle the edge of the mandala anti-clockwise with your left ring finger and recite: "The outer iron mountains encircle the perimeter..." and consider it to be equal in size to the three-thousand-fold universe.

When you recite: "King of mountains..." place one large heap in the centre and imagine this to be Mount Meru surrounded by the seven golden mountains and the seven lakes of enjoyment. Following this, as you place heaps in the cardinal and intermediate directions one by one, it does not make any difference if you take east to be facing you or facing the direction of offering.

Starting in the east, move in a clockwise sequence and place a heap in each of the cardinal directions: The eastern continent of Videha is semi-circular in shape and formed of crystal. The southern continent of Jambudvipa is quadrilateral in shape and formed of lapis lazuli. The western continent of Aparagodaniya is circular in shape and formed of either ruby or coral. The northern continent of Kurava is square in shape and formed of gold.

The sub-continents are the same shape as their main continent. Reciting: "Deha and Videha..." place heaps either side of each main continent, first left then right. Then place the precious mountain in the east, the wish-granting tree in the south, the bountiful cow in the west, and the spontaneous harvest in the north. Then place the seven royal attributes plus the vase of treasure, making a total of eight, one after another in the four cardinal and four intermediate directions.

Place the four outer goddesses, starting with the goddess of beauty, in the four cardinal directions, and the four inner goddesses, starting with the goddess of flowers, in the four intermediate directions. Place the sun, formed of fire crystal, in the east, and the moon, formed of water crystal, in the west. Place the precious parasol in the south and the banner victorious over all directions in the north. When you recite: "All the wealth of gods and humans..." pile the heaps one on top of the other until there is no more space left, and finally place on the top an ornament such as a wheel of Dharma or an equivalent.

Following this, first make the offering of the ordinary mandala of the nirmanakaya. Bring to mind the seven royal attributes and so on, the wealth of gods and humans without exception, everything that exists within the entire three thousand-fold universe of a hundred million worlds, whether owned by someone or not. In addition, take your body, all your possessions and your entire accumulation of merit, and visualise offering all this to your nirmanakaya master and the host of deities.

THE EXTRAORDINARY MANDALA OF THE SAMBHOGAKAYA:

On top of this great array, mentally create inconceivable clouds of offerings, including the pure realms of the five Buddha families with the five aspects of excellence, perfectly-arrayed temples adorned with numberless offering goddesses of the senses, including the goddess of beauty, and offer it all to the sambhogakaya master and the host of deities.

THE EXCELLENT MANDALA OF THE DHARMAKAYA:

Upon the basis of unborn mind itself, visualise arranging as adornments the unimpeded arising energy of the five wisdoms, represented as five heaps. Alternatively, arrange upon the Dharmadhatu unborn ground of primordial purity, the unceasing spontaneously present four visions in the form of four heaps. With these key points of visualisation in mind, recite: "OM AH HUM. The cosmos of a billion universes..." etc.

When accumulating many recitations, sometimes offer an extended thirty-seven point mandala, as detailed above. Be sure to complete one hundred thousand repetitions reciting the seven point mandala offering: "The ground is anointed with perfumed water..." As usual, this practice should be done complete with the opening, main part and conclusion.

NINETEEN

FEAST OFFERING OF THE BODY

The kusali's accumulation, otherwise known as the beggar's accumulation of merit or 'Chod', is linked to the mandala offering and is another means or path for accumulating merit. It is a particularly skilful means for completing the two accumulations, whereby the physical constituents of our body, which we cling to and cherish so dearly, are transformed into pure nectar and all kinds of riches and delights, whatever is desired, and offered as a feast to invited guests.

Generally what is called 'Chod' or 'cutting' is exemplified by cutting a tree at its roots, whereby the branches and leaves are also automatically severed. Similarly, using skilful means and wisdom, we cut through the four demons in the expanse free from description, imagination or explanation, beyond conceptual thought: the basic space of the Dharmakaya Great Mother. In this way, confusion is clarified from its very foundation, and dualistic and mistaken conceptualisation is liberated into its own natural state.

In this context, the four demons are: 1) the tangible demon, 2) the intangible demon, 3) the demon of elation and 4) the demon of conceit.

1) The tangible demon refers to dangers caused by the four elements, such as earthquakes, fear of fire and so on, and also anything which harms our body and mind, such as enemies, thieves, poisonous snakes, wild animals, and fear of flesh-eating demons, ghosts and evil spirits.

2) The intangible demon refers to the inner eighty-four thousand afflictive emotions, such as attraction and aversion and so on, which give rise to the suffering of samsara.

3) The demon of elation refers to fixating on and being attached to any slight inner feeling of progress or potential in concentration meditation.

4) The demon of conceit refers to the root of the previous three demons; this is taking pride in 'I' or 'mine', or the concept that the five aggregates really are 'me' or 'mine'. For this reason the demon of conceit is the root of all the demons.

Therefore, the realisation of selflessness specifically crushes all things we dare not approach, for example demons, etc., totally smashing obstructions and adverse conditions, and transforming them into spiritual attainment. Maintaining the uninhibited and spontaneous extraordinary yogic discipline of transforming negative signs into fortunate ones, we wander around barren places and lonely mountains.

In addition, maleficent ghosts and demons need to be brought under the influence of great compassion and overwhelmed by vast wisdom. To this end, we give away our body without any feeling of loss or attachment, to whichever beings want it, for the fulfilment of whatever desires they have. In this way we cut through clinging to our physical aggregates.

For the kusali's accumulation of merit, which follows on from the mandala offering, we make offerings and gifts of our body to four kinds of guests. These may be classified as the 'four great feasts': the white and variegated feasts, and the secondary red and black feasts.

THE VISUALISATION

In the centre of your heart, visualise the essence of your mental consciousness as Black Vajra Yogini, swaying in a dance. In her right hand she holds up a curved knife pointing skywards, and in her left she holds a skull-cup full of blood to her heart. Grunting behind her right ear is a black pig's head. Her attire is that of a wrathful goddess.

The syllable P'ET is the union of method and wisdom. As you cry out the syllable, short and sharp, your awareness becomes Machig Troma Nagmo, and in an instant your awareness flies up the hollow central channel, out through the aperture of Brahma at the crown of your head, and arrives high in the sky. At that moment, your previous body collapses to the ground as an unconscious corpse, which instantaneously becomes as large as the billion-fold universe, overwhelmingly fatty and succulent.

Meditate you, as Black Vajra Yogini, are huge, with thick limbs and eyes bright as the sun and moon. With the curved knife in your right hand, which cuts through the root of dualistic perception, slice off the dome of the skull, which is as large as the billion-fold universe. With your right hand pick up the dome and place it, with the forehead facing you, on a hearth formed of three human skulls each equal in size to the King of Mountains, representing the three Buddha bodies.

With the curved knife in your right hand you, as Vajra Yogini, skewer the corpse and place it in the dome of the skull, now a cup. In the sky above the skull-cup visualise a cool white inverted HANG syllable, and underneath the skull-cup a hot red inverted short AH. Visualise flames burning from the AH which simmer the corpse in the skull-cup into nectar. Steam rises from the nectar which melts the HANG syllable above it, causing a stream of white and red nectar to flow down and mix inseparably with the nectar in the skull-cup.

Then recite many times: OM AH HUM. OM purifies all the nectar's impurities, AH multiplies the nectar many times, and HUM transforms it into whatever is desired. Meditate the nectar of uncontaminated wisdom produces all that is desired, and fulfils all wishes from the inexhaustible fully-arrayed great clouds of the sky treasury.

THE WHITE FEAST

Then, in the wide and vast space in front of you, visualise the recipients of your offerings. Your gracious Lama is at the front, together with the Three Precious Jewels, the Three Root Refuges, guardians and oath-bound deities, together with their ocean-like assemblies. Below them on the ground, visualise the recipients of your generosity: obstructive spirits, karmic creditors and all six types of sentient beings of the three realms.

Above, your root Lama and the Lamas of the lineage, together with the Buddhas and Bodhisattvas, have tongues of vajra tubes. Between them and the ground, the hosts of blessed yidam deities have tongues of tubes the shape of their particular symbolic instruments. Visualise they draw up and partake of the essence of the nectar, by which means all your obstructions to practising the holy Dharma and attaining realisation are cleared, and all favourable conditions and the positive accumulations to which you aspire are increased.

After this, still visualising yourself as Vajra Yogini, countless activity-performing dakinis radiate from your heart centre. The dakinis are identical, but white, yellow, red, green and blue in colour, and they offer a skull-cup full of the essence of uncontaminated nectar to each sentient being of the six kinds in the three realms, including karmic creditors and obstructive spirits, thus satisfying them all.

THE VARIEGATED FEAST

Again, from the steam of simmering nectar radiate inconceivable clouds of offerings of the wealth and enjoyments of gods and humans, including the five desirable objects and symbols of the eight auspicious articles, and so on. These are offered to the guests above, gracious recipients of offerings. Consider the accumulations have been completed and obscurations purified for you and all sentient beings.

For the guests below, the six kinds of wandering beings, visualise whatever wealth or enjoyment each of them desires, showers down on them like rain, so they all become happy, content, satisfied and delighted. Consider debts accumulated through beginingless lifetimes by you and all other sentient beings are extinguished. Karmic debts are resolved, flesh debts of the body are cleared, and negative actions and obscurations are purified.

Finally, the remains of the feast are given to all the pitiful beings of the six realms: the feeble, weak, crippled, deaf, mute and so on, in the form of whatever each of them most longs for. The feast's remains become medicine to cure fatal diseases, miraculous limbs for the crippled, wisdom eyes for the blind, blessed ears for the deaf, wisdom tongues for the mute, and so on, contenting and satisfying them all.

Consider all the six types of beings are liberated from their individual karmic perceptions. All males attain the level of Avalokiteshvara, and females the level of Noble Tara. Finally, in a state of mind with no conceptualisation of any aspect of the offering or its recipients, rest in meditative equanimity. This cuts the root of the self-grasping demon of conceit and is the supreme realisation of the consummate and ultimate Chod.

TWENTY

THE DIRECT PATH TO SUPREME ACCOMPLISHMENT

'Accomplishment' is understood to refer to attaining and achieving our intended objectives, and also success in our wishes. Additionally, in terms of spiritual practice, accomplishment carries the meaning of attaining, by means of any suitable sadhana ritual, the protection and refuge of deities and yidams, and so on, by pleasing them with offerings, in order to fulfil the aims of the practitioner. Accomplishments are divided into two kinds: common and supreme. Common accomplishments include simple powers of illusion and magical display, and limited and temporary clairvoyance. Supreme accomplishment refers to the achievement of complete omniscient wisdom knowledge, or the attainment of the body of unity.

Here we come to the stage of the practice for attaining the supreme accomplishment which is known as 'Lama Yoga' or 'Guru Yoga'. In Tibetan the word 'Lama' means 'high' or 'superior' and is apposite because there is no one more worthy of receiving offerings. If you were to say, "What about the Buddha and others?" we see in the teachings that it says:

"Without the Lama, even the name *Buddha* would not exist."

Therefore, enlightenment comes through the Lama, and in the one Lama the Three Precious Jewels are complete. For these and other reasons, seeking, finding and relying on a genuine Lama is of crucial importance for all those who wish to be liberated, both in this lifetime and in the future.

There is no guarantee that someone with the name 'Lama', or the title of such and such a holy incarnate Lama or Tulku, or with powerful influence, is definitely a genuine master. There are false Lamas, fake adepts, fraudulent treasure revealers, and others.

One time when I was a child, I heard an eccentric man from another region had come to a village close to Dzogchen Monastery, saying he was a treasure revealer. He made a public declaration that on a particular date he was going to reveal a hidden treasure or terma. The day before the treasure was due to be revealed, he was spotted in the distance by a herdsman doing something peculiar at the foot of a cliff. When the strange man had gone away, the herdsman went to have a look at the place where he had just been. In a mud-filled crack in the cliff the herdsman saw a statue had been hidden. He took the statue out and in its place left a turd. Filling the crack up again with mud, the herdsman returned home without telling anyone.

Next day, when the time arrived to reveal the treasure, the strange man turned up looking very dignified, followed by many local onlookers. Arriving at the crack in the cliff, he thrust his hand into the mud and pulled out a handful of stinking shit. Laughter filled the valley as everyone fell about with mirth. The fraudulent treasure revealer was humiliated and ran away, never to return.

Charlatans and con artists like this bring discredit on the Buddha's teachings, and their type can appear anywhere. There are also some who hold the name 'Lama' who have studied the Dharma but, instead of taming their minds with the Dharma, they have become coarse and savage, greedy for everything, displaying tremendous attachment and aversion. I have heard of such people and how they disparage great masters such as Padmasambhava or the Incomparable Lord Tsongkapa. By doing this, the Dharma actually becomes the cause for rebirth in the lower realms.

An authentic Lama and teacher of the path will first have completed their own practice of the path and attained the signs of accomplishment, possessing the enlightened qualities of progress on the path. The time then arrives for them to benefit others by taming their minds. Such masters are in control of their own experiences, by which means they are enabled to overwhelm the experiences of others. Someone merely looking into such a master's eyes will develop the wisdom of realisation in their mind stream. This is the kind of master we need.

In my experience, I have never met a master more exalted than my own root guru. My supreme root guru had the name Jigme Dadrin Yonten Gonpo but, as was customary among Khampas in Tibet, he was known affectionately as 'Gonre'. Very dignified, he had an overwhelming presence about him. His deep voice was melodious and vivid, and just seeing his face would bring happiness and a change in perception. Because his mind was full of love and compassion, everyone who met him would experience a change in perception; filled with indissoluble happiness and faith, a feeling of bliss would grow, making you long never to be apart from him.

Khenpo Gonre never once had any attachment or desire for illusory worldly wealth or possessions. Whatever objects came into his possession he would immediately give away to whoever was around at the time. He was particularly compassionate to poor, helpless people, being like a parent to everyone who was desolate. Everything he did was practise of the Dharma, and for the benefit of sentient beings, never otherwise. It was rare anyone of that period maintained such perfect ethical discipline or upheld monastic conduct as he did.

Around Khenpo Gonre's body a fragrant aroma of ethical discipline, indefinable and unlike and unrivalled by any incense made by mundane processes, permeated for a distance over three arms' length. Especially from the direction of the prevailing wind, the scent that wafted was even more fragrant.

My supreme Lama was the spiritual tutor to Dzogchen Rinpoche. He was expert in the general teachings of Sutra, Tantra and auxiliary subjects. In particular, he was an effortless practitioner who had attained conference of the lineage blessings through the practise of luminous Dzogpa Chenpo. From the age of ten until my precious Lama passed into nirvana, I stayed together with him and Dzogchen Rinpoche Jigdral Changchup Dorje in the same hermitage, almost every day and night without separation. Because my master and we two students lived in the same accommodation, we were closer than members of the same family. I parted from my parents when I was ten years old and turned to these two Lamas to take the place of my parents, and so was brought up on the sweet milk of the sacred Dharma.

In the early evenings, my precious Lama would tell amazing stories and legends from the Dharma. Usually early morning, late morning and the evening were practice sessions. In the afternoon, teachings of Dzogpa Chenpo were given. My supreme Lama would sit cross-legged in a square box day and night, without loosening his belt, in meditative equipoise. Never separate from the wheel of luminosity, for him meditation and post-meditation were undifferentiated. He had control over the subtle mechanism of channels and winds, and the fetters of the winds, so he never became sick. Additionally, by pinpointing the essence of the completion stage vajra body, he purified the movement of the karmic winds in the central channel. Having freed all the knots in the subtle channels of his throat chakra of enjoyment, spontaneous vajra songs arose unimpeded and everything experienced arose as symbols and scriptures.

My precious Lama's father was a tantrika called Kyabmo Menla, an emanation of Padampa Sangye and accomplished practitioner of the Pacifier Chod lineage. Long ago, when another accomplished Lama was living in a remote practice cave, lots of local spirits came to him. They said, "Today, Kyabmo Menla gave us a beautiful zi onyx whip," and showed it to the Lama. The Lama looked and said, "It's a piece of wood with zi patterns drawn on it with paint." This demonstrates Kyabmo Menla, by the power of meditative concentration, could emanate whatever anyone wanted and had control over the magical display of the sky treasury. There are a great many legends spoken about how Kyabmo Menla demonstrated signs of his accomplishment.

My precious Lama, the supreme Jigme Dadrin Yonten Gonpo, being the son of Kyabmo Menla, would on occasion teach Chod in eerie places and charnel grounds. In the middle of the night, and at other times, he would sometimes shout out P'ET very loudly, and as a child, thinking ghosts and evil spirits were close, I used to grow afraid! Additionally, during his sleep in the wheel of luminosity, he could be heard speaking mantras for two hours or so, in a voice different from his usual one.

When I was thirteen, with these two great masters, Dzogchen Rinpoche and Khenpo Gonre, and a large number of attendants and followers, we formed a large caravan together and, mounted on horses and mules, set out on pilgrimage to Central Tibet, visiting chiefly the sites and sacred places which the Lotus Born Master visited and blessed. In those days we relied on horses, yaks and mules for transport and travel took an extremely long time. In the early dawn we would pack up camp and move out, stopping at noon when we would set up camp again and rest.

We travelled through hundreds of beautiful meadows, and over thousands of high mountain passes, rolling hills and valleys, great rivers and gentle streams. We saw the wild asses and yaks of the high ranges and the nomads' white and black herds of sheep and yaks living together. We enjoyed many views of white snow-mountains piercing the azure sky and beautiful mirror-like turquoise blue lakes, compelling vistas those who remained at home could not witness. The pure atmosphere and clear, refreshing breeze brought feelings of happiness and well-being.

When travellers used to make camp for the night, they pitched cloth tents. In our camp there were never less than fifty cloth tents. Sometimes in the dark of night, many people would witness the tent which was occupied by my master and us two students brightly illuminated, as if many butter lamps were burning within, although not one was lit. I also saw, half asleep and half awake in the middle of the night, the entire inside of the tent suddenly filled with light.

My holy Lama personally taught me how to write Tibetan letters and gave me tests. When I was small and we ate tsampa, he used to mix it and give it to me. He was also my ordination master. During midday breaks in practice, when we three, master and students, made retreat in the same hermitage together, he would give Dzogchen Rinpoche and myself quintessential instruction teachings on the Seven Treasuries of Longchenpa, the Trilogy of Natural Ease, the Four Heart Essences, and other key texts, teaching both explanatory and hearing Tantras in the manner of scriptural transmission.

One time we three stayed together in silent retreat. Every day, before the break of dawn, having finished my practice session of Manjushri, one of our two assistants would help me put on my robes and accompany me to visit the toilet. One day it was the turn of an assistant who enjoyed having fun to lead me to the toilet. For a joke he took away the only lamp and left me there in the dark. I was young and so afraid I could not help but let out a scream. I still remember how afraid I felt!

Above the door of our hermitage was a Dharma horn made from rhino horn, which Khenpo Gonre said had been the Dharma horn in the lifetime of his master Zhenga Rinpoche. When he was not in retreat, Khenpo Gonre would blow this horn and many students would gather from all around, to whom he would regularly give instructions in the Dzogchen preliminaries and main practice teachings.

Dzogchen Rinpoche Jigdral Changchup Dorje was five years older than me and he possessed wisdom innately in his mind stream. Particularly, he was expert in the meaning of the Tantras and endowed with mastery of the ritual practices of the visual transmission. From him I received many empowerments and transmissions, including the Scripture of the Great Assemblage empowerment and the Excellent Wishing Vase. Together as Dharma fellows we received many empowerments, teachings and oral instructions from both our precious Lama tutor and the Second Jamyang Khyentse Chokyi Lodro, who was a student of the Fifth Dzogchen Rinpoche. We went together many times to his seat at

Dzongsar, each time staying for one or two months, and received a vast number of profound teachings from him. The previous incarnation of this Khyentse, the First Jamyang Khyentse, was a student of Dzogchen Pema Banza (my previous incarnation) and teacher of the Fifth Dzogchen Rinpoche.

At that time there were many great holy masters with us to receive empowerment, including Katok Situ and Moksa Rinpoche. Khyentse Rinpoche's consort was the daughter of the Lakar family who were not only special Dharma patrons to Dzogchen Monastery, but their district fell under Dzogchen Monastery's ordination jurisdiction. For these reasons, we have a strong and longstanding special connection with the Khyentse Lama palace.

In the summer of the Fire Monkey year, 1956, Khyentse Chokyi Lodro, Dzogchen Rinpoche, Khenpo Gonre and I spent a long and happy summer's day together in conversation in a breezy tent pitched in a garden near the Copper Temple of the Three Realms in Samye Monastery. We parted on that day forever.

Another day in that year, our precious tutor Khenpo Gonre, Dzogchen Rinpoche and I, together with our attendant caretakers, assistants and monks, visited the holy city of Lhasa and the sacred Jowo Rinpoche statue. As we circumambulated around the Jowo and Dzogchen Rinpoche was about to touch the crown of his head to the left foot of the statue, an unknown monk made an offering of a parcel which smelled of medicinal herbs, placing it in his hands. Rinpoche passed it to me and I felt heat radiating from it. The following day was the auspicious tenth day of the month and we held a feast offering. Dzogchen Rinpoche opened the parcel to find it contained a holy statue called Source of All Accomplishments. This represented the form of Guru Rinpoche as Guru Mahasukha, Guru of Great Bliss; a palm's width in height, with a demon's skull-cup as its base. It was amazing, unlike any other statue, made from medicinal powder mixed with clay and with pieces of gold, silver and other kinds of precious substances.

Also in the parcel was a yellow scroll, inscribed with symbolic script which embodied enlightened speech. The support of enlightened mind was similar to the material of the statue, together with precious gems and various medicinal substances mixed with something like sindhur, red pigment. It had a wonderful fragrance like nothing I had ever smelt before. The time for what is called a 'treasure' to be revealed had actually arrived, and we had the great fortune to actually witness with our own eyes the guardian of the treasure give it in the manner of making an offering. In this way both these two holy masters, Dzogchen Rinpoche and Khenpo Gonre, spontaneously revealed a vast number of Dharma treasures of the sky treasury from the expanse of enlightened realisation.

When we made pilgrimage to glorious Tsari and circumambulated the peak of the Pure Crystal Mountain, Lamas and students all had to walk. On the banks of the Blood Red Lake, my precious tutor Lama, dancing and gesturing with his arms, sung a melodious vajra song, which caused the appearance of amazing signs, so obstructions of local deities became naturally pacified. Suddenly, without hesitation, our precious Lama strode into the lake, but some of his attendants grabbed him, preventing him from going in any further. Dzogchen Rinpoche's father and my great-uncle, Adro Kechog Ngawang Norbu, were with us at the time and said because Khenpo Gonre had been held back, the auspicious circumstances were slightly discordant and the merit of his students was low. They said, "If the auspicious circumstances had been excellent, then he would have certainly revealed an extraordinary lake treasure that day."

We three, master and students, went on a vast pilgrimage to White Skull Snow Mountain, Yarlung Crystal Rock, Drak Yangdzong Caves, Yerpa Moon Cave, Chimphu Red Rock Cave, Ke'u Ri Yangdzong Cave, and other places, and made huge feast offerings. In the Great Secret Flower Cave in Chimphu, and the Inner Guru Rinpoche cave in Yangdzong and others, Dzogchen Rinpoche undertook strict solitary retreat. In Khradruk Monastery, he opened the mandala of the Ocean of Dharma of the Gathering of all Teachings and performed the sadhana of making sacred medicine for seven days, with a gathering of over one hundred practitioners. It was a great spiritual assembly complete with the four aspects of ritual service and accomplishment. Following this, we held one-hundred thousand celebratory amendment feast offerings and butter lamp prayers of aspiration, and finished by casting the coloured mandala sands into the river, thereby effectively bestowing the important rites of the general and specific teachings.

At that time many amazing signs of accomplishment appeared which everyone witnessed: nectar flowed from the accomplishment torma and nectar boiled from the accomplishment skull-cup. Medicinal fragrance filled the surroundings for a kilometre, and so on. Generally speaking, the miracle of nectar flowing from the accomplishment torma is unique to the lineage of the Dzogchen Lords of Accomplishment, Drubwang Dzogchenpa.

Every year in Dzogchen Monastery, when the Great Vase Consecration Ceremony of the Month of Miracles is held, nectar drips from the accomplishment torma of the three roots, as well as from the great food offering torma. This miracle continues to manifest every year in Dzogchen. In 1996, when I first established the Saga month Manjushri Throne Ceremony in Shira Sing Buddhist University, due to the time and circumstances we could not hold an elaborate and extensive assembly like the great gatherings which were held in the past. However, nectar still spontaneously flowed from the accomplishment torma.

Equally miraculous is the representative statue of Guru Rinpoche Mahasukhakaya, body of supreme bliss, also known as 'Dzogchen Mardoma'. It has been made by each successive Dzogchen lineage master and has been famous for centuries all over Tibet for protecting all those who carry one from sickness, negative influences and fear of harm or attack. These days the Dzogchen Mardoma is famous all over the world, and appreciated by many people regardless of their faith in Dharma.

My extraordinary, precious and supremely gracious Lama Gonre had no feelings of pleasure or sorrow, joy or anger, but was always profoundly spacious and open, regarding the myriad activities of samsara with a smile, like an old person watching a child playing.

In 1959, during the time when everything fell into turmoil, Lama Gonre accomplished his escape from the violent conflict. He dismounted from his horse, sat as straight as an arrow in meditative equipoise, and became enlightened in primordial inner basic space. At that time the sky was filled with rainbows and a latticework of lights. The following day at sunrise his precious body had disappeared; mother dakinis had taken it. There are many other amazing stories like this.

At the same time, among terrible fighting and turmoil, Dzogchen Rinpoche Jigdral Changchup Dorje, under a pretext of having been slightly injured and reaching the point of death, uttered the sound HIK!, clear and pure a few times and merged inseparably with enlightened mind of the ground of emanation. I managed to keep hold of his precious relics throughout the period of the Cultural Revolution and beyond, guarding them with my life. Afterwards, to enshrine his relics and demonstrate my faith in Rinpoche, I built a great gold reliquary dharmakaya stupa of enlightenment which liberates on sight. This is now enshrined in the main temple at Dzogchen Pema Tung Great Perfection Retreat Centre.

Inside the golden reliquary I placed Dzogchen Rinpoche's precious relics as consecration objects, along with some of All-knowing Jigme Lingpa's flesh, Jigme Yonten Gonpo's hair, as well as many other absolutely extraordinary support substances, including a spontaneously multiplying relic of the Buddha. To say merely prostrating to this stupa with devotion, even from a distance, will bring an end to our samsaric rebirths is, I believe, not an exaggerated claim of its spiritual power.

It is necessary to speak a little of the lives of holy masters, because in order to transfer the realisation of the wisdom lineage, the blessings of the lineage masters are extremely important. These in turn depend on uncontrived faith and devotion, so for this reason here is a brief summary of the names of the victorious Dzogchen Monastery lineage of the Great Perfection Heart Essence of the Great Expanse, Dzogchen Longchen Nyingthig:

From Samantabhadra to Vajrasattva, Garab Dorje, Shirasingha, Padmasambhava, and so on, the three lineages, mind, symbol and hearing, were passed to All-knowing Longchenpa. Following this, the Great Chariot of the Heart Essence of the Great Expanse was transmitted to All-knowing Jigme Lingpa by the Mind Lineage of the Victorious Ones. Jigme Lingpa realised the inconceivable essence of enlightened mind inseparable from all Buddhas; the expanse of vast enlightened wisdom mind unfolded to him. He received the Symbol Lineage of Awareness Holders from the wisdom light body of Longchenpa in a total of three visions. He also received the Hearing Lineage of Great Individuals, receiving the transmission by listening to the oral hearing lineage which liberates through hearing. Thus Jigme Lingpa received all three transmissions.

Of his students, the Four Jigmes from Kham, the lineage passed through Jigme Gyalwe Nyugu to the Fourth Dzogchen Rinpoche Migyur Namkhar Dorje, then Orgyen Tenzin Norbu and Great Khenpo Shengar Rinpoche, and was given to my master Jigme Dadrin Yonten Gonpo. This is the extremely close lineage. Jigme Yonten Gonpo also received the lineage of Dodrup Kunzang Shenpen, Gyalse Shenpen Tharye and Patrul Jigme Choki Wangpo; thus he unified both transmissions. Through my Lama's graciousness I then received this root lineage.

Another of my teachers was Dzogchen Pema Tsewang. He kept pure discipline, maintaining the outer vows of individual liberation. He was a realised Bodhisattva, replete with the inner nature of bodhichitta, and he was a master of rigpa awareness, having reached full realisation of the secret great esoteric path of Vajrayana. Dzogchen Pema Tsewang was rich in the qualities of learning, discipline and nobility. He was a renunciate yogi who maintained the qualities of training. Staying with him, I received gracious and detailed instruction in the thirteen major philosophical texts including auxiliary teachings.

Another of my teachers was Dzogchen Thubten Nyendrak. He possessed the qualities of the nine holy modes of conduct. In particular, he was famed throughout Amdo, Central Tibet and Kham for his scholarship. Also my great uncle, Dzogchen Adro Ngawang Norbu, was a master. He was a Lama of the region and his vows were those of a mantra-adept vajra holder. He was renowned for his learning of the Sutras and Tantras, as well as the general sciences, and had attained signs of accomplishment. He gave me the transmission of the Hundred Thousand Tantras of the Nyingma School and detailed teaching on the Treasury of Precious Qualities.

The teacher who taught me how to read and write was the learned, disciplined and noble Dzogchen Khenpo Chojor. In particular, he was extremely expert in the Paramita teachings. It was in 1958 that he had just received the throne of Head Khenpo of Dzogchen Monastery. Such excellent Lamas and spiritual masters are like a range of golden mountains, and as rare as stars in daytime sky.

Here in this section, I have used my holy Lamas as examples to talk about the qualities of spiritual masters, the source of accomplishments. Having found a spiritual master of this kind to show you the way, if you train in the realisation and conduct of the Lama with faith and devotion, together with diligence, there is no doubt you will attain supreme accomplishment in this lifetime. Especially, having received profound secret mantra empowerment, it is very important to maintain the vows and sacred commitments, just as if you had arrived at a junction of two roads, one leading to advantage and the other to danger.

So, on this crucial point, we arrive at the stage of actual Guru Yoga of the Dzogchen Essence of the Great Expanse preliminaries. This is what to do:

In one Tantra it says:

> "Better than meditating on a hundred thousand deities
> for ten million kalpas
> is to think for a single moment
> of your Lama."

For all of us who strive from the bottom of our hearts for liberation, first it is vital to seek out a Lama and spiritual master who has the suitable attributes to show us the way. Following that, it is vital to train with them and receive instruction. Finally, it is vital to train in the realisation and conduct of the Lama and unify your mind with theirs.

It is important to understand, at this stage of ultimate yoga, effortless Dzogpa Chenpo, we are not taught at some point there is hope results will arise through concepts and discernment, or through analysis of logical arguments. Additionally, it is not the case, by relying on sadhana practice and with great effort, the common and supreme accomplishments are attained in stages. Neither is introduction given by means of examples that elicit partial and dualistic truth.

In Dzogchen practice, by praying with fierce, unfeigned devotion and faith to a Lama who has supreme realisation and seeing them as an actual Buddha, the power of the Lama's familiarisation with true realisation will unify the student's mind with the Lama's. The blessings of the lineage, the wisdom of realisation, will develop in the student's mind, and by these means liberation will be accomplished. In this way blessings will come with swift energy; this is meditation on Guru Yoga, the ultimate heart of the path. We can be certain this is so.

Visualise the Guru Yoga field of accumulation in the following way:
You are in a vast and open plain, your entire vision filled with the pure realm. Visualise, in the centre of the full-sized and vastly arrayed Palace of Lotus Light, perfectly complete in all its attributes, you yourself, in essence the Dakini Yeshe Tsogyal, in appearance Jetsun Vajra Yogini. She is red in form with one face, two arms, and three eyes which gaze longingly at the heart of the Lama. In her right hand she is playing a damaru skull-drum, held aloft in the sky, which rouses beings from the sleep of ignorance. Her left hand rests on her hip and holds a curved

knife with a vajra handle which cuts the root of the three poisons. She is naked, adorned with the six bone ornaments and garlands of flowers. Visualise her as present but empty in essence.

In the sky above her head at the distance of an arrow's length is a ten-thousand petalled lotus flower in full bloom, formed from myriad precious substances. Upon this lotus are sun and moon cushions. In the centre, in nature your gracious root Lama, is the form of the Precious One from Oddiyana. He is white in colour with a red radiance and sits in the royal posture. He is wearing a brocade robe, monastic robes and a gown, and he wears the lotus hat on his head. In his right hand he holds a gold vajra at his heart in the threatening mudra. Under his arm he holds his consort Princess Mandarava in hidden form as a khatvanga trident.

Surrounding him, within a lattice of five-coloured lights and encircled in spheres of light, are the Eight Awareness-Holders of India, the Twenty-Five: Lord and Subjects of Tibet, and so on, an oceanic assembly of the Three Roots and oath-bound guardians. Visualise them gathered around the Great One from Oddiyana. With intense longing and devotion, pray to them and recite the words of invitation.

As you do this, meditate the wisdom deities, including the Glorious Copper-coloured Mountain and the Palace of Lotus Light, together with all their temples and deities, actually appear in reality. They dissolve inseparably into the commitment deities which you have just visualised.

Now we offer the seven branches. As we have seen, the path of the secret mantra has many skilful means and is without difficulty. It is the practice for those with sharp faculties. For this reason, accumulations which take many hundreds of thousands of aeons to gather in the lesser approaches become consolidated in a single moment in the Vajrayana and liberation is attained in one or more lifetimes. Of these, the most supreme is the making of offerings to the Lama. All the different methods for gathering the accumulations are included in the seven branches.

FIRST OF THESE IS THE BRANCH OF PROSTRATION:

Visualise your body multiplied numberless times and, together with all sentient beings infinite as the sky, meditate you prostrate together. We need to unite as one body, speech and mind: prostrate with physical devotion, pray with devotion of speech, and with mental respect have the devotion which sees everything your master does as enlightened.

The Branch of Making Offerings is as Follows:

Make offerings to the Buddhas and Bodhisattvas of clean and pure, actual and mentally-created offerings. Follow noble Samantabhadra's miraculous manifestations of offerings and offer the wealth of gods and humans from all the heavens and all earthly places, including drinking water, bathing water, flowers, incense, lamps, perfumed water, food and music, as well as celestial mansions, pleasure gardens, the sixteen vajra goddesses, and inconceivably more.

The Branch of Confession:

Feel tremendous remorse and regret for all the negative actions, obscurations, faults and failings you and all sentient beings have accumulated with body, speech and mind in all lifetimes since beginingless samsara. Openly admit and lay them aside, promising never to do such things again. Confessing, complete with the four powers, visualise all your negative actions and obscurations gathered as a black heap on your tongue. Rays of light shine from the bodies of the assembled deities of the field of accumulation and touch the black heap. Meditate this cleanses and purifies everything.

The Branch of Rejoicing:

Rejoice in the magnificent undertakings and aspirational prayers the Buddhas, Bodhisattvas of the ten directions and their students, as well as you yourself and all other sentient beings have done, will do, and which are currently being done. Whatever positive accumulation of virtues there is, included in both the two truths, defiled and undefiled, rejoice from the bottom of your heart for everything.

The Branch of Requesting the Buddhas to Turn the Wheel of Dharma:

Pray to whichever Buddhas, Bodhisattvas and those appearing in the form of spiritual masters who have yet to turn the wheel of Dharma, by emanating your body numberless times and offering golden wheels, right-spiralling white conch shells, and other such things, so they may turn the wheel of Dharma in accordance with the minds of the three kinds of beings to be tamed.

THE BRANCH OF PRAYING TO THE BUDDHAS NOT TO ENTER NIRVANA:

By multiplying your body numberless times, pray to whichever of the Buddhas and Bodhisattvas in any of the pure realms who, having completed the task of benefitting sentient beings and taming their minds, are ready to pass into nirvana. Beseech them to stay until samsara has been emptied and continue to benefit sentient beings. As you recite the words remain mindful of their meaning.

THE BRANCH OF DEDICATION:

Take this merit to represent the entire roots of merit which exist and have been accumulated by yourself and all other beings throughout the three times, all gathered together, and dedicate it in order for all beings to attain enlightenment with the seal of non-conceptual wisdom. Do this in just the same way as Noble Ever-youthful Manjushri, Samantabhadra and others dedicate. Think in this way and dedicate.

If we do not dedicate in this way to attain full enlightenment, the merit can be destroyed by negative actions, for example by anger and, if the result of virtue does ripen, once we have experienced the result it will be exhausted. By dedicating in this way, the merit will never be lost. Even after experiencing the result one hundred times it will continue to increase more and more.

Currently we are ordinary beings and unable to make a dedication with unsullied wisdom which realises the nature of the threefold aspects of the dedication, the dedicator and the object of dedication not to be truly existent. However, it is taught if we have the intention to dedicate in whichever way the Buddhas and Bodhisattvas dedicate, then we will effectively dedicate with the threefold aspects perfectly pure.

Having offered the seven branches combining the recitation with the visualisations, once again pray to the essence of all the Buddhas of the three times, the unequalled treasury of compassion, the glorious protector, your holy Lama. All your wants and desires are spontaneously fulfilled. "You are like a spiritual wish-fulfilling jewel. I rely on you, practise with you alone; I have no other hope but you. You are all-knowing!" You pray, thinking this with devotion which brings tears to your eyes. Recite the prayers and then the 'vajra guru' mantra several times.

Having done this, from a white OM syllable at the point between the eyebrows of Guru Rinpoche and your Lama, inseparable as one, rays of light shine forth, sparkling like crystal. They touch the crown of your head and purify the three negative karmic actions of the body, and the obscurations of the subtle energy channels which give rise to the physical body. You receive blessings of vajra body, receive the vase empowerment, and become a vessel of the development stage. The seed of a fully mature awareness-holder is established. The fortune to attain the level of the nirmanakaya is placed in your mind stream.

From Guru Rinpoche's throat, a red AH syllable shining like a ruby emits light rays which touch your throat centre. Obscurations of the four negative karmic actions of speech and obscurations of wind are purified, as it is the subtle energy winds which give rise to speech. You receive blessings of vajra speech, the secret empowerment, and become a vessel of mantra recital. The seed of an awareness-holder with power over life is established. The fortune to attain the level of the sambhogakaya is placed in your mind stream.

From Guru Rinpoche's heart centre, a sky-blue HUM syllable emits light rays which touch your heart centre. Obscurations of the three negative karmic actions of mind and obscurations of the subtle drops are purified, as it is the subtle drops which give rise to mind. You receive blessings of vajra mind, the knowledge-wisdom empowerment, and become a vessel of bliss-emptiness fierce heat meditation. The seed of an awareness-holder of the great seal is established. The fortune to attain the level of the dharmakaya is placed in your mind stream.

Again, from the HUM syllable at Guru Rinpoche's heart, a second HUM syllable shoots out like a shooting star and merges inseparably with your mind. It purifies the karma and cognitive obscurations of the ground of all. You receive blessings of vajra wisdom, the ultimate empowerment which words describe, and become a vessel of primordially pure Great Perfection. The seed of an awareness-holder with spontaneous presence is established. The fortune of the ultimate result of the Svabhavikakaya is placed in your mind stream.

With devotion, follow the words of the preliminaries text and recite and meditate in unison accordingly, finally merging your mind inseparably with your Lama's and remaining in meditative equipoise. When you come to close your practice session, pray once more to your Lama with intense devotion. Guru Rinpoche smiles and, with joy in his eyes, a fiery hot ray of red light blazes from his heart and touches yours, as you visualise yourself as Vajra Yogini. The moment it touches you, you are transformed into a sphere of red light and, shooting like a spark from a fire, merge into Guru Rinpoche's heart. Remain in meditative equipoise.

Following this, experience all that appears and exists as a manifestation of the master and dedicate the merit for the benefit of all sentient beings. It is necessary to recite the Guru Yoga mantra ten million times. It is taught just by practising this one practice with perfect devotion and pure sacred commitments, we will be drawn up to the abode of Guru Rinpoche and reach the level of Samantabhadra.

The teachings of the Great Perfection are supreme among other spiritual approaches; they obviate the need to rely on countless aeons and numberless lifetimes of gathering the accumulations and striving. These teachings provide crucial points of profound instruction for attaining enlightenment in one lifetime, one body. However, like the rungs of a ladder, the preliminaries and main practices must be traversed one step at a time. In the same way a container must be cleaned thoroughly before a precious substance is poured into it, first we must purify our mind stream by means of the preliminaries. Having done that, we may enter into the main practice. This is like constructing a building upon firm and stable foundations. The preliminary practices are like a protective escort to accompany us along a fearsome path. Without a capable guide we will not be able to pass along a road thronged with armed enemies and bandits. Without the preliminaries, even if we know some points of the main practice, we will not be able to integrate it into personal experience and the essence will elude us.

First we train our mind with the Four Mind Changers and then proceed with general training in the Common and Extraordinary Preliminaries. Crucially, the complete essence of both the preliminaries and the main practices is the profound path of Guru Yoga. From my heart I give this vital advice to benefit all who yearn for liberation: take Guru Yoga as the core of all practice.

TWENTY ONE

UNION OF MERGING AND TRANSFERENCE
AT THE POINT OF DEATH

The Buddha taught many different kinds of Dharma teachings. Subsequently, numerous scholars have studied these teachings and elucidated them in terms of both words and meaning. However, the essential point is someone who, by means of practising the holy Dharma, has found the courage and confidence necessary to overcome fear at the moment of death, is called a Buddhist. On the other hand, however many teachings, Sutras, Tantras, transmissions and direct instructions someone has learned, even if they can recite them by heart as fluently as the ceaseless flow of a river; if, at the moment of death, they have not been able to assimilate into their mind stream one word of instruction for the benefit of themselves or others, it is as if they had set out to fetch water and returned home with the bucket completely empty: a complete waste of human life.

Once I met someone stricken with disease, on the brink of death. The doctor had confirmed his imminent passing, and so his wife and the nurses knew there was no other path for him except the one which confronted him: death. However, the doctor was concerned about depressing the sick man, so did not tell him the truth. Similarly his relatives avoided confrontation, crying secretly, and no one explained his situation clearly to him. In view of all this, it took the sick man a while to understand his present illness was terminal, but eventually he saw when death comes, everyone, including Buddhists, feel afraid. Day by day his breathing became ever more laboured and his pulse weakened. On the brink of death, the dying man's eyes sank into his skull and his nose began to droop. His teeth became stained and grimy and he kept struggling with his clothing. He would beg to be propped up in bed, or asked to be lowered down again, and so on.

As these signs of immanent death appeared, the sick man and his wife lost all hope and were forced to face up to the circumstances which would confront them after his death. Then the dying man began panting swiftly and harshly; tears streamed from his eyes, and his face grew grey with misery. In a weak despairing voice, rasping from the back of his throat, he cried out the names of the doctor, influential family members and his relatives. "Don't let me die!" he sobbed, begging and pleading, his voice full of suffering. Witnessing his suffering, I felt terrible pain. It was as if the people around me, even those I have no connection with, became like thorns in my heart. The determination arose in me that, if I were actually able to save him by sacrificing myself, I would be prepared to die in his place.

At this point, all the dying man's past actions arose in the reflection of the mirror-like memory of his mind. When this man was growing into an adult, he never gave death a moment's thought, and he even went so far as to rob other beings of their precious lives. As an adult, his fierce tyrannical commands pelted down on weak and completely innocent people like thunderbolts, bringing great suffering. He destroyed and demolished representations of Buddha's body, speech and mind, criticised the holy Buddhist teachings and masters, and committed many other such negative acts. Remembering all this, the dying man suddenly became terrified, almost fainting, in a state of mental and physical agony. I could see from his appearance he was having visions of the sky falling to earth as his breathing ceased, and he died.

Someone possessing blessed insight, or clairvoyance, would be able to perceive clearly the even more terrifying experiences which this man encountered after his death. The eyes of ordinary people like us would recognise, from that day on, he was not only separated forever from this world, but also eternally separated from all his loving family and friends. All that remained was what we call a corpse, terrifying, unclean and malodorous, left together with a lifeless name. Apart from this, there would be nothing else to see. After a few days, the corpse would be cremated, buried, cast into a river or given to the vultures and so on, according to the regional custom. Following this, over many years, the dead man's name would also gradually fade from memory and eventually be forgotten.

We cannot witness what happens after a dead person's final breath has been expelled, however we can witness the unbearable suffering of those left behind. Members of the dead person's family who held them dear pray to the Precious Ones, beseeching that their beloved one may be protected from the terrors of the intermediate state as they pass down the path to the next life. An ignorant few lament and cry, saying, "Where are you going, leaving us behind like this?" beating their chests, pulling at their own hair, and similar behaviour. However, the dead person's consciousness has either swooned or already left the confines of the physical body, so how can anyone remain to give an intelligible reply; and how can any of that be of the slightest benefit to the dead?

In many regions of Tibet, after someone has died people avoid mentioning their name and, if someone else in that area has the same name, it is customary to change it and give them a different one. The reason for this is as follows: if the dead person is not attached to their family, friends, home and possessions, and has already practised Dharma in preparation for the next life, that merit will accompany them and bring about rebirth in the higher realms and liberation, so neither temporary nor long term suffering will come about. If that is not the case and they did not practise holy Dharma while alive, then there will be no positive karma to welcome them at death. Moreover, after the person has passed away, if those conducting the funeral services also do not undertake any meritorious practices which will be of benefit to the dead, then merely burning paper money, giving flowers, or making solemn speeches is of no use.

In particular, if the dead person grasps at or is attached to the experiences of this world, then the perpetuation of previously accumulated non-virtuous negative actions will act as karmic causes which will come together with the karmic conditions of the objects which the deceased grasps at and is attached to, and bring about negative results. Just as a magnet attracts iron, the samsaric state is once more brought about, and again the deceased enters the samsaric prison of suffering. In the Buddhist land of Tibet, it is for this reason people refrain from saying the name of someone recently deceased. If family or friends call their name it could cause the dead person, who retains a mental body, to develop grasping and attachment and therefore cause them harm; so it became the custom to refrain from calling the names of the dead. If it becomes impossible not to refer to the dead, then it is customary to refer to them as the 'peaceful spirit'.

It is taught generally of the three: 'life force', 'vital basis' or 'la' and 'mental consciousness', life force may be severed by a negative force, and mental consciousness follows karma. La remains when the dead body is disposed of or buried. What is known as 'la' is the basis of the life force, and is the subtle essence of the life and life force. If it were to go away, dissipate, or flee and so on, at that time the signs are discomfort, loss of radiance and lustre of complexion, and insomnia. Before someone dies their la diminishes. Signs of this include a stopping of the la pulse. In the secret mantra of the Nyingma tradition of Tibetan Buddhism there are many methods to revive the la by means of ritual and meditative concentration, including summoning or ransoming the la. After death it is said what is known as the la remains when the body is discarded and can be understood as being a person's innate guardian or ancestral gods. Actually, the la is a part of a person's perceptions and not some powerful non-human entity which can benefit or harm us.

If the la is comfortable at death, then all those left behind will also be comfortable, but if the place where a body is discarded is not suitable and so on, then the la will be uncomfortable and those left behind will experience loss of livestock or other misfortune. There seems to me to be an unmistaken connection here between observable phenomena. It is said there are innate negative forces, or messengers of death, demons and negative spirits which can impersonate the form of a dead person to cause misfortune to others. Also, some kinds of demons can even possess living beings whose la and strength are diminished and bring harm to other living creatures in this way.

In Tibet, when someone has died it is not good for the family to cry. Traditionally it is said if someone cries over a body, the tears will become a hail of red hot iron upon the deceased. This is said by those with not particularly high levels of education or understanding in religion, but if we investigate carefully it is clear there is a valid reason for this. The deceased is a hundred times more anxious and miserable than those left behind, being completely isolated, and full of despair and terror. At that time the consciousness is unsupported but for a mental body, which depends solely on the smell of nourishment for food. Without protection or refuge, friends or help, time passes in fear and terror. When driven by the winds of karma, the deceased returns again and again to the vicinity of their previous home and family. At this time, if the living have no guidance or solace to offer and just sit around crying, it will make the deceased that much more depressed and attached, the influence of which will increase the risk of taking a negative rebirth. For these reasons, the harm caused by mourners' tears is comparable to being showered by a hail storm of red hot iron.

For the first few days after death, relatives cry and weep, but following that they start debating how to divide the wealth and possessions and then they argue and fight. There is nothing more harmful to the deceased than this and it is a terrible thing to do. A mental-bodied being in the intermediate bardo state has no corporal enclosure of flesh and blood but has very clear memory recollection and also a minor level of clairvoyance or higher perception, therefore if those left behind engage in negative actions in relation to the deceased, the deceased will be angered and this will propel them into a lower rebirth. Just as even the heaviest of ships can be steered easily when it is floating on water, great benefit and great harm can be brought to a being while in the bardo state.

Moreover, it is common for Tibetans to take an oath in the presence of the corpse saying, "To increase your positive merit, I promise to do positive actions and give up negative ones." If they manage to do so, these actions become beneficial both to themselves and the deceased in the future. In particular, paying service and respect to representations of the Buddha, Dharma and Sangha, or a site of assembly of the spiritual community: a monastery or nunnery etc., giving to the poor, making regular offerings, restoring great Buddhist universities and doing other such meritorious work, brings swift benefit.

Most especially, on the brink of passing away, at the point between life and death, a spiritual master can be invited to perform the Phowa transference of consciousness and, by means of this profound practice, the consciousness can be drawn directly and forcefully to the Blissful Pure Realm of Sukhavati. For the deceased person it is better to receive this than be offered all the world's riches. At the time of death, even if they had all the riches in the world, not only would it be impossible to cheat death, but the wealth itself would become a source of attachment and a cause of suffering.

As this is case, if we consider carefully we realise there is no certainty how many years of life we have left or when we will die, therefore not only those on the brink of death but all of us should make haste to receive at the very least this single spiritual instruction. Any biped who does not do this is no different from a four-legged animal.

The swift path instruction of the Phowa transference is a special fast track means of the secret mantra Dzogchen Great Perfection. It is one of the five practices for attaining buddhahood without meditation. It is numbered among the practices to attain buddhahood without meditation because it is taught that this method does not to require a long time, many lifetimes or aeons, or the difficult development or perfection stage meditations of other paths. However, it is not taught that the stages of visualisation of the transference are unnecessary; but, because it is a swift path of practice, many people with sharp faculties and thin karmic obscurations can practice for just seven days and gain signs of accomplishment.

If someone on the brink of death has previously received instructions on the transference and practised them until gaining signs of accomplishment, then at the time of death, when the spiritual master recites the introduction and stages of visualisation, they themselves can focus with one-pointed faith. They recall their previous familiarity with the practice and together the power of both Lama and practitioner makes the attainment of liberation easy. Even for a very average practitioner, if the spiritual master has great realisation, he or she will certainly be able to propel them with great skill like a shooting an arrow into the pure realm of Sukhavati, to become inseparable with Protector Amithaba's enlightened mind.

The transference is one of the teachings by which means those with great negativities may be liberated through forceful methods. The teachings say: "Receive those without sufficient training by means of the transference."

There are many varieties of instruction for the transference of consciousness, and many different means of transmission. If we take the example of the highest dharmakaya transference, for an already familiarised practitioner, a master or friend with pure vows will talk them through the process, giving introductions and visualisations. They will say, "The signs of death will appear to you as follows..." and, "You are about to experience changes in your perception, so you will see such and such a vision." "The stages of dissolution are like this and that, so pray with devotion, and in this and that way rest in equanimity." By means of quintessential instructions in the practices of Trekcho of primordial purity and Todgal of spontaneous presence, they become liberated in that lifetime.

In the dying phase, the luminosity of the dharmakaya is recognised, like a child meeting its mother, and liberation occurs. Similarly, there is the middling transference of the sambhogakaya and the modest transference of the nirmanakaya. There is also the ordinary transference of the three metaphors, and so on, and according to the instructions of one's tradition there are differences between these practices of time, metaphor and methods of liberation etc.

The transference to care for the dead is a forceful method for liberating even those with no spiritual practice and heavy negative karma. For this it is absolutely necessary the Lama has seen the truth of the path of seeing and achieved the first of the Bodhisattva levels of realisation. Without having realised the supreme mind of true bodhichitta the Lama will be unable to draw another's consciousness to a pure realm. This kind of master with supreme realisation unifies their subtle winds, awareness and their mind, with the consciousness of the deceased and thereby instantaneously conveys him or her to the ultimate sphere, the actual blissful pure realm in a direct ascent to enlightenment.

Alternatively, there are histories of some accomplished masters who would summon the consciousness of the deceased into an object or ritual inscription as a support to focus attention and give the deceased Dharma instruction. After this, by means of the visualisation stages of the transference practice, they were able to move the consciousness in the manner of a physical object. There is a historical account which describes this: The first Dzogchen Rinpoche Pema Rinzin, together with two of his students, went to perform the transference for a dead person. Rinpoche summoned the deceased's consciousness to reside under a saucer and then instructed each of his students to attempt to move the consciousness. When the students sounded the HIK they were only able to wobble the saucer slightly. Then the master himself did the transference, and with one single HIK the saucer was thrown aside.

In Tibet, funeral rituals for the dead are performed for forty-nine days after death. The reason for this is generally the lifespan of a being in the intermediate state is forty-nine days. Counting from the day of death, every period of seven days is the weekly anniversary when it is customary for a large gathering of monks and nuns to assemble to perform various rituals to purify obscurations, guide the dead, and send them to a pure realm. The reason for this repetition is because every seven days the being in the intermediate state re-experiences the suffering of dying.

However, the most important time of all occurs during the death process when the outer breathing has ceased but the inner breath has not. During this time it is considered very important an extraordinary Lama is invited to perform the transference practice. This is because there is a short time, a few seconds, which is incredibly decisive and crucial in determining whether or not the consciousness of the deceased can be transferred.

In the nomad regions of Tibet, there is a custom of making plentiful offerings to the master who performs the transference, beginning with the horse the deceased rode or the best horse of the household, together with a saddle, bridle and saddle blanket. In other places it is also the custom to offer a tinderbox, bellows, water ladle, copper cauldrons, bowls, foodstuffs etc., as well as cooking supplies, travel provisions and other useful articles, all packed into saddle bags and strapped onto the back of the horse to be given as additional offerings.

Three days after death is generally the time when the consciousness awakens from its swoon, and this is an important time for introduction to the experiences of the intermediate state, so that day is when an eminent master is invited, who carefully creates positive merit for the deceased. On the final day, when forty-nine days have passed, a ritual entitled 'Completion' is performed and on the following day 'Indicating the Path' is performed, again by welcoming an outstanding master. Usually, in accordance with the means and needs of a family, introduction to the instructions of Liberation Through Hearing in the Bardo is given every seven days, or throughout the full forty-nine days, as well as the profound teaching of the Self-liberated Mind of the Peaceful and Wrathful Ones, Liberation Sutra of Vajrasattva, Confession of Misdeeds, Aspiration of Excellent Conduct and so on. In addition, it is customary for masters and incarnate Lamas to be invited, regardless of their tradition, to perform by means of rituals the rites for the deceased, including rituals to send them to a pure realm, purification rituals and various recitations to remove obscurations.

Immediately on or following the forty-ninth day, a blessing is given to the bones of the deceased by means of a Vajrasattva ritual. The bones are then ground into powder, mixed with clay and moulded into small stupas which represent the mind of enlightenment of the one gone to bliss, the Buddha, and which are called 'tsa tsa'. The following year, on the anniversary of the death, the equivalent of one year's share of food which would have been the deceased's is used to hold an elaborate commemoration offering.

Because religious and social customs regarding the purification and disposal of corpses vary according to different cultures, all kinds of different methods have developed. In the Buddhist land of Tibet, there is a method which is not widespread in other lands, that of giving the body to the birds, which I will now say a little about. At this point some people become terrified, shuddering with fear. This reaction is just the very tight bindings of your attachment to self grasping; other than this, after this body has become a corpse it is no different to earth or stone, so where are its feelings of pain? If it were the case a corpse has feelings, how much suffering it would experience being buried in a hole in the ground!

It is important the site where a charnel ground is established is blessed. Tibetans invite a holy master who has the completed the appropriate amount of mantra recitals and practice of the generation and perfection stages, to a place which has been determined to possess excellent qualities, to consecrate the land. Following this, the site is blessed with the mandala of the peaceful and wrathful deities and it becomes a sacred charnel ground. Stupas of the enlightened one and mani walls of one hundred thousand stones are erected. Mantric syllables are printed on cloth and hung as prayer flags, and all these are also consecrated.

In such a charnel ground, a practitioner of the Chod with extraordinary experience and realisation will, in the preceding evening, free the corpse from the negative force which brought about death. The astrology of death is calculated to determine the direction in which the 'hal khyi' spirit will be moving, and so on. According to the time and direction indicated by the calculation, and at approximately the break of dawn, from a pure direction the corpse is taken to the charnel ground.

The Chod practitioner will lead with preliminary prayers of going for refuge and arousing bodhichitta and ritual texts from the Chod tradition. The corpse is then turned over and, beginning at the top of the spine, the flesh is chopped up with the great cross cuts of the peaceful and wrathful deities, together with the liberation offering of Heruka cross cut. The body parts are then blessed as offering substances of wisdom nectar and become a feast offering. Wisdom, activity and worldly dakinis are invited in the manner of those doing service. An assembly of skeletons and messengers who gather to receive the leftovers is also summoned. All these come in the form of vultures according to the 'calling the birds' visualisation ritual, which is accompanied by the drums, bells and thigh-bone trumpets of the recitation ritual. The corpse is then chopped up and given to the vultures, which consume everything down to the last scrap.

When a corpse is cremated in Tibet, the appropriate yidam deity mandala is practised and the associated wisdom fire deity is invoked. This wisdom fire deity merges with oneself, the samaya being, and resides, whereby the elements of self-grasping are offered and burnt as offerings and gifts in the fire of wisdom, thus purifying them.

By conducting this kind of virtuous, effective and authentic funeral service, it not only leaves the living in a good state of mind and the la of the deceased at peace, but sees the deceased on a path leading onto more and more happiness in each successive series of lives. Having seen others off, we ourselves also need to prepare to go down that same path. Not only is the transference practice very profound at the time of death, but prayers of aspiration made at the point of death also make it easy for the aspirations to be accomplished. "For the sake of myself and all sentient beings, may I provide food for those who hunger, water for those who thirst, may I protect those without a protector, and be a refuge for those with none", and so on. By praying to the Three Precious Jewels, prayers of aspiration will be actualised accordingly.

On the verge of death, confess negative actions and failings accumulated since beginingless time. Dedicate all merit to great enlightenment. Think at the time of death: "I have met with this opportunity to rely on the outstanding instructions of the profound path of transference and attain perfect enlightenment, may all mother-like sentient beings be liberated from the suffering of samsara." Generating this aspiration with courage and confidence is one extraordinary quality of Buddhists.

I once met an old Tibetan monk who had no wealth or possessions. He was alone and on the brink of death. He had not received extensive education and was not very learned; however, since the time he was young he had done prostrations, circumambulations and purified his obscurations. When he was young he had received the preliminary and main practice teachings of the Dzogchen Heart Essence of the Dakini from a master and had engaged in the appropriate practices.

He always enjoyed joking and playing around. He was really good at telling hilarious stories, and other people could not help but fall about laughing. He was one to ridicule others' inappropriate behaviour and improper situations by mixing in pointed observations with his humorous tales. He was still making fun as he came close to death, not even giving it as much thought as one would do when going out of the door. Having eaten his fill of the food of this world, he was satisfied. But he said he still had the desire to drink a bowl of milk for the sake of making an auspicious connection, because it would be good to make himself clean and white inside. He drank the milk, removed his old clothes and put on his Dharma robe. He entered meditation with a small smile on his face as his subtle elements began dissolving. A surprising thing happened then; a coil of warm steam emerged from the crown of his head and wafted off into the air. Some corpses are frightening and repellent while others do not evoke fear. As the movement of his breath stopped his face was still smiling, as if he has fallen asleep, and his corpse did not frighten anyone.

The old monk had no one to cry for him, and also there was no one to hold an elaborate funeral for him afterwards. He possessed nothing except a small amount of tsampa mixed with dried cheese, enough to live on for about a week, and a little butter. He lived by training in the twelve good qualities and was contented, with few desires. This kind of person had no horse to offer for the transference recitation and no one to perform it for him, but still he entered the pure realm as naturally as a person enters their own home.

When I was thirteen years old, my mother, who was thirty-seven, passed away in what was astrologically her year of obstacles. That year I was living in the secluded Long-life Retreat Centre in Dzogchen and it happened when I was studying the Five Collections of Middle Way Reasoning with Khenpo Pema Tsewang. When my mother fell ill, my eminent uncle Dza Mura Tulku immediately sent several messengers from my home region of Dzachuka to request I should be given one month's leave from study and come quickly. I interrupted my Dharma studies at that point and, riding quickly, was able to make the four or five day journey to my place of birth to arrive at my uncle's monastic seat, Gelong Monastery. At that time, except for experiencing a little pain around her left ribs, my mother seemed healthy and had not changed. My mother was known for her beauty and could sing beautifully from memory the Legend of King Gesar, a hundred pages at a time, naturally distinguishing the different melodies which marked out each of the heroes. Even at that time she was the same as she had always been, never showing any signs suffering.

Gathered together were my parents and all my brothers, sisters and uncles in the midst of the beautiful nomadic meadow pastures. There were herds of livestock; white, black and mottled horses, sheep, yaks and other animals, with many four-eyed dogs (dogs with two round markings below their real eyes), some black with white chests, some mottled grey and so on, about the same size as baby yaks, wandering around wearing red ropes of yak hair round their necks.

In the centre of all this was our square tent made of black yak hair. The men stayed on the right side, and on the left were the women. In the centre was a large stove, roaring with flames, upon which we boiled tea and milk and cooked our food. At the upper side of the tent our fuel was stacked up and covered by a long striped cloth. Heading the line of men was the family shrine, arrayed with offerings and lots of burning butter lamps. On the women's side were great copper pots full of milk, yoghurt and food, where my mother and sisters prepared to receive guests. On a square white woollen mat the men would sit cross-legged and the women would sit kneeling with their legs tucked under them to one side. Generally, this is how the north-eastern nomads of Tibet like to live.

At that time our large nomad family sang joyful songs, and we amused ourselves while enjoying delicious milk, yogurt, butter, sweet cheese and so on. This was the last time all our close and distant family members were gathered together, and it seemed half-a-month passed by in a brief instant. I still have not forgotten the joyful time we spent together, and sometimes memories arise in my dreams at night.

Following that, according to the arrangements of my precious uncle, Mura Tulku, I went with him as part of a group of about one hundred of his followers and like-minded people from other districts. We rode to visit temples and monasteries, in places including Lap Monastery, for almost a month before returning to his monastery, at which point we heard my mother had suddenly fallen ill and was confined to bed.

From Gelong Monastery my uncle and I forded the Dza River on horseback and crossed the northern meadow. On the ridge between Madod and Dzachuka, in a place near Dzagyud, we arrived at our family camp by evening time. My mother's health had deteriorated and I could tell just from looking at her that she would not live long. My eminent uncle sat by my mother's pillow and, together with myself, began to recite the transference practice of the Dzogchen Heart Essence. While I accompanied him in the recital I sat close, staring at my mother's face.

At one stage during the recital my mother put her hands together and slowly recited a few words from Chagmey Rinpoche's aspiration prayer to be reborn in Amitabha's pure realm; at this time my eminent uncle sounded five additional HIK sounds; before he uttered the last one her breathing had stopped. I was taken aback for a moment and my mind became blank. After the recital was finished and I had an opportunity to think about what had happened, I could not bear the sadness of being separated from my gracious mother forever. However, when I thought about it carefully, she received the transference and was shown the way by an emanation of Avalokiteshvara, my eminent uncle Dza Mura Rinpoche, who guided her to a pure realm. More than that, my mother was herself the daughter of the yogi master of awareness Dzogchen Adro Sonam Chophel, who was the teacher of many holy masters including Katok Ngagchung. There was a naturally-occurring AH syllable on her tongue which was plain to see, and she was from a noble family well-respected in the locality. These thoughts made me less anxious. Later we asked Dzogchen Rinpoche Jikdral Changchup Dorje for divination of her rebirth, and he said, "The signs are good."

In this same way, death will definitely befall us all. When this happens, if we do not think ahead and prepare now, we will not be able to deal with it on our own. There is no telling when the signs of death will appear, so if at that time we suddenly panic, then it is down to bad planning and lack of foresight. We will have the same regret as if we had paid a fortune and received something completely worthless. To avoid this I am now going to say a little about one of the five Dzogpa Chenpo teachings for attaining buddhahood without meditation, the transference instructions for attaining buddhahood without meditation at the moment of death.

To distinguish the different types of transference: first, the superior transference to the dharmakaya by the seal of the view requires generating and familiarising one's mind stream with the unmistaken view of the natural state of Great Perfection in this lifetime; so at the point of death, by the direct path of Trekcho of primordial purity, through the technique of uniting basic space and rigpa awareness, one transfers to the expanse of the dharmakaya.

By familiarising oneself in this life with the yogas of the generation and perfection phases, as the confusing visions of the intermediate state arise, one is transferred to the wisdom body of unity. This is the middling transference to the sambhogakaya by uniting the generation and perfection phases.

Having entered the path of maturation and liberation, and possessing the instructions of the intermediate state in the bardo of becoming through taking the incarnated nirmanakaya as the path, one is transferred to a pure realm. This is the modest transference to the nirmanakaya through immeasurable compassion.

The method of using metaphors of the central channel as a path, the drop of mind consciousness as a traveller, and the pure realm of great bliss as the destination to which one transfers, is called the 'ordinary transference of the three metaphors', or the 'self-motivated transference of the three metaphors'.

Someone with supreme realisation can perform the transference for someone else, either at the moment of death or while they are in the intermediate state. This is called the 'transference for others by the hook of compassion', or 'transference performed for the dead with the hook of compassion'. However, it is taught one should not to perform the transference until one has seen the truth of the path of seeing. The time to do the transference is when the outer breath has ceased but the inner breath has not yet stopped. It is said this practice is like befriending a traveller on their journey.

The main instructions of the transference, both for training and for putting into practice at the moment of death, are as follows:
Seated on a comfortable mat, keep your body straight according to the seven-point posture of Vairochana. The ordinary physical components of your body instantly become Vajra Yogini, red in colour with one face and two hands, the right hand holding a curved knife, the left a skull-cup full of blood. In the crook of her left arm, she embraces a trident which is in essence the father Heruka. She is ornamented with silks, jewels and bone ornaments. Her right leg is slightly bent, the left outstretched in the striding stance, and she is standing on a lotus, a sun and a human corpse. The clear form of her body is like a thin film filled with air, or a red silken tent. In the centre of her body is the central channel as wide as a middle-sized bamboo arrow, a completely hollow tube of light. It has five characteristics: it is blue like the essence of pure lapis and its walls are as thin as the petals of a lotus. It is as luminous as a sesame oil lamp, straight as the trunk of a plantain tree and empty like the tree's hollow centre stripped of bark. Its upper end is open at the aperture of Brahma on the crown of the head like an open skylight. Its lower end is closed four finger widths below the navel. At the level of the heart centre, upon a knot like that found in bamboo, is a light green drop the size of a pea, which is the essence of the subtle wind, and it is quivering slightly. On this is the essence of awareness visualised as a red HRIH syllable burning like the flame of an oil lamp. Visualise all this as manifest.

High in the sky, one forearm's length above the top of her head in the basic space of phenomena, the ultimate unexcelled pure realm Akanishtha, in a limitless effulgence of rainbow lights and spheres, upon lotus and moon seats, is the embodiment of all refuges, indivisible from your gracious root guru, the world-honoured protector Amithaba. He is red in colour with one face, and his two arms are placed in the mudra of equanimity, upon which he is holding an alms bowl filled with the nectar of immortality. He is wearing the three Dharma robes and blazes with the majestic splendour of the marks and signs. He is sitting in the full lotus position. Amongst others, on his right is the Bodhisattva Lord Avalokiteshvara and to his left the Bodhisattva Vajrapani, all surrounded by an immense retinue of Buddhas, Bodhisattvas and victorious ones of the three roots, who gaze lovingly upon you and all other sentient beings with smiling eyes and joyful hearts.

Pray to the great guide Amithaba who leads us to the pure realm of great bliss, by reciting the liturgy together with visualisation.

With intense heart-felt faith and devotion, recite seven or so times the names of Amithaba: "Bhagavan, Tathagata, Arhat, utterly perfect Buddha..." Having recited this however many times, then recite: "EH MA HO! This spontaneously appearing place..." from our tradition of the Dzogchen Heart Essence. Then hold in your mind the HRIH syllable basis of mind awareness and, from the back of your palate, say HRIH five times together, moving the quivering light green drop of subtle wind up the path of the central channel, thus also driving the red HRIH syllable essence of mind upwards, like wind blowing a piece of paper upwards. With the final HRIH, the syllable touches the aperture of Brahma and you sound a powerful HIK! like shooting off an arrow, and your consciousness dissolves into the heart centre of the inseparable guru and Buddha Amithaba. Meditate that your mind mixes inseparably with the mind of your master. Once again, visualising and concentrating on the HRIH at your heart centre, repeat the process five or seven or more times, reciting HIK! many times, and so making your concentration more stable.

Following that, repeat seven times the names of Amithaba: "Bhagavan..." etc. After this, recite the familiar prayer, known as 'Inserting the Grass-stalk'. This is a transference practice of the Dzogchen Monastery lineage, so-called because the signs of training come easily, enabling one to insert a stalk of grass into the aperture of Brahma. It is appropriate to recite any one of the full, medium or summarised versions: "I prostrate to Buddha Amithaba..." etc. Then as before, recite the propelling recitation shooting one HIK! for every five HRIH.

Again recite the names of Amithaba: "Bhagavan..." etc. Then recite from the transference practice of the Sky Teaching: "EH MA HO" Most marvellous..." etc. Follow this, in the same way as before, by the propelling recitation.

In summary, practice this over and over again until you are ready to finish the practice session. Then place the seal of the space of the five kayas: recite with mental concentration the unborn syllable AH five times, after which recite P'ET! once. Repeat this sequence five times, then rest in equanimity in an unelaborated state beyond concepts.

To end: The retinue of assembled deities above the crown of your head dissolves into the central deity, the deity melts into red light and dissolves into you. In an instant you transform into the Bhagavan protector Amithaba, red in form, with one face and two hands. His two arms are placed in the mudra of equanimity, upon which he is holding a long-life vase filled with the nectar of immortality. He is adorned with silken robes and jewellery set with precious gems, and blazes with the majestic splendour of the marks and signs. Visualise the upper end of your central channel is now closed off with a moon mandala and a crossed vajra. Visualise clearly all these details.

Once again, from your heart centre multi-coloured lights emanate outwards and invite all the life essence of samsara, nirvana and the path in the form of light and light rays, which permeate into you. Imagine you become the immortal vajra body as you recite: "OM AMARANI JIVANTIYE SVAHA" one hundred times. Then recite the dharani for longevity, and others.

Not only does this practice cause your life no harm, it also reduces obstacles to life. Signs of accomplishment are: headaches, exudation of serum, a mound appearing on the crown of the head, being able to insert a stalk of grass into the aperture of Brahma, and so on. Practice until these kinds of sign appear. However, it is only necessary to actually put this into practice when signs of death are irreversible and the stages of dissolution have begun at the time of death. Except for this, to end one's life at an inappropriate time is a very serious negative action and not something which should be done. However, when the elements of the body are in balance and the subtle channels, winds and drops are flourishing, it is not easy to complete the transference. In advanced age, or at the moment of death, transference becomes easy, just as the mature fruit of autumn falls readily.

Therefore, practice from this time onwards and at some time, when it becomes necessary, you can trust you will have confidence. Also, when you suddenly experience terrible fear, focus your mind on the crown of your head and visualise you Lama residing above your head. If you can become skilled at doing this then, if death should come suddenly, it will be extremely useful. In general the training of continually visualising your master on the crown of your head is a very important practice which is highly praised.

TWENTY-TWO

DEATH OMENS IN THE MIRROR OF TIME

This body of ours, which we cherish and care for, passes through stages of birth, growth, development, weakness, decline and increasing frailty, and then this drama of human life comes to a close. All these stages are included within the categories of birth, ageing, sickness and death. All living things experience birth and death, but it is not certain that everyone will experience obvious ageing or suffering. There are many who die prematurely, not long after birth, or in youth, without having time to grow old. Similarly, many healthy people also die suddenly from various conditions. Therefore, we need to do some research and investigate carefully both birth and death, the doors of our suffering.

If we were not born, the suffering of this life would not happen and there would also be no death. If we did not die, we would not experience suffering after death and there would be no taking up of future rebirths. If we could prevent birth, this would automatically put an end to death. If we trace the source of birth, it comes from death in a previous life. But death this time is different from our deaths in previous lifetimes; when we find the confidence of liberation into the dharmakaya at death, the machinery of samsara will be destroyed, so we will not need to experience suffering in the future.

To illustrate this point: a river flows along an established course, but we can use methods, such as building pipelines etc., to divert the water somewhere else. In the same way, from beginning-less time up to now, ignorance or unknowing has caused desire and attachment, under the influence of which we circle through samsara. Therefore, this time round, if we open the eyes of awareness and wisdom and look for an alternative to the path of samsara, a path beyond suffering, we can find it. That being the case, first, the great undecided issue facing all living beings is death. If we knew approximately when the great enemy death was coming, we could prepare to retaliate. In the same way, if we are able to gain knowledge of an enemy's troops and weapons, and make a map of the terrain, we can find a way for our forces to gain an advantage. It is exactly the same with death.

Death comes through an exhaustion of life, karma and merit. Because our life force and our strength depend on our body, by examining our body, our psychological state, omens in dreams etc., we are able to estimate approximately when death will come. In the Tibetan medical tradition, by using the palpable pulses and urine diagnosis, various illnesses of the physical elements and constitution can be recognised. In the same way, by examining the channel of the la vital basis, the seven wondrous channels, and so on, illness and death, and other undesirable negative circumstances, encountering an enemy, for example, or a parent's sickness, can be known and anticipated.

Also, some estimate can be made as to the likelihood of future events by making 'mo' divinations and 'mirror' divination, and by casting 'inquiry rolls', and so on. Mo divinations can be done with a mala, dice, crown or cords, and there is also the Mongolian mo, in which the right shoulder blade of a castrated ram is used; all these methods have many variations.

Generally, divinations are performed to determine all kind of things, including the extent of someone's support from the gods (luck), the fortune of the teachings, the political outlook, business and harvests, the outlook regarding enemies and opposition, fortune and luck regarding earnings etc., circumstances to foretell a problem free pregnancy and delivery, and so on. These sorts of methods of divination and fortune-telling are not to be taken as one hundred percent reliable. If you climbed to the top of a nine-story building and made a divination as to which direction you should choose to jump off, one direction is bound to come out as being good; this example shows why divinations cannot be relied on.

However, I cannot say divinations and predictions are completely false. If there is an issue which we as human beings cannot understand and, to help us, we invoke the truth of the Three Precious Jewels by praying to them with total conviction, without the slightest doubt; because the ultimate nature of phenomena is inconceivable and the law of cause and effect of the provisional nature of phenomena is infallible, then, due to the power of the truth of the Precious Jewels, they will never deceive us.

Additionally, the indications of a mo divination which an outstanding master performs in reliance on a personal yidam deity, should be considered suitable for us to rely on for guidance. In the same way, the methods of divination: 'churning the golden vase' and 'food wrapped indications' etc., are also the same as asking guidance from the Three Precious Jewels, and so can also be relied on. With the combination of an outstanding means of divination, an outstanding ritual and an outstanding master, there will be an undeceiving, reliable and clear outcome. But to do a divination carelessly, like a childish game, is nothing but cheating yourself and others.

There are two types of 'mirror' divination. In one, reflections are seen in the face of a mirror. The second is called 'mind mirror divination', where divinations arise in the mind of the diviner. In all of the revealed treasure texts, there are a plethora of divination texts which depend on many various kinds of yidam deity. To do these one first must receive the empowerment, transmission and instruction. Then one completes the designated number of mantra recitations required. One then specifically needs to practise the divination practice to accomplishment. Only then it can actually be put into practice. If one just 'has a go' at divination, the results will have no affinity with secret mantra.

Some diviners do not see their divinations themselves. There are those who, having recited the mantras and ritual, get someone who has a pure subtle constitution to look into the face of a mirror to investigate any good or bad signs. There are also those who use certain astrological and numerological calculations to indicate whether upcoming events will be favourable or unfavourable. Using calculation in accordance with the elemental constituents: the life force, physical body, power, wind horse and la, and also the year, the eight predictive trigrams, and astrological indications including date and time of birth, the planets and stars of a person are studied, and the resulting calculation brings a clear indication of whatever happiness and suffering are likely to arise, as well as an indication of lifespan, and so on.

Also, changes in a person's psychological state can indicate death; this is because everyone has their own personality. For the kinds of people with a surly disposition which causes them to be wild and savage, the beneficial medicine of the holy Dharma has no power to change their body or mind; but if suddenly they do have a change of character, this is a sign that death is imminent. If someone of good character with a gentle nature suddenly takes a dislike to others, becoming angry and hostile; this again is a sign of approaching death. Dreaming repeatedly of the sun setting and darkness falling, empty valleys and plains, empty towns, being alone and living miserably, leaving familiar surroundings and searching for a place to stay, wearing red clothing, travelling to the west, meeting and talking to dead people, riding a donkey backwards, and so on, are all signs that one is going to die within three years.

Basically, all these methods for predicting future happiness and suffering are in essence used because of our fear of dying; we want to know whether or not there is any danger of death coming unexpectedly. Of all the methods I have discussed, the method to determine time of death by studying the body is the most profound, because birth and death are both connected with this present body.

This body is characterised by the assemblage of the four elements, therefore in the Dzogchen teachings there is the 'form indication of lifespan', based on the appearance of the reflection of the elements. Here, any shortage or surplus in the body's reflection indicates the time of death. The shape of the reflection indicates whether, by means of 'cheating death', reversal can or cannot be made and, from the colour, the presence of negative entities can be examined.

Firstly, the method to indicate the time of death through shortage or surplus is as follows: When the sky is very clear, in a secluded place, naked or wearing thin clothing, face away from the sun, stand up holding a stick or a mala etc., and stare at the heart level of your shadow without moving your eyes, or letting your mind wander. Stare like this for a long time. When your vision becomes blurred, stare at the sky in front of you, at which point a vision of the shape of your whole body will arise. If all your limbs are intact, together with the object you are holding in your hand, if everything is totally complete, then it indicates there is no problem.

If the object you are holding in your hand is not visible, then this is known as 'being separated from the supporting deity', and death will come in seven years. If the right hand is not visible, death will come in five years and, if the left is not visible, death will come in three. If the right leg from the knee downwards is not visible, death will come in two years. If the whole right leg is not visible, death will come in eight months. If the left leg is not visible, death will come in one year. If the right side of the head is not visible, death will come in nine months. If the left side of the head is not visible, death will come in eight months. If nothing above the neck is visible, death will come in five months. If the neck is also not visible, death will come in three months. If the upper body is not visible, death will come in two months. If the lower body is not visible, death will come in one month. If there is only half of the body and the right side is not visible, death will come in nine days. If the left side is not visible, death will come in twenty-one days.

Looking at the shape indicates whether, by means of 'cheating death', reversal can or cannot be made. If a square, rectangle, circle or semi-circle appears, it is possible death can be averted by 'reversal'. If a triangle or a human corpse bound up into a ball appears, it is said there is no reversal.

The presence of negative entities can be determined from colours which may appear. When you look at the sky as before, if from a perception of whiteness the vision fades from the centre outwards, then one is possessed by naga or gyalpo negative spirits. If from a vision of blackness it fades from the right, one is held by demons or mamo. If a vision of redness fades from the left, then one is held by naga tsen or gongpo spirits. If a blue vision fades up from the legs, one is held by naga or tso-men spirits. If the appearance is insubstantially black, one is possessed by mamo or yama, if clear yellow, one is held by 'owners' of the locality, and if the appearance is mottled, one is possessed by a death demon.

With these colours, if a time comes when the vision of your body is missing some part or has changed shape, swiftly identify which negative spirit is harming you, and use protective measures to oppose this negativity, applying means to cure yourself. At a time when the vision of your body is not missing any part or has not changed shape, is to identify the innate negative spirit.

Examining the connection between sky and earth:
At midday face south, squat down and place your elbows on your knees, raise your hands to between the eyebrows and with both eyes look straight at your wrists. If they look very thin, there is no problem. If they appear separated, then it is a sign of death, and it is said that death will come in nineteen days.

The indication of the person riding a lion by Mt. Meru:
At sunrise, on the western side of a pool of water, stand beside a high wall and look at your reflection which arises in the water. If two transparent shadows are on the wall, there is no problem. If there is no upper shadow, it is said death will come in sixteen and a half days.

Indication of film on water:
At sunrise, urinate in a vessel which is not white and not black. Investigate the steam. If it is purplish there is no problem. If there is none, death will occur in fifteen days. If it is faintly black, death will occur in eleven days. If it is red with dots, it is said death will occur in nine days.

Indication of the spiritual practitioner:
When the sun begins to rise, empty your bowels. If there is steam, there is no problem. If there is no steam or it is red with circles, it is said that death will occur in nine days.

Investigation of the sun at the peak of the great mountain at sunset:
Looking sideways, apply pressure to your eye. If there is the 'lamp of the eye', there is no problem. Without this, death will come in three days. Pressing the ears, if there is a sound like drumming, there is no problem. If the sound is like a great wind, then it is taught that death will come in seven or eleven days; and if there is no sound death will come in five days.

SIGNS OF IMMINENT DEATH

It is taught the stages of the dying process are as follows:
Earth dissolves into water and the body becomes heavy. Water dissolves into fire and the mouth and nose drip. Fire dissolves into wind and heat dissipates. Wind dissolves into consciousness, the outer and inner breath cease and consciousness is lost for a moment. Consciousness dissolves into sky and one remains in non-conceptuality. Sky dissolves into luminosity and wisdom vision arises.

We cannot ignore the great enemy; death is right in front of us. Through fear, some people do not dare speak of death. Others consider speaking of death inauspicious, so they sit without mentioning a word of it. This is even more stupid. We cannot find a place to hide from death. By mentioning the word we do not die any sooner, and avoiding thinking about death does not avert its coming. Therefore, we need to understand the secret mysteries of the great unseen path in front of us. For this reason, as I mentioned previously, death is connected with our current body, so begin by examining this.

Despite taking advantage of advanced modern medical technology to examine and test our bodies and reassure us death will not arrive in the foreseeable future, we should remember if unexpected obstacles do arise, this can cut short our lives. We can be killed by others, involved in a fatal accident, develop a fatal disease, or other opposing conditions can occur which we never anticipated. Therefore, if you understand the various means which indicate imminent death, you can protect your body in this life and ward off untimely death. Such understanding is very beneficial. If death is inevitable, knowing and thinking about it in advance will give you time to prepare yourself for dying. I think the process of examining the signs of death is important knowledge, and we cannot do without this aid for attaining happiness in this life and the next.

TWENTY THREE

CHEATING DEATH WITH ADDITIONAL LIFE

If someone were to ask me, "Has a person ever come to the world who has faced up to the great enemy called death and been victorious?" then, without hesitation, I would be sure to answer that many such people have come. If asked, "How did they do this?" I would reply many have come who triumphed over the enemy, death, and so had no need to die. By means of meditating on the path and the method of arousing the compassionate mind of bodhichitta, all sorts of people have conquered death; there are those who attain the rainbow body, some dissipate into subtle atoms, and a few do not abandon their bodies and live as long as an aeon. Through mastering the holy teaching of the Great Perfection, the supreme yoga, pinnacle of vehicles, the result is the attainment of this kind of physical basis, and it occurs in the following way:

In the lineage of the Great Perfection, of the three sub-divisions, the first teacher of the Sign Lineage of the Vidyadharas was Garap Dorje, who received the six hundred and forty thousand tantras of Dzogchen from Vajrasattva himself and compiled the texts of the scriptural transmission. By actualising the wisdom of the union of no more learning, he disappeared in a mass of light by the Dentig River. At the time of his passing, his principle student Manjushrimitra prayed with great longing, and from a precious chest the size of a thumbnail Garap Dorje's testament, 'Three Phrases that Hit the Key Points', fell from the sky. By merely seeing this, his realisation became equal to the master's and he lived for one hundred and twenty nine years. Finally, in the Sosaling charnel ground, Manjushrimitra passed away into a mass of light.

At that time, Manjushrimitra's student Shirasingha called with great longing and down fell Manjushrimitra's testament, 'the Six Meditation Experiences', in a precious chest. Through practising these instructions, Shirasingha passed away into a mass of light in the Siljin charnel ground. At that time his principal student Jnanasutra cried with longing and Shirasingha's final testament, 'the Seven Nails', fell in a precious chest. Jnanasutra practiced this and in the great Basing charnel ground passed away into a mass of light. At that time his principal student Vimalamitra cried in despair and Jnanasutra's final testament called 'the Four

Methods of Resting' fell in a precious casket. By practising it exactly, he attained the deathless transition-less permanent holy body, and up to this day he himself works to benefit beings and can be seen by those with pure karma.

Also from Shirasingha, as Vajravarhi prophesied, Master Padmasambhava received the empowerments and texts of direct practice instructions of the Dzogpa Chenpo most secret and unexcelled Heart Essence of the Dakini, plus the supporting transmissions of the Seventeen Greatly Esoteric Essence Tantras, together with the ancillary practices. He entrusted these to Padmasambhava as keeper of the teachings who practised in the Sosaling charnel ground. Abandoning both birth and death, Padmasambhava attained the level of a deathless master of awareness of longevity and mastered great miraculous power. This is the Sign Lineage of the Vidyadharas.

Those who practise the direct instructions of the three sections of the Dzogchen Teachings belong to the oral lineage of people. Of this, masters Vairochana, Pang Mipham Gompo, Ngenlam Changchup Gyeltsen, Zadam Rinchen Yik, Khugyur Selwei Chog, and so on, attained the rainbow body or dissipated into subtle atoms. From the earliest times up to the present day in the Amdo, Central and Kham regions of Tibet there have been countless such masters. By means of the swift path of the secret mantra hundreds of thousands of gods, nagas and human masters of awareness have actually attained enlightenment.

Padmasambhava passed into the essence body of the great transference and attained the level of a master of awareness with power over life. The Dakini Yeshe Tsogyal did not abandon her physical basis and passed into the sky. There have been a great many others like them, including many former lineage holders: the twenty five, lord and subjects, and the accomplished masters of Yerba and Chuwori Monasteries etc. In later times, in the monasteries of Gatok, Palyul, Shechen and Dzogchen etc., hundreds and thousands of accomplished masters, and those who attain the rainbow body, continue to appear.

Additionally, there are inconceivable numbers of people in former and later times who have attained accomplishment by practising the respective paths of the Tibetan Eight Chariots of Spiritual Accomplishment and freed themselves from fear of death, the details of which can be found in their individual biographies.

In this way, if you receive the blessings of the lineage but do not master a degree of realisation of the direct instructions, realise the view, or develop supreme meditative absorption, simply by entering the path of these teachings, receiving empowerments, keeping pure vows, and with the proviso that at the time of death you combine this with positive prayers of aspiration, then you will be able to transform death into something joyful, and will be content to be sick and happy to die. By this means, making the great enemy, death, into a friend is one way to face up to him.

Alternatively, spending this life accumulating a plethora of positive and negative karma and then when death comes crying out in despair, does not evoke any pity in the Lord of Death; he will not release you. Power, status, force or weapons are impotent against the Lord of Death. There is no chance of using your influence to pay death off with a bribe and flee out of a back door via a secret escape route. Therefore, when that time comes, American dollars or gold and silver will be useless as protectors and friends, and of no value in making provision for the journey to the next life. We need the holy Dharma and nothing else. Therefore, if you had only one day left to live and you spent it practising the holy Dharma, then the karma would be sure to ripen and the virtuous merit would be ready to benefit you in the next life. Moreover, the closer to death you are, Dharma practice becomes that much more valuable. Tibetan people have a saying: "mani recitations at death are worth a horse."

At the time of death, the holy Dharma is more valuable than any wealth, and it has immediate application. The basis of practising the holy Dharma is this human body with the freedoms and advantages. This body is like a boat which takes us to liberation, therefore we need to make great effort to avoid it coming under the influence of any causes of untimely death.

The condition of untimely death occurs if one of three things is exhausted: life force, karma or merit. If the life force becomes exhausted, conduct longevity rituals. Generally these rituals are found in the Tantra and sadhana sections of the new and old traditions; more specifically, in the transmitted and hidden treasure teachings of the Nyingma tradition. Practice these rituals in reliance on whichever yidam deity is suitable, each with their varying ritual practices of various mandalas; practise the phases of approach and accomplishment until signs of accomplishment are gained. You also need to receive the supreme empowerment of immortal life, and its relevant practice, the number of times that corresponds to your age, or any different number of times. This empowerment should be received from a Lama complete with appropriate qualities and who possesses the power through having been empowered.

A short life is the fully-ripened result of accumulating the negative karma of killing in a previous life. To exhaust this karma, ransom the lives of many animals. To do this it is necessary to ransom living creatures marked out for slaughter, ransoming them from the blade of the knife with money or goods, and making sure the creatures will remain alive by restoring them to their individual habitats and placing them on suitable ground or in water etc. Ransoming lives is the same as doing any virtuous Mahayana practice, so use the three practices for the opening, main part and conclusion. First, begin with refuge prayers, then take the Bodhisattva vows and recite the seven line prayer. Recite the long life prayers, the dharani for longevity and also the particular recitation for saving the lives of creatures. Having completed this, recite the confession of downfalls Sutra, names of the Buddhas and Bodhisattvas, mantras to purify lower rebirths and others, so the creatures may hear them. Feed the creatures special holy substances such as Dharma medicine nectar which liberates through taste, and so on. Finish by sealing the practice with prayers of dedication and aspiration. Make an absolutely pure aspiration prayer for the long life especially of your glorious and supreme Lama, together with all masters of the teachings, wherever they are. Doing this will benefit the teachings and beings in general, as well as pacifying adverse conditions which threaten your own life, and so will once again be helpful in prolonging your life.

If your merit is exhausted you need to accumulate positive merit. Generally speaking, this is helpful not just for a long life, but for whichever Dharma or worldly activities you want to undertake. If you have not previously accumulated merit, you will not be able to accomplish very much. Just as it is taught: "Someone with merit accomplishes all they wish", so this can be understood to mean someone with no merit will achieve none of the things they wish for. We need to increase our merit both by making offerings and being generous. According to how much we have, that which we offer needs to be pure and excellent, without taint of avarice or attachment.

If you have no wealth, visualise offerings and offer them to a pure object. Generally, one's parents, the sick, teachers of Buddhism and 'last birth' Bodhisattvas who will be enlightened in their next life, are powerful objects to make offerings to. Therefore, by paying homage to those with marvellous enlightened qualities, a great accumulation of merit will quickly be amassed. Giving impartially to orphans without refuge, the aged without protectors, the crippled, the deaf and mute, and so on, will increase merit. If merit increases, life will be long and hopes and wishes will be fulfilled, and so it will be possible to avoid life-threatening conditions and adverse circumstances.

Conditions which bring about deterioration of lifespan include: receiving secret mantra Vajrayana empowerments but impairing the commitments, or meeting others with impaired commitments and closely befriending them, being in a state of mental agitation or always miserable, being depressed or always suffering from deep regret, experiencing great terror and fear, becoming extremely angry and letting anger consume your mind, and being struck by weapons and arrows aimed at you by those who practise sorcery or black magic; these and other things bring about deterioration of lifespan.

Signs of the deterioration of lifespan are a swift change of personality, behaving in an uncharacteristic way, getting angry with those around you for no reason, always moaning that things are no good, changes of expression and losing lustre, improper behaviour, loss of appetite, and so on; all these can occur. This kind of deterioration of life causes our 'life support' to split, or become crooked or broken. In addition, our la vital basis can deteriorate, become scattered, or flee etc. in which case we need to perform an authentic 'ransoming the la' ritual.

To do so, in a clean wooden bowl mould a 'la sheep' complete with sense organs from white butter. In its heart place unbroken grains of white rice, the number of which corresponds to the age in years of the person to be protected. Place the la sheep and wooden bowl together into an un-rusted copper bowl marked with the eight auspicious symbols and filled with water. A practitioner with pure vows follows the ritual and, while reciting mantras, the wooden bowl floating on water is gently spun with a longevity arrow until the la sheep comes to face the direction of the person to be protected. Signs of achievement are the number of white rice grains increasing beyond the number of years and the life-summoning longevity arrow becoming longer than before.

Similarly, there are all kinds of rituals for cheating death. There is 'clearing a treacherous path', which involves actually clearing away stones and obstacles from roads and paths, and also 'building a golden bridge'. To perform the latter, in a suitable section of river arrange stones with long life prayers, the dharani for longevity and other mantras carved onto them, from one side of the river to the other. This is taught to bring about the speedy reversal of negative conditions.

Another outstanding way to ransom death and accumulate merit is to amend any impaired and broken vows in relation to your root guru, and make feast offerings. The fire offering of the dakinis and the fire puja of the four activities: pacifying, increasing, magnetising and subjugation are also profound. By meditating on the truth of the generation and perfection phases and working the key points of the subtle channels, winds and drops, train in the direct instructions of dispelling hindrances. In addition, by means of the Dzogchen three unwavering states and the four methods of settling and so on, enter meditative equipoise in a state of stillness and insight. This unwavering state is the most supreme of all the ways to accumulate merit.

Also from our tradition of Dzogchen, the following is taught to ransom death by means of interdependence: On a piece of paper draw circles with four spokes and a rim. In the centres write the syllables RAM YAM KHAM LAM E. Together with this, write individual syllables on the spokes, and the vowels and consonants of the Sanskrit alphabet around the circumferences. Colour them with the colours of the five elements. Visualise the deities of the five elements, make offerings and consecrate them with the Essence of Interdependence. Make prayers of auspiciousness, put them in five upturned skull-cups and wrap them up with woollen threads of the five colours.

With tsampa dough mixed variously with earth, water, fire, wood and wind, and exposed to the breath of various species of animals: horse, cow, etc., make an effigy as high as the length of your forearm. Place the written syllables as follows: RAM at the eyes, YAM at the ears, KHAM at the nose, LAM at the tongue and E at the heart centre. Make other substitute effigies coloured red, yellow, white, black, green and multi-coloured, and arrange them in a row. Between them place various grains and precious jewels. Affix sky symbols, wooden objects, five colours of woollen threads, and feathers of the bird of bad omen as ornaments to both the effigy and the substitute effigies. Place your own urine, hair and nail clippings, snot and saliva among the effigies and cut up pieces of your clothing as sleeves and edging. Place in front of each effigy a pinch of food and small ball of dough. Arrange ritual offering torma according to each individual colour. Take sticks of birch and willow and score them with a mark for every year of your life and put them under the arms of the effigies. Then, consider the items you arrange are empty by reciting RAM YAM KHAM. While reciting OM AH HUM visualise the five desirable qualities.

Think of the elemental divinities, the eighty thousand classes of obstructive spirits, the Lord of Death, together with guests who are karmic creditors, and recite the seven lines to repeat: "Take this, take this!..." etc. Afterwards, place all the effigies together into a container and send them down the middle of a river. It is taught that by this ritual we can free ourselves for three years from untimely death resulting from conflict of the body's elements and harm from negative spirits.

Additionally, the following are taught as special methods to reverse the changes which herald approaching death (see chapter 22): If no implements, your mala etc., appear with your visible life form, make one hundred and eight feast offerings to your Lama. If the right arm is not present, with dough made from various grains make an effigy of a lion's head. Into the centre of its open mouth stick the number of feathers corresponding to your age in years, and take the effigy down a path leading to the north. If the left arm is not present, place tiger, pig and dog teeth in a weasel-skin bag with an effigy which has been rubbed on your skin, and cast the bag into a river.

If the right leg is not present, in the west at evening time light fires of juniper wood according to your years of age. If the left leg is not present, at the heart centre of an effigy the length of your forearm in height, place a birch stick marked with your age in years and take it to a temple at dawn.

If the right side of the head is not present, form a small box from nine kinds of earth from places in ruins and the seeds of black trees. Inside this, place your hair and nail clippings etc. and twelve pieces of willow. Write to the kings of the years: "take this tiger..." etc., including each of the names of the twelve years and, inserting thorns, take the box to a charnel ground at midnight. If the left side of the head is not present, make an effigy with twenty five kinds of grain and place in its heart human, horse and dog bone, rolling it in pieces of cloth. Conceal it in a hole at dusk on the eleventh day of the month, eighty paces to the south, and call your name three times with wailing cries.

If nothing is present above the neck, in a south-easterly direction burn triangles of thorns according to your years of age, and recite RAM the same number of times. If nothing is present above the waist, in the centre of a piece of paper four fingers in size write the years of your age, and the name of your animal year with the syllable LAM. In the east write YAM, south RAM, west E and north KHAM and hang the paper on your nose.

At midnight, naked and with your hair tied up, run in the four directions and, saying many meaningless phrases, such as: "...carry you to the mouth..." and "...leopard look at fox..." etc., take the paper to a charnel ground.

If there is no upper torso, burn the names of the twelve years in a fire. If no lower torso is present, go to a charnel ground and burn all kinds of bones. If the right side of the body is not present, make tsa tsa and recite the mantra of Ushnishavijaya according to your years of age. If the left side is not present, it is said you should recite the five dharanis according to your years of age. If the connection between sky and earth is cut, read the teachings and strive at virtue. If this does not help, perform the mandala rites according to your years of age. If the 'tree' is broken, seek medical attention and meditate on the subtle wind.

Urine Indications
If the scum of urine disappears, draw the forms of each of the twelve years in the colour of your element. At the time of the setting sun, with a tsa tsa, effigy and triangle of birch for each, send them to a north-easterly charnel ground. If the urine is vaguely black, mix iron or copper filings with various grains and scatter them in the four directions. If there are red drops in the urine, stab effigies according to your years of age with porcupine spines and, at an easterly crossroads, mix them with various bones and send them off there. If there is no steam on fresh urine, on a horse skull-cup write the syllables of the five elements and, when sunset is approaching, send it off to the west making many horse noises.

If your hearing fails, visualise YAM in the heart. When the eyes turn upward, someone else should perform a cleansing ritual from the crown of your head with a vase of water blessed by the recitation of mantras. If a single hair is raised at the back of the head above the neck, work hard at making feast offerings and torma; so it is taught.

If inner signs of death appear, hold the vase breath and do as many virtuous activities as possible. If secret signs of death appear, if you do three times more virtuous activities, ransom lives and work hard at making longevity tsa tsa and other longevity practices, then death will be averted.

The length of our life is determined by our previous karmic activities and immediate circumstances. The basis of our life, the subtle essence of heat and breath resembling a hair from a horse's tail, resides in the life channel of the body. When conditions opposing our life occur, this life basis can become split, crooked, broken or weakened. By means of longevity practices, 'extracting the essence' practices, and medicinal compounds etc. the subtle essence and wind will flourish, and this will ultimately increase lifespan. What we call merit is positive karma and acts as the cause for our lifespan to increase. It is taught that if all three: life, karma and merit, are exhausted together there is no possibility of restoration.

Twenty Four

The Great Path of Impermanence and Death

Death comes at the moment when having exhaled, releasing our last breath, we are unable to breathe in again; or when the circulation of the blood ceases and the blood flow through the heart stops, in the same way as a machine stops working when its power supply is cut off. Everyone knows this.

As all living beings go down the path towards death, the generations of people gradually change. This is something we can observe happening all the time. Seeing this as an everyday phenomenon, it does not strike us as being of any great importance. However, if we analyse it carefully in terms of our own mortality, we realise if a machine develops a problem we can change its components and switch it back on again, but if the human body develops a disease of the vital organs then, although surgical treatment may be successful, healthy function may not be restored completely.

If a disease has a karmic cause then, even if all the global medical experts were consulted, they would have no means of bringing about a cure. Not only that, but there is no one on this earth whose lifespan is exhausted but who has not yet died. Therefore, if suddenly my heart stops working, all my work in this life will come to a halt. My plans for the future and my future aims and wishes will all be destroyed together. If that happens, does everything for which I worked so hard throughout my entire life completely go to waste? Even more uncertain is the overwhelming unavoidable experience approaching us all, the terrifying manifestation of appearances which occurs in the period which separates death and the next life.

Of all the work we do in this life, careful investigation of what will happen after we die should be considered of primary importance. In the same way, just as when we visit the tailor to order a new suit and, as the first step our measurements are taken, it also makes sense that the length of life and the amount and achievability of activities in that lifespan are tailored to fit with each other. Moreover, in the same way that today we make preparations for tomorrow, if we neglect to prepare now for our journey down the great future path of death, it would be an oversight of terrible importance. So, whatever we undertake, it is crucial to prepare in advance, and therefore, we are now going to do some research about death.

In general, everything that is born naturally dies, so the first herald of death is birth. Reckoning from the evening of the baby's birthday, first he becomes one day old; death is already approaching. This is a distant indicator of death. In particular, the lifespan in our human world is uncertain, so whether we are growing up, in our prime, or growing old, these are all signs of death to come. Inevitably at the end, the imminent signs of death will occur, and in stages the elements will be subsumed so the life sense faculties cease. This is death, which terrifies us all. The great enemy called death, whose dreaded name no one dares to utter, has descended upon us.

This body is formed from union of the five elements. If there comes a time when one element becomes the enemy of another, sickness occurs. When one element dissolves into another, death occurs. During the process of dying, in the gross dissolution phase, earth dissolves into water, the body becomes heavy and we are unable to sit up. Form dissolves into sound and our vision of forms becomes less clear than before. Water dissolves into fire, we dribble and mucus drips from the nostrils. Sound dissolves into smell and our hearing becomes confused; we cannot distinguish sounds as we did before. Fire dissolves into wind and body heat reduces. Smell dissolves into taste and the nose cannot detect any odour. Wind dissolves into consciousness and the eyeballs turn inwards, the outer breath becomes laboured, rapid and panting. The legs and arms flail. Taste dissolves into touch and the tongue cannot detect any taste. At that time the rising wind escapes and the body cannot be supported; it is heavy, the limbs unable to move. Speaking becomes very difficult. The wind which generates lustre of complexion escapes and black grime forms on the body and around the mouth and nose. The mouth becomes dry. The eyes become faded. The noxious stench of death is all-pervading. The refining wind escapes and we have no appetite for food or drink. All physical strength is lost.

The fire-equalising wind escapes and body heat is gradually drawn in from the feet to the centre. It is said those with training in the teachings of the Great Perfection become liberated at this point, and the teachings state this is also the profound time to perform the transference practice. After this, the karmic wind of the great kalpa escapes and our awareness becomes confused and disordered. Blood in the small vessels converges into the main artery. At this time a heavy darkness encroaches on our outer vision, as happens when night falls. Awareness gathers at the centre of the heart and we lose consciousness. At that time a drop of blood from the main artery is propelled into the centre of the heart and the eyes become white. When the second drop is propelled the head slumps, one breath enters and then is expelled with an 'hhhhha', shooting out as far as an arrow's length. The third drop is propelled and with a 'yik' sound the breath is expelled out the distance of about an arm's length. Then the outer breath ceases with an 'ugh'.

The body loses the sense of touch. Wind dissolves into awareness and the inner breath ceases, the union of the gross channels, drops and wind breaks up and the subtle stages of appearance, increase and near attainment proceed. The life-holding bodhichitta drop which was inherited from our father descends and awareness dissolves into appearance. A perception of whiteness arises, like the light of the moon rising in an autumn sky, and the thirty three thoughts which come from aggression cease. The rakta inherited from our mother moves upwards, appearance dissolves into increase, a perception of redness arises, and the forty thoughts which come from attachment cease. The two seminal drops meet at the heart centre and increase dissolves into near-attainment. Like the descending of darkness in the autumn sky, a perception of blackness arises and the seven thoughts which come from ignorance cease. Consciousness is lost in the underlying basis of all for the time it takes someone to eat a meal, but those whose calm abiding is stable or whose channels are clear will remain in this state for a longer time. Those whose negative actions are great or whose channels are blocked only remain for the time it takes to click the fingers. For most there will be no awareness or thoughts for four and a half days. This is called wind dissolving into the wisdom central channel and is the period when mind and wisdom separate.

Additionally, during life the channels of the lungs, which are the size of wheat-straws, are filled with wind and provide the basis for all the breath increasing. They reside in connection with the heart centre. The wind is likened to a blind horse with four strong legs and the manifestation of awareness is likened to a fully-sighted cripple, the two are like travellers, journeying together. The manifestation of awareness and wind are connected at the heart centre, and their combination is designated as mind or thought. At death the continuum of wind coming and going is cut, so the fleet blind horse disappears, at which time the manifestation of awareness, which is likened to a fully-sighted cripple, dissolves into the mother-like awareness and so basic luminosity arises, or mind and wisdom separate; thus it is described. The physical aggregates, the basis of self-grasping, are lost, and so the conditions break apart; therefore, as crystal light is subsumed into crystal itself, the dynamic energy of wisdom - discursive thoughts - dissolves into wisdom itself. This is the moment when the luminosity of the actual nature of awareness's own manifestations becomes apparent.

Once again, recovering from the faint which resulted from the separation of the eight life-holding winds, we regain some consciousness, and now in the intermediate state of the dharmata, primordial manifestations arise of that which is termed the 'consciousness dissolved into sky'. Here luminous unceasing visions of primordial purity arise from the ground of being in the manner of appearances, like light rays radiating from the sun, and this is perceived as being like a cloudless autumnal sky. Unelaborated luminosity arises resplendently and this is called the luminosity of the first bardo. Again, the length of time this lasts is indeterminate but depends on whether or not one has any training in concentration practice.

If liberation does not occur at this time, the extremely subtle part of wind-consciousness arises in reverse order. From the point of view of our sense faculties, when the perception of increase dissolves into sky-like luminosity, there is no perception of substantiality, but until the time when we regain belief in substantiality, changes in perception occur; and in the experience of pure dharmata, everything perceived arises as visions of five-coloured lights, brilliant and lustrous, like looking at sunbeams shining through gauze. In the light, the natural sound of the dharmata resounds as the great roar of a thousand dragons, or thunderclaps exploding simultaneously. After that, luminescence dissolves into union, at which time a grain-heap mandala of the five Buddha Families, their consorts and the assembly of peaceful and wrathful deities arises in immeasurable brilliance and lustre.

When residing in the five days of concentration meditation, the corresponding five wisdoms gradually arise. The first day, the entire sky dawns as sky-blue coloured light and the Bhagavan Vairochana mother and father appears. A blue light appears, shining from Vairochana's heart centre, pure, resplendent and brilliant, which connects to our heart centre. If we recognise this blue light to be the wisdom of the Dharmadhatu, we will be liberated. Alongside this, a dim white light of the gods comes forth. At that time, frightened by the natural blue light of the wisdom of the Dharmadhatu, if the concept of attraction towards the dim white light of the gods grows, we will wander in the god realms and continue to circle among the six classes of being.

The second day, the white light of the utter purity of the water element arises. White light shining from the heart centre of Buddha Akshobhya, the natural light of mirror-like wisdom, arises with a dim smoky light of the hell realms. The third day, the yellow light of the utter purity of the earth element arises. Yellow light shining from the heart centre of Buddha Ratnasambhava, the natural light of wisdom of equality, arises with a dim blue light of the human realm. The fourth day, the red light of the utter purity of the fire element arises. Red light shining from the heart centre of Buddha Amitabha, the natural light of discriminating wisdom, arises with a dim yellow light of the hungry ghost realm. The fifth day, the green light of the utter purity of the air element arises. Green light shining from the heart centre of Buddha Amoghasiddhi, the natural light of all-accomplishing wisdom, arises with a dim red light of the demigod realm.

The periods of these days are called 'days of concentration meditation'. To explain the five 'days': if when we were alive we practised concentration meditation, one 'day' is the length of time we are able to remain in non-distraction without a thought arising, so each brief period of concentration meditation counts as one day. If we have previously trained in this, now is the crucial time to put it into practice. Accordingly, it is taught for an ordinary person with no meditation training, one day is merely the time it takes for a person to open and close their hand, or a shooting star to speed across the night sky.

Following that, at the time when union dissolves into wisdom, extending from our heart centre into the sky above is the expression of awareness manifest as the appearances associated with the four wisdoms: blue, white, yellow and red light. These are ornamented by five clear drops matching each individual colour, within each of which are five tiny drops. Above this also shine globes of light like parasols of peacock feathers.

After that, when wisdom dissolves into spontaneous presence, the wisdom appearances dissolve into the circular lights above. At this moment, from the state of the appearances of primordial purity, clear as a cloudless sky, all directions, above and below appear instantaneously as the pure realm of the peaceful and wrathful deities and the entire impure appearances of the six kinds of being. Those who do not recognise this as their own true nature, or have doubts will, as before, be unable to attain liberation from samsara. Together with the great wind of life, the consciousness comes forth from whichever of the nine doors of the body is most fitting.

Then the second intermediate state, the intermediate state of becoming, arises like appearances in dreams. Here there are no corporal senses but, just as someone in a dream has the sense faculties of touch, sight, hearing, etc., the apparent mental body of the intermediate state has complete sense faculties. In this state beings also possess minor miraculous powers and can move anywhere without hindrance, except into the womb of their future mother. However, they have no power to stay in one place for even a moment and are overwhelmed by fear. However long they remain in the intermediate state, for the first half of their time their form appears in accordance with their habitual tendency. In the latter half, they appear in the form into which they will be reborn. During this time they cannot be seen by anyone except for others in the intermediate state, or those who possess pure sight. Possessing a little clairvoyance, the minds of beings in the intermediate state are seven times clearer than they used to be. They drift around like wool blown by the wind and arrive at any destination in a mere moment.

Beings in the intermediate state of becoming see their home and family as if in a dream and continue to do things they used to do due to habitual tendency but, because they have no basis of a physical body, they have no control over themselves. They see their family but the family cannot see them. They feel unhappy and lonely, angry, hateful and anxious. The four elements are like an enemy; wind buffets them, earth crushes them, water carries them away, fire burns them and, with other frightening appearances of great suffering, they come to realise they have become separated from their physical body. The tremendous suffering of realising they are dead causes them to faint, and they experience further, lesser deaths. If they see others happy and laughing, they think: "They're enjoying themselves while here I am, in this wretched state!" and become terribly angry.

These beings feel desire and attachment to the family's wealth and possessions. If they see others using what was once their own money or possessions, they begrudge them the wealth they still covet and unbearable anger grows. Apart from that, based on the conditions of the multitude of things they see and hear, their accumulation of afflictive emotions grows and their mind stream becomes extremely chaotic. Because in this intermediate state lifespan is uncertain, this can last for seven days or so, but it is absolutely unpredictable. Every seventh day, however they died, they re-experience dying in the same way each time.

Exhausted from not having a gross physical basis, they think: "Wouldn't it be nice just to get any kind of body."

Sometimes a terrifying, unbearable pitch blackness welcomes them forward. Large numbers of karmic bloodthirsty, carnivorous demons wielding weapons and shouting, "Kill her!" and "Strike him!" chase after the bardo being, and they will chase after you too.

Terrifying blizzards and wild animals appear and pursue you. Mountains collapse, oceans swell, fires blaze and hurricanes billow violently. At these times you shelter briefly in grass huts, stupas, or temples etc., but only for a moment, because awareness has separated from the body. Merely by thinking of a place you find yourself there. You consume the scent of food which is dedicated to the dead and burnt. Your innate deity and your injurious demon accompany you in the same way as a living body is accompanied by its shadow.

Additionally, if you see karmic visions of the three poisons: unbearable redness, greenness and blackness, that is a sign you will fall down to the three lower realms. Or if you are to be reborn in either the god realm or the human realm, the signs are your body will be adorned with white light shining out as far as your arms can reach, or covering many miles, or that you hold your head erect. If you are to be reborn in the demigod or animal realms, you see visions of yellow light, you hold your head to the side and you see tempests of rain and snow like blood and digestive refuse. For the hell and hungry ghost realms your visions are black and you see yourself shuffling with your head bowed down. Appearances arise like dark spots, black cotton wool, or smoke and so on.

Other signs of entering individual places of rebirth are as follows: temples and pleasure parks indicates rebirth in the god realms. Wheels of light indicates rebirth as a demigod. Foggy sky indicates a mere human rebirth. Among many people indicates a precious human rebirth. Living in a hole in the earth indicates an animal rebirth. Barren places and blocked tunnels indicates rebirth as a hungry ghost. Darkness and torrential dark rain indicate rebirth in the hell realms. Thick darkness and being driven by blizzards indicate rebirth in the cold hells. These and many other signs can appear.

Wherever you are going to be born will seem enticing, your longing for it will increase and you will yearn to go there to have a look. Alternatively, driven by terrifying appearances, you see a place as a refuge in which to hide. By remaining there for even a brief moment you take rebirth. You become encased in the seed of your future parents, and in your mother's womb experience a little pleasure before losing consciousness for a moment. Recovering, you experience all kinds of suffering, followed by the suffering of birth. Now, you are in a different body from before. You may have taken rebirth as a dog, but there is no turning back now.

In this rough outline I have written about the experiences, from the intermediate state of dying to the intermediate state of dharmata, and the intermediate state of becoming. When experiencing these states, so we have no fear of the hallucinations and avoid taking another rebirth, there are profound instructions on how we can achieve liberation into the pure realms of the dharmakaya, sambhogakaya and nirmanakaya, from the instructional teachings of the main practices of the Great Perfection. These divide the intermediate states into four or six: the bardo of the place of birth, of dream, of meditation, of the moment of death, of dharmata and of becoming.

There are instructions for the intermediate birthplace state, which are like a swallow entering its nest without hesitation. There are instructions for the intermediate dream state which are like raising a lighted lamp in a dark house. There are instructions for the intermediate concentration meditation state which are like an orphaned child reunited with her mother. There are instructions for the intermediate state of dying which are like a king granting the right to passage. There are instructions for the intermediate state of the dharmata which are like a child going to his mother's lap. There are instructions for intermediate state of becoming which are like fixing guttering to a section of aqueduct with a broken support, and so on, too many to be mentioned.

Someone with modest faculties who enters the door of the Dzogchen teachings, firstly may not be able to achieve liberation because of lack of training in the instructions for the intermediate state of dying, which are like a beautiful girl looking into a mirror. Those with modest faculties may have no confidence in the instructions of the consciousness riding the horse of the subtle wind, and so be unable to transfer either by entry into another body or the transference of consciousness. With the cessation of the outer wind when mind and wisdom separate, if such people gain no recognition by means of the direct instructions of emptying out the intermediate state then, in the intermediate state of the dharmata, when the appearances of the ground which arise from the ground are not transformed by the technique like a child going to his mother's lap, then those with modest faculties will not be liberated in the great inner basic space of primordial purity. Not recognising the sounds, light rays, subtle drops, forms and reflections of the peaceful and wrathful deities as their own manifestation they will become scared and afraid, so these appearances pass in a moment, and they will wander in the intermediate state of becoming. At this time, because they have little aptitude in training for their bodies to emerge in the sambhogakaya by means of the instructions like fixing guttering to a section of aqueduct with a broken support, those with modest faculties are unable to become enlightened.

For these people, though their Dharma lineage is that of the Great Perfection, they themselves have not attained Great Perfection. However, it is taught if this kind of person recognises the death process so, when death does come, establishes their devotion to the guru as a firm support and upon this, recalling the instructions the guru has taught, they think longingly: "Now I am going to the naturally emanated pure realm", then it is taught just by doing this, by the truth of the inconceivable dharmata and the blessings of the Lama, they will be miraculously reborn inside a lotus in whichever pure realm they aspire to reach.

The qualities of the natural nirmanakaya pure realms, known as the 'five great sighs of relief of complete liberation', are as follows:
To the east is the pure realm called Manifest Joy where nirmanakaya Buddha Vajrasattva resides in an immeasurable mansion wrought from precious crystal, ornamented with pediments, windows and staircases of precious jewels, and so on. The entire ground is made of precious crystals. It is vast and wide, and so incredibly beautiful and attractive that beings never tire of gazing at its glory. Outside the mansion there is a river, the waters of which possess the eight qualities of purity, and if the sick drink these waters they are cured of all their ills. On the outskirts of the river there are eight great lakes. On the lakes dwell flocks of birds of multitudinous colours, each singing their own beautiful melodies. Beyond the lakes are walls built from seven precious materials.

In the centre, upon a Dharma throne made from the seven precious materials sits Vajrasattva. In the evening he teaches the causal Dharma teachings. At midnight he teaches the Dharma of the outer secret mantra. At dawn he teaches the Dharma of the inner secret mantra. At midday he teaches the unexcelled Dharma of resultant Dzogpa Chenpo. All the Bodhisattvas living in this pure realm will become enlightened after one lifetime, without exception. The riches and wealth here are comparable with the heaven of the thirty-three gods and all who dwell here live for five hundred and fifty years. In this pure realm, merely thinking of food or refreshment assuages hunger and thirst. Here there is no suffering of birth, old age, sickness or death, so it is supremely joyful. Merely thinking of wished-for objects of enjoyment causes them to appear, so in this way flowers and myriad other offerings are made to the nirmanakaya.

Similarly, to the south is the Glorious Pure Realm. In the westerly direction is the Stacked Lotus Pure Realm, to the north is the Accomplishing the Highest Action Pure Realm, and in the central direction is the Densely Arrayed Pure Realm. Each realm is individually arrayed with limitless marvellous qualities. Each retinue of Bodhisattvas listen to the Dharma of their teacher and will become completely enlightened Buddhas in one lifetime, without exception. Those who take birth in this kind of pure realm enter the door of this Dharma teaching of the Great Perfection, but they are the kind of person who is of modest faculties, or not very hard working in this life, so this is the way for them to become liberated.

Depending on the superior, middling or modest faculties of individuals, each of them has their own conceptual understanding of death and their own methods of dealing with it. For practitioners of Dzogchen, death is the time to attain enlightenment, so they are extra happy about it. For those who have the Dharma, death is like a swan flying from one lotus lake to another, so they are not afraid. For others with negative deeds, the nearer death approaches the more afraid they become. There is nothing to add to their lifespan, so they are like a pool lacking any fresh source of water to re-fill it, or an emptied granary; they are of the nature of extinction. Like an animal led to the slaughter, each step they take leads them closer to death.

Our human life is also like this. Death dwells beside us, everyone with a mind needs to grasp this fact. We must prepare ourselves now, with fearless confidence, making provision for that time while we have the freedom and leisure to do so. Now is the only time we have; later will be too late. All of us, bound for death, must consider this fact over and over again and do so unflinchingly. Otherwise, when death comes you will beat your chest when you can no longer breathe and, lying on your death bed, you will weep. Your friends and family will gather round sobbing and moaning; but at that time regrets are useless.

When the last hour comes, when neither restorative medicine nor a skilful doctor can add even one more minute to your lifespan, the negative and miserable activities on which you wasted your life, and which you still have not completed, will be not the slightest help. Therefore, forget your pointless, insignificant labours, merely preparing for retirement which there is no knowing whether you will live long enough to enjoy, and give priority to consideration of the only certain key event your future definitely holds. In that way you are certain to be successful in attaining the fearless confidence bestowed by the instruction that recognises the nature of illusion.

TWENTY FIVE

PURGING THE CHRONIC DISEASE OF ILLUSORY DUALISM

The true nature of the body, speech and mind of all sentient beings is neither presently nor forever inherently impure. However, with our illusory adventitious perceptions, we see 'me' and 'you' as separate, and it is these dualistic concepts, labelling things 'mine' and 'yours' which give rise to happiness and suffering, and in addition 'beautiful' and 'ugly', 'clean' and 'dirty', 'true' and 'untrue' and so on, as limitless illusory dualistic appearances come forth. We are confused in this way for life after life, from time without beginning to time without end. We experience the individual physical manifestations of each of the six kinds of beings, uttering each of their particular vocal sounds, and having all the different thoughts of each various mind; each rebirth brings us a plethora of discrete suffering.

We continue on this round of suffering which has no end, circling through each realm, which is why it is termed in Sanskrit 'samsara' or 'cyclic existence'. The pointless suffering of this cyclic existence is vast, with no limits of depth or breadth; therefore the simile of an ocean is used, and so it is called the 'oceanic suffering of samsara'. Liberation from this suffering is called the 'transcendence of sorrow', or 'nirvana' in Sanskrit. What we distinguish as 'good' and 'bad' is the product of the dualism of confused mind. Accordingly, the chronic disease of dualistic confusion is diagnosed in the Sutric Paramita spiritual approach, and the correct view is resolved by scriptural authority and logical reasoning; in this way the sublime wisdom which realises the nonexistence of identity of both self and phenomena eliminates self grasping from the root. Subsequently, by means of remedial vajra-like samadhi, the extremely subtle latent karmic obscurations of knowledge are quelled.

The sublime esoteric Great Perfection is a swift path with many methods and without difficulty. Building upon the foundation of the paths of the Middle Way and Mahamudra teachings, the Great Perfection is shown to be a profound and extraordinary resultant vehicle. In the essence of the single sphere of the basic space of phenomena there is no differentiation of good and bad, and so this is the path we need to practise. As long as the disease of dualistic confusion is present in a person's mind stream the root of suffering has not been cut, so there will be no end to the continuum of suffering experienced. If the confusion of grasping at duality is cut from within, then at that time suffering will cease.

The way to vanquish the demon of confusion requires making a distinction between confusion and non-confusion. For example, if someone is afflicted by a mental disorder, the first step in treatment is to diagnose the condition correctly, after which it is possible to treat its cause. If we recognise a latent mental disorder, then the nature of the disorder can be examined, and the difference between mental health and the disordered state will become apparent.

Similarly, if we desire to put a stop to this miserable confusion, first we need to recognise our delusion and take it to the point where we cannot become any more deluded. Once a delusion has reached its height and cannot become any more confused, it becomes tired and exhausted, so exposing the true nature of the delusion. Having become exhausted, delusion fades away on the spot. In this way, by disappearing, delusion has put an end to delusion. Left behind in the absence of delusion is nothing but non-delusion. The name of this instruction taught in the Dzogchen texts is 'Rushen' or 'making the distinction', and the aim is to cut the root basis of being reborn in samsara in the future. In actuality, we are separating dualistic karmic latency into purity and refuse within the expanse of the single dharmakaya sphere.

Now we have a rough understanding of the meaning of the Dzogchen view; but, just as calling a drawing of a circle 'the moon' cannot be compared to the experience of seeing the actual moon, we have not developed any of the three: comprehension, experience or realisation. However, when we embark in training on the higher path of the main Dzogchen practice, we will master the meaning of what has been indicated by examples. It is said: "if an auspicious connection is made with the body, realisation will arise in the mind." Similarly, in reliance on this kind of preliminary teaching, the root of delusion will naturally be released. If we can arrive at our own fundamental state, then certainty and conviction is determined from within our mind.

Alternatively, reading tens of thousands of scriptures and studying closely with hundreds of geshes and teachers does not bring progress, but makes delusions more pervasive. However, until a new seedling has grown strong, we need to be that much more wary of the enemies of frost and hail. In this same way, however much we utter words like emptiness, non-duality, evenness, equal taste, and so on, in truth if we prick our hand on a thorn it hurts, and if we eat candy it tastes sweet etc.; our perceptions cannot be reversed. As long as we are not free from the bonds of this illusory body of delusion there is no way of blocking these sensations of pleasure or pain.

Similarly, there are also the 'illusory' visions of hindrance and obstacles. Therefore, until we are free of the fixation that conventional things have true existence, we must certainly direct our efforts on the basis of conventional dependent origination: the undeceiving cause and result of virtuous and negative actions, and also by gathering accumulations and purifying obscurations.

Based on this, so we are not affected by hindrances and obstacles, first we need to meditate on protection circles and so on, and to embark upon the extraordinary view and meditation of the Mahayana; going for refuge and arousing bodhichitta must be done as a preliminary to practice.

Together, the impure environment and inhabitants of the three realms are called samsara. The Buddha bodies and pure realms are nirvana. Of these two divisions, samsara and nirvana, all illusory vision of the impure three realms of samsara is the karmic latency of dualistic perception subsumed within the pure expanse of great nirvana in which we grasp at or separate purity from refuse. To be free from this, in order to train in seeing naturally arising wisdom in all its nakedness, first we realise the implicit faults of the things to be abandoned. If this is done, attachment will automatically be disengaged. This forms a path which accords with karmic perceptions of samsara.

To become free of grasping, like cutting iron with iron, the method and the instructions to engage in dispelling discursive thought with discursive thought are taught as follows:

In a secluded place, visualise your body as a flaming vajra and, upon the crown of your head, visualise your Lama as in guru yoga practice, or wear the armour of the eight syllables. Visualise your Lama's form as dark blue with a wrathful countenance and his hair tied up upon his crown. He is baring his teeth and rolling his tongue. Upon his crown is a yellow LAM syllable, on his forehead a blue E syllable, at the chin a yellow SER syllable, at the throat a smoky KHAM syllable, at the two breasts white HA syllables, at the heart a light blue HUM syllable and a black P'ET syllable, at the navel a red RAM syllable, and on the soles of both feet green YANG syllables.

From your Lama's heart centre a blue HUM syllable is emanated and this enters the student's heart; meditate on becoming a HUM syllable. Consider all actions of body, speech and mind are the display of your Lama's body, speech and mind. Please the local deities of the place by giving them ritual torma offerings. Following this, first complete the physical activities:

Strip off entirely except for an 'ong ruk' loincloth, get up and run around, jump and leap about, hunch over and stretch out, roll around, dance about, etc. Whatever physical movements come to mind, do them freely without hesitation. Then change this into prostrations and circumambulations, adopt the postures of the deities, form mudras and perform dances of the deities, etc. At night, rest by sleeping in a comfortable bed. Signs of making the distinction will come; these include having no attachment for the body, no longer thinking you are hot or cold, hungry or thirsty, and feeling you are blazing with blissful heat and soaring in the sky, etc. This practice will pacify obstructions of the body, purify negativities and obscurations, bring liberation into the nirmanakaya, and ultimately transform you inseparably into the vajra body of all Buddhas.

Next with your speech, copy all the different sounds uttered by the six kinds of beings: deities, naga, yaksha, humans, or jer and vicious demons. Sing melodious songs, recite the consonant letters, and make the forceful sounds of HUM! P'ET! and RE LE! Utter cries of sorrow and wails of suffering, joyous laughter and miserable lamentations. Alternatively, make the noises of animals, horses, cows, goats and sheep etc., and the sounds which accompany human birth, old age, sickness and death. Make whatever sounds you can think of. Sometimes shout P'ET! forcefully many times, and finish up with the sounds of Dharma recitation. At night go to bed in complete silence.

The signs of making the distinction of speech are the welling forth of Dharma recitations which were not known previously, speaking in Sanskrit, not wanting to say anything, and experiencing blissfulness. This practice will pacify obstacles of speech, purify negativities and obscurations, bring liberation into the sambhogakaya and ultimately transform you inseparably into the essence of vajra speech of all Buddhas.

After that, contemplate the happiness and suffering of the six kinds of sentient beings, those with Dharma and without, samsara and nirvana, and so on, as much as you can bring to mind. Propel your mind to the centre of the sky, the bottom of the ocean, into mountains and rocks and so on, places you have and have not been, the habitats of the six kinds of beings, pure realms and pleasure gardens. Think about Buddhas, Bodhisattvas, temples and stupas, enemies, friends and those in between. Think about whatever comes to mind. Proliferate attachment and aversion, and train in leaving no trace.

To finish, bring to mind the meaning of Dharma teachings, and in this state reside in the absolutely pure view, meditation, action and fruition, so confused mental thoughts cease and concentration meditation of non-conceptual bliss-clarity comes forth and develops of its own accord. The timeless freedom of sky-like realisation arises as a natural condition. It is taught this practice will pacify obstacles of mind, purify negativities, bring liberation into the dharmakaya and ultimately enlighten you inseparably into the essence of vajra mind of all Buddhas.

In this way, by training the three doors in the nine practices described above, the outer distinction is made, and there is no attachment or aversion, nor suppression or promotion of physical heat or cold, etc. Wisdom arises from meditation and exceptional words and meaning arise in speech. You need to meditate until ceaseless clarity and emptiness arise in the mind, and there is experience of bliss. If these things happen, the fundamental point has been reached and you will be able to gain the benefits mentioned. Because of this, it is crucial all who desire to expose the faults of samsaric suffering should first strive to train in this kind of path.

TWENTY SIX

THE MACHINE OF NO THOUGHT WIND

The mind of sentient beings abides in the body. This body also comes into being by the mind's confused grasping and by the power of clinging. In this experience of life these two: mind and body, exist in manner of support and supported, but initially it is from the confused aspect of mind that the body comes into being. The mind, having come under the influence of unaware confusion, acts as the cause. The conditions are the seeds of our parents and the consciousness from the intermediate state coming together; after this, the six elements of earth, water, fire, wind, sky and wisdom assemble to form the body. The subtle channels gradually form and the foetus passes through the stages of development: 'creamy', 'quivering', 'oval', and so on. When the months of growth and development are complete, karmic winds turn the baby upside down and it is born.

The mind which depends on this body is combined with subtle wind. Appearances of the mind are left outside. Awareness dwells within. Between these is the mount of karmic winds which become like a horse to the mind which rides them, and in a state of the grasped and the grasping they roam about.

The profound swift path of the secret mantra Great Perfection relies on methods to bind and act upon the karmic winds which move back and forth, and in this way address the delusions of successive samsaric lifetimes without beginning or end. Unlike the methods of the lesser spiritual approaches, the swift path does not depend on spending a long time using concentrated logic to reason through the mesh of confused thoughts from the outside, but uses direct instructions of a forceful method to identify innate genuine wisdom from within.

Generally speaking, there are five winds within the channels: life-sustaining, ascending, downwards-voiding, fire-equalising and pervading wind which, together with subsidiary winds, perform their own individual functions. The strength of life is generated by the winds connecting through all the channels. In the twelve periods of time in one day, the breath is exhaled through the nose and mouth twenty one thousand six hundred times. There are two types of wind: karmic wind and wisdom wind. Using the power of meditation, the yogi purifies all karmic wind, transforming it into wisdom wind to attain enlightenment.

Wind and awareness associate together, one acting as the cause, the other as the condition. Wind then moves consciousness, placing it on the objects of the five sense doors and so on, and so we wander in samsara. Wind is an element and consciousness is clarity and awareness. These two are likened to a disabled person, unable to walk, riding around on a blind horse. By cutting the continuum of karmic wind and retaining wisdom wind, the illusory perceptions of samsara can be turned aside. Therefore it is extremely important to practise in training the winds. For this reason, here I am going to teach from Dzogchen Heart Essence of the Great Expanse the Yantra of applying the wind activities, the three no thoughts. First is fixing the mind on the no thought of bliss and emptiness:

In a secluded place, sit in the seven point posture of concentration meditation. Visualise your body as hollow and clear like an inflated balloon, in the centre of which is the central channel which has four particular attributes: it is straight like a slender trunk of a plantain tree, as thin as a lotus petal, blue like a cloudless sky and bright like a sesame oil lamp. At the crown, the upper end of the channel, visualise a white HUM syllable, and at the lower end below the navel a red AH syllable. With the four applications press down the upper wind and draw up the lower wind, so the AH syllable at the navel burns with fire. Gradually the HUM syllable at the upper end of the central channel melts and from it drops of nectar flow down. The nectar fills all the four chakras, together with the fine subsidiary channels. Think the wisdom of bliss and emptiness arises. Focus your mind singularly on a white AH syllable at your heart centre, one pointedly cutting the continuum of subtle thoughts and so resting. This enables the use of bliss as a means to give rise to the wisdom of sublime knowing and emptiness. It is taught to practise this frequently for short periods of time until competence is reached.

The second mind training, the no thought of clarity and emptiness, is taught thus:

Breathe out the stale air from the lungs in three or nine sets of exhalations, because it is necessary to expel the impure poisonous wind. Following that, when you breathe in, all outer appearances, fixated as being true and completely solid, melt into shimmering light and mix with clear blue sky. As this blueness enters your body, think your body fills up entirely. Press down the upper wind and draw the lower wind up slightly. Seal these together and, by meditating on this, an experience of clarity and emptiness will grow. Also, according to the teaching, it is important if you are too cool you should meditate this wind feels hot and if you are hot meditate it is cool. It is taught this vase-breathing practice is the source of all good qualities.

> "Because the central channel is supreme, it does not show in visual experience."

This time, until you breathe out, hold your breath in this way, so the breath passes into the paths of the left and right lateral channels and enters the lower end of the central channel, which is like the lower half of the Tibetan letter CHA. By means of the breath entering the central channel, realisation of the first Bodhisattva bhumi irreversibly arises. Regarding the arising of each of the signs of the three states: entering, residing and dissolving, as the first knot of the central channel is released and wind enters, the qualities of the first bhumi arise. Then, when wind and mind reside in the central channel, the qualities of the second bhumi arise. As wind and mind completely dissolve, thoughts of subject and object are purified like the expanse of sky. Also, all good qualities of knowing develop in their entirety, so for the present, life is long, sickness is rare, the body is comfortable and swift like a bird. These and other good qualities are the excellent attributes of reaching the essential point of the vase-like breath.

It is taught the Great One from Oddiyana said: "All good qualities of wind need to be developed by practising the vase-like breath, so Tsogyal, apply the vase as the key point in all meditation on the winds!"

The third method of mind training, the no thought of dharmata, is taught thus: Relax both body and mind. Without moving the eyes, in a state free from all recollection and thinking, proliferation and subsidence of thoughts, without making any particular effort to hold the wind, fill the middle wind out straight from below the navel. This is an extremely profound instruction.

The Great One from Oddiyana taught: "Listen, Tsogyal, sit crossed-legged, draw up the lower wind slightly, press down the upper wind slightly, and fill the middle wind out from the navel. This is the wind practice of wisdom residing in its own state."

This is helpful for the body meditating on the generation stage, the mind meditating on luminosity, and so on, whatever the practice. It is a wind practice which spontaneously accomplishes all of the three: holding, drawing and spreading the drops. It also spontaneously purifies thoughts of subject and object. This practice removes problems of awareness, such as becoming drowsy, dull or agitated during meditation, and prevents problems of the sense faculties occurring, including the onset of blindness etc. It prevents the development of diseases of phlegm and gall bladder. It heals bloating and griping pain in the stomach, and both contagious and infectious diseases. This is a wind practice of long life, enduring like the sun and moon.

Visualise your own body as the yidam, sit straight not leaning to one side or hunched over, then press and fill out the wind below the navel. Look into the space in front of you with an open gaze. Place your awareness in a state of original purity. This is called the wind practice of great wisdom. It is also called the wind practice of dividing mind and rigpa awareness. During this practice, slightly arch your back at the waist. Fill out your abdomen at the level of the navel. At full in-breaths and all times of wind activities, fill out your abdomen. By applying the key points of this one pointedly, the upper and lower winds are naturally drawn in. By always filling out the abdomen at the level of the navel, the focus of attention also becomes the filled out navel.

Meditate on yidam deities by also focusing on filling out at the navel. When reciting essence mantras, also naturally draw in the winds by filling out at the level of the navel. Meditate on dharmata no thought wisdom also by extending at the navel level. While doing any of the four activities: walking, moving around, lying down or sitting, it is taught we should not leave this great secret wisdom of practice. It is also taught this kind of middle wind should be extended, not only while training the mind as in the preceding practices, but on all steps of the path to accomplishing Bodhisattvahood. It is an excellent supportive condition and most important.

From beginingless time, this ownerless entity called mind, lost to free rein, fabricator of multitudinous random thoughts, wild as an untamed horse, can through various means, using methods to train and tame, gradually become workable. To do this, train the mind with the three practices of no thought, so awareness can be held wherever it is placed and can remain for increasingly long periods of time in a sky-like state of no thought. This is the measure of individual mastery.

TWENTY SEVEN

UNWAVERING PEACEFUL CONCENTRATION

Of the three doors, body, speech and mind, mind is the most important. From beginning-less time until now, we have been wandering in samsara. This is motivated by confused mind's afflictive emotions which, together with body and speech, cause the accumulation of non-virtuous karma; the result of this is endless roaming within the three prison-like samsaric realms. To turn away from this state and hope to achieve complete liberation and perpetual contentment, merely by going through the motions of doing spiritual practices of body and speech will bring little progress, so it is essential to make sustained effort in the single meditation method of concentrating the mind.

As it says in a Sutra:

> "Mind is chief.
> Mind is extremely swift.
> Mind goes at the head of all Dharmas."

However, body, speech and mind have the connection of support and supported, so when meditating all three are important. That being so, first the body sits in the unwavering seven point posture of Vairochana. If the body is straight the channels are straight. If the channels are straight the winds are straight. Because the winds are straight, the drops are straight. Because the drops are straight, awareness comes to rest in a natural state and meditation naturally arises.

When a beginner meditates, none of the following activities should be engaged in: physical actions, activities like business, work and so on. Dharma activities such as prostration, circumambulation etc., and esoteric physical exercises should also be avoided. Generally the physical posture should be like this: place the legs in the full lotus position. Place the hands below the navel in the mudra of equanimity. Straighten the spine like an arrow. Join the abdomen to the spine. Slightly bend the neck. Touch the tongue to the upper palate. Look forward into space with the gaze directed in line with the tip of the nose.

During the Dzogchen Heart Essence practices, the pith instructions tell us to keep the lips and teeth slightly apart and breathe through the mouth. Additionally, there are key points of posture and gaze, as well as many Yantra yoga exercises that are mentioned in the quintessence instruction guidance of the main Dzogchen practices, all of which need to be known at that stage.

As for speech, when meditating put a stop to conversation and confused chatter. Also cease recitations and discussion of the Dharma. Eschew mantras and verbal recitations so, like a vina with broken strings, speech is overcome and discarded.

During meditation do not employ the mind to investigate confused mundane thoughts. Cease meditation on deities and yidam. Do not pay attention to concepts of view or meditation but let the mind self-settle. Allow body, speech and mind to come down to a genuine state and become refined.

Generally speaking, in the instruction guidance of the Great Perfection, two approaches to meditation are taught: the entry point guidance of calm abiding and the entry point guidance of insight. Of these, in order to avoid obstructions and hindrances, we follow the entry point guidance of calm abiding and meditate on calm abiding.

The mind of a beginner is like an untamed horse. If you sprint to catch hold of such a horse it is sure to bolt, and you will fail to catch it. But if you use various methods to lure the horse close and gradually attempt to grasp it, then you will be able to catch it. Similarly, if you strive to hold this untamed mind by force, the level of thought activity will only increase. Therefore, through methods using various reference points, the mind slowly comes down to a genuine state and authentic calm abiding will develop in the mind stream.

Before beginning meditation, arouse the mind of bodhichitta by thinking: "For the sake of sentient beings as numerous as the sky is vast, in this life and body, in order to attain the unexcelled level of buddhahood which accomplishes the two-fold benefit, I am meditating on the Dharma of the Mahayana." Also precede meditation with guru yoga practice.

To begin, meditate on calm abiding with defined attributes. Let the three doors, body, speech and mind, come down to their natural state and assume the seven point body posture of Vairochana. Upon this posture as the base, place a small object in front of you, something like a stick or a stone. Gaze directly at it without letting your mind wander to anything else, just rest on it in stillness. From time to time, make sure you do not seize on the object with piercing intensity, rest naturally, but do not allow your mind to wander, place it only upon the support of non-distraction. When you have become serene, slowly release and loosen into relaxation. During relaxation do not engage in various streams of thought but, as before, stop your mind from wandering.

Short practice periods help prevent the mind sinking into dullness and sleep, and also prevent the arising of hindrances and obstructions, such as discursive thoughts proliferating out of control, and so on. By practising frequently, problem-free meditation will develop, so train like this again and again. Having finished the practice session, be mindful and do not lose the state of meditation. Slowly integrate it with all your activities and take it as the path of practise.

After having mastered this training, again enter the session of practice as before and, in the sitting posture, bring the three doors down together to their natural state. Now visualise in this way: Think at the mid-point between your eyebrows is a white drop bright and clear, luminous and brilliant, the size of a pea, apparent but without self-nature. Focus your attention upon this without letting the mind wander. Within this clarity, as before, released and loose, let your mind self-settle. Do not let thoughts cut in. Meditate in the same way as before, in the same way training for numerous short sessions of practice.

Again, meditate your body is empty and clear. At the level of your heart is a red drop of light, essence of wind and mind mixed, the size of the flame of a medium-sized butter lamp, shining and brilliant blue in colour, hot to touch. Focus your awareness on it. Rest in clarity and cut distractions as before.

If calm abiding still does not grow in your mind stream, visualise in the space in front of you the form of Vajrasattva, about the length of your forearm in height, apparent but without self-nature, possessing the nature of brilliant white light. Focus your awareness on Vajrasattva's heart centre and repeat this practice numerous times for short periods as before. Also, you can focus your mind without wandering on the Bhagavan Lord Shakya, whose form is blazing with brilliant golden light, or Bodhisattva Avalokiteshvara, whose form is white and radiant with a white HRIH syllable complete with ঃ at his heart centre.

It is taught at first thoughts will become more numerous, but in the end they will become fewer, and this is an experiential sign that meditation is gradually developing. Whatever focus we hold, if the latencies of negative thoughts proceed from the mind, whichever latency of negative habituation arises: attraction, aggression, and so on, place the mind upon it, release and relax. Sometimes, when a thought arises, identify it and by doing so the thought self-liberates, naturally vanishing without any trace. As another thought arises, identify it and simply by not following after it, arising and liberation or disappearance occur simultaneously. Relax in an unmodified state and break up your thoughts in this way. Become extremely familiar with these quintessential instructions.

Following this is the instruction for training the wind:
Sitting in the seven point posture of Vairochana, first in order to remove the poisonous wind, expel from the right nostril the wind of aggression three times. From the left nostril expel the wind of attraction three times, and from both nostrils expel the wind of ignorance three times, making nine in all. Alternatively, expel once from the right, once from the left, and once from the centre, making a total of three cleansing exhalations. At the same time, think that all your negativities and obscurations emerge from your nostrils in the form of scorpions and are burned in a fire of wisdom in the space in front of you. When you breathe in, hold the breath below the navel for as long as you can before expelling the air again.

Following this, the practice of reciting the three unborn vajra syllables is as follows:
Clear the stale wind and sit in the essential physical posture as before. As you breathe in, in the form of the syllable blessed by the bodies of all the Buddhas, white OM syllables gather together. Press down the upper wind, draw up the lower wind and hold it below the navel. As long as the wind is conjoined, it is the essence of the speech of all the Buddhas in the nature of red AH syllables. Rest for as long as awareness remains, during which time hold the wind as long as you can. When you breathe out, it flows out in the form of blue HUM syllables, essence of the minds of all Buddhas. Think it radiates uninterrupted emanations to benefit beings.

In this way, breathe in OM, which remains as AH, and is exhaled in the nature of HUM. To hold this in mind one-pointedly without wavering and meditate like this continuously is called the 'recitation of the unborn vajra'. Every day the wind of a healthy person moves twenty one thousand six hundred times. To accomplish this number of recitations of the three syllables of the unborn vajra will be to develop inconceivable good qualities, and so needs to be done as a regular practice.

Now, the training in calm abiding without attributes is as follows:
In the essential physical posture as before, gaze directly into space without meditating on any reference point whatsoever. Focus your awareness unwaveringly on the space in front of you. As you remain in this presence, rest in it. From time to time investigate the nature of the awareness of who is focusing. Again focus, then again investigate, and so on in turn. Post-meditation, cultivate unwavering mindfulness in your mind stream in everything you do.

After having trained like this, lower your gaze. Relax both body and mind, and remain without any reference to anything to be meditated on. When you are present in mere unwavering non-meditation, in a state of self-settled fundamental nature, unspoiled and unadulterated, interrupt it, and then again allow yourself to relax as before. Sometimes look at the nature of who is focusing and who is interrupting. If you find it is mind, then look at its essence and relax. Train until good calm abiding has developed.

Following this, from time to time again focus your awareness without wavering. Again relax loosely, remaining in uninterrupted spaciousness. In this way, alternate between focus and release. Move your gaze up and down, right and left in turns, and in the times in between remain relaxed. Sometimes look at who is engaging intently in practice and who is changing focus. By turns, bring your mind down to the centre of your heart and release your mind to the all-pervading sky, and so on, changing your gaze in various ways in turn. If it comes about that, wherever you place your awareness, it is vivid and present, and wherever you release it, it is directly there, if your awareness is able to go where it is sent and remain where it is put, then calm abiding has been developed.

If impediments of dullness and agitation occur then, according to quintessential guidance, visualise the face of your guru. The example of flawless calm abiding is likened to the steady flame of a butter lamp sheltered from the wind which does not quiver. Wherever awareness is placed, it is stable and unmoving. Untouched by faults, it is lucid. Unshaken by adventitious thought patterns, awareness remains true.

If water is not stirred up, it becomes clear. In the same way, the three doors become clear when placed on the underlying basis of all, so one has no desire to move physically, and no desire to speak. All the proliferations and subsidence of thoughts in the mind are purified in their own place, and so it comes about that one naturally resides in a state of concentration. Developing extraordinary calm abiding, which has with it the experience of no thought of clarity and emptiness in your mind stream, overcomes gross suffering and afflictive emotions.

Due to this, in the short term no circumstances giving rise to diseases caused by disharmony of the elements will occur, and the constitutional elements and sense bases will remain where they are, so the mind of enlightenment develops. Ultimately, inexpressible truth will grow in the mind stream and all thoughts will be liberated where they are; whereby the insight of primordial purity's natural condition will reside self-settled in the state of natural great perfection beyond conception and expression. Therefore, it is crucial that all those who wish to attain the result by travelling the path gradually should strive at these practices.

TWENTY EIGHT

POWER OF THE CHANNELS, WINDS AND DROPS

That which resides dependent upon the vajra body are the subtle channels, the subtle wind that moves, and the dependent subtle energy drops. Discussing these, the aspect of mind which comprises its essence, primordially pure and unsullied by confusion, is called 'wisdom'. However, by the power of mind under the influence of confusion, karma manifestly compounds, by which the causes and conditions assemble to produce a body, and thus rebirth in samsara comes about. At the same time, an assembly of the parents' seeds and a consciousness of a being of the intermediate state and the five elements: earth, water, fire, wind and space join together, and body, speech and mind develop.

How does a human body form? In the centre of the five properties of the assembly of the five elements is the eight-fold group of consciousness; of which, except for the ground of all, the other seven remain indistinct. Then, from the ground of all, afflicted mind arises and produces the life-wind which gives rise to the formative forces. By these conditions, the karmic wind is instantly produced and, through the powers known as mixing, gathering and supporting, the stages of growth and development of the first week in the womb occur.

On the first day of the fifth week, the subtle life channel which connects with the mother is cut. On the second day, the channels of the heart, including the subsidiary channels, form to create a place for the winds to arise. Following this, gradual development continues each day. Then, during the remainder of the nine months in the womb, seventy two thousand channels come into being. Of the three well known channels and five chakras, the main channel is the central channel, which has been given many names, including 'avadhuti' in Sanskrit, ever-pulsing, life-channel, 'kaga muga', and so on.

These names indicate the central channel is the base for the life-wind, and connects the secret place to the crown of the head. The upper end of the central channel is closed by a HUM syllable with the nature of the white element. The lower end below the navel is closed by the red element short AH syllable. Between these the central channel is filled with the life-wind, the basis of the consciousness of the ground of all, and is sky blue in colour. It is said there are two channels either side of this central channel: the residing channel and the meditation channel. The right channel is called 'rasana' and white, the left is called 'lalana' and red. In females these are reversed. The three channels are connected below the navel and split from that point.

Within the three channels reside the syllables OM AH HUM which, in an impure context, form the basis of the three doors and the three poisons, and accumulate karma of the three realms. At a time of purity, they form the basis of the three Buddha bodies. From the aggression element in the rasana, clarity and method are produced. From the aversion element in the lalana, bliss and wisdom are perfected. The ignorance element in the ever-pulsing central channel forms the basis for no thought inseparable union of the former qualities to arise.

These three subtle channels act as posts for the umbrella-like spokes of the four chakras, which are connected inside the body to their outer petals, with channels arranged like a web. Of the four groupings, the crown chakra of great bliss has thirty two channel petals, the throat chakra of enjoyment has sixty channel petals, the heart chakra of Dharma has eight channel petals, and the navel chakra of emanation has sixty four channel petals. The four chakras form the basis of the four Buddha bodies and the five wisdoms. In the centre of these reside the syllables of purifying wisdom OM AH HUM SO and, if the secret place chakra which guards bliss is added, HA is included making five.

In the vajra body there are seventy two thousand channels; these include the burning fire chakra of the six channels which hold the fire element, and the inflaming wind chakra of the six channels of completely pure wind. It is taught there are thirty five million fine channels which bring growth in even the finest hairs.

The residing wind moves within the channels that are present. The essence of wind is the wind of the five elements. In addition to the five main winds there are five subsidiary winds. The first basic wind is the life wind or karmic wind which resides in the heart centre inseparably with rigpa awareness in an expressive manner. This thereby brings about the generation of the dualistic thought activity of grasping and fixating. If the life wind is faulty it can cause fainting and bring about mental disorders. At worst a problem with the life wind causes death.

The second main wind is the ascending wind which resides in the upper body. This wind functions to move breath in and out of the lungs, and in the throat to facilitate speech. If faulty, it produces disease of the upper body. Third is the downwards-voiding wind which resides in the lower body and works to remove waste. If faulty, it produces disease of the lower body. Fourth is the fire-accompanying wind which resides in the stomach and separates the nourishing part of food from waste. If faulty, it produces stomach diseases. Fifth is the pervading wind which generates body strength. If faulty, it causes problems of paralysis etc.

There are five moving subsidiary winds of the five physical sense faculties. The naga wind apprehends form. The turtle wind apprehends sound. The lizard wind apprehends smell. The devadatta wind apprehends taste. The king of the wealth-gods wind apprehends touch. If these are faulty they cause diseases which oppose their respective functions.

All the basic and subsidiary winds move through all the channels of the body, as well as the twelve houses of the navel, generating their functions before passing out through the nose. In the average person in the prime of life, one whose elements are not conflicting, the outer wind element will move twenty one thousand six hundred times during the twelve time conjunctions of one day. It is taught the wind which moves in the inner subsidiary fine channels will move one hundred and twenty thousand six hundred times per day. In each large movement of breath the wisdom wind moves fifty six times and in each small movement of breath it moves one fifth of that.

Regarding the subtle drops which depend on these moving winds, the arranged bodhichitta drops reside in all the channels of the body in just the same manner as oil pervades a sesame seed. In the rasana channel, from the moon or the white element, an inverted HUM, subtle drops fall which develop all the body constituents, as well as the brain, marrow and bone. In the lalana channel, from the sun or red element AH subtle drops fall and develop flesh, blood and lymph etc.

From the central channel, drops of luminosity, the very essence of the essence, arise and mix with the root of utterly unchanging luminosity: an unelaborated drop of dharmata, life-holding bodhichitta, essence of the blood from the centre of the heart, which is present in the manner of a ball of light, piercing both eyes like a luminous channel of light. Its essence is empty, lucid and ceaseless, residing in the manner of the three Buddha bodies. This is indicated by the nature of objects not leaving the sphere of emptiness, but currently appearing in this way, which is the sign of the dharmakaya.

The sign of the sambhogakaya is that the unity of basic space and awareness is actually evident to the senses. The indication of the nirmanakaya is the power of perception of objects by the six-fold group of consciousness without mixing as they arise in all their variety. Subjective wisdom is the essence of mind itself connected with these, free from conceptuality and unconfused.

If the channels and winds are mastered and one is trained in the essential drops, then limpid clarity without affliction, knowledge realising non-conceptualisation, will begin to blaze from within. Ignorance of one's own nature causes impure confused drops with aspects of purity and refuse to come forth. The pure white element resides in the nature of a HUM syllable in the central channel at the crown, and the red element resides below the navel in the nature of a short AH at the juncture of the three channels. The refuse, the essence of food and drink, by passing through the four channels of the liver, is turned into blood. The essence of blood becomes flesh. The essence of flesh becomes fat. The essence of fat becomes bone. The essence of bone becomes marrow. The essence of marrow becomes regenerative fluid. Regenerative fluid provides bodily strength and the refuse of this drops from the lower doors.

True enlightened mind, essence of the empty and lucid dharmakaya, abides in relative mind. That mind depends on bodhichitta in the form of essential drops. That in turn depends on wind, which in turn depends on the channels, which in turn depend on the body. Therefore, our own body is a mandala of pure deities primordially and spontaneously residing. Regarding this, the body is a mandala of channels. The channels are a mandala of syllables. The constituents are a mandala of nectar. The winds are a mandala of wisdom, and rigpa awareness resides in the manner of a mandala of enlightened mind. As it is taught in our tradition of Dzogchen, the soles of the feet are associated with wind, the three-way junction of channels is associated with fire, the navel is associated with water, and the heart is associated with earth; so the body, an assembly of the four elements, is a mandala of deities, an immeasurable mansion, complete with a circumference and pediments.

The four channels in the heart where the wind moves are the four doors of the immeasurable mansion. Consciousness is Heruka. The eight-fold group of consciousnesses are the eight gauris or wrathful deities. The eight objects of consciousness are the eight tramen. This, connected with other such pure divinities and complete with the three seats, is the vajra body. By applying the key points of the vajra body, the channels, winds and drops are used as the path in order to actualise the ultimate result.

In addition to this, concerning the ordinary and extraordinary preliminaries, take guru yoga as the path and receive the four empowerments with longing devotion. Visualise yourself as Vidyadhara Vajradharma. Distinct in the centre of your body is the central channel with the four characteristics, the dharmakaya, the right rasana channel, the sambhogakaya, and the left lalana channel, the nirmanakaya. The rasana and lalana are joined below the navel, at the lower end of the central channel, with the upper ends curving at the nape of the neck. Visualise clearly both channels extending into the nostrils. Expel the karmic winds from the right and left nostrils in turn, seven times each. When the winds of the five elements and five poisons have come out, consider the channels to be free of problems, relax and let consciousness settle into a natural state.

In the centre of the maroon heart tent, visualise Samantabhadra father mother, blue, in meditative equipoise, the size of a pea. Their sense bases are extremely clear and distinct. In their heart centre is a drop of five-coloured lights, whirling around; inside this visualise limpid and clear the unborn life-syllable AH, brilliantly white, as if drawn by a single hair.

Following the key points of the four wind trainings, bind together wind, the syllable AH, and rigpa awareness, and pass through the paths of the rasana and lalana to convey them to the centre of the heart. By striving, through the personal clarifications of the key points of direct instruction, the two life and downward winds merge into one, and in the central channel, by perfecting the inherent potentiality of the three: entering, abiding and dissolving, inconceivable enlightened qualities are attained. In particular, by releasing the navel knot of channels, the realisations of the first bhumi will arise. The truth of dharmata will be seen directly. If you do not have the key points of direct instruction and karmic winds enter the life channel, there is a risk of madness.

This is the quintessence of all perfection stage practices. Holding wisdom wind in the central channel is the supreme tummo inner heat practice. The nature of mind purified as the dharmakaya is the supreme practice of luminosity. The core falsity of appearances collapsed in upon itself is the highest degree of illusory body training. Day and night arising as a wheel of luminosity is the ultimate peak of dream manifestation transformation. The three doors possessed of the three vajras is the most excellent transference. Therefore, the essential aspects of Mahamudra and the Six Dharmas (of Naropa) are complete in this practice, and it is the result of all secret mantra.

Visualise the three channels as before. Distinct at the top of the central channel is the white element in the nature of a HUM syllable, and at the lower end is the red element in the form of an AH stroke. Breathe in through both rasana and lalana channels and, from the short AH at the navel, the flickering fire of wisdom-knowledge burns. Its essence is bliss, its nature is clarity and in appearance it is blazing heat which fills the navel chakra. Now meditate that blissful warmth develops. Visualise the crown chakra of great bliss, the throat chakra of enjoyment, and so on, and hold the wind in each of them. As the flame touches the HUM syllable, bliss begins to quiver and the drop melts to fill all the channels and petals of the crown. Offerings of bliss-emptiness nectar are made to the heroes and dakinis of the subtle constitution. The two accumulations are completed and the two obscurations are purified. Similarly, the throat and the navel fill as before. Think you attain the vase empowerment, secret empowerment, wisdom-knowledge empowerment, together with the precious word empowerment and you experience joy and supreme joy, together with extraordinary wisdom.

When the essence touches the short AH below the navel at the juncture of the channels, fire and nectar burn indivisibly and all appearance and existence is filled with fire. All discursive thought and latencies grasping at the container and contained are burnt. Finally, your own body together with the flame becomes smaller and smaller and, subsumed in a state free from elaboration, remain in luminous emptiness. Perform dispelling hindrances, HA shakes, and small bangs. In this way, if you arrive at the crucial point, bliss-heat will burn like fire and clothing will not be needed. You will be able to control the five elements. By purifying the impure karmic wind, you attain miraculous powers and higher knowledge. If you cling to this as real or hindrances have not been cleared, you will become a powerful demon (mistake the view) and fall into error; disease and problems can develop in this life and so on. The benefits and harm are great, so be extremely careful.

TWENTY NINE

THE VITAL IMPORTANCE OF MATURING EMPOWERMENT

The exact meaning of the words 'to give an empowerment' is simply: someone who themselves has power, confers this upon another person who does not have it. In this way, at a suitable time, a powerful reigning monarch will establish his son the prince as heir to the throne of the kingdom by holding elaborate ceremonies and bestowing symbols of power, including a crown made of gold and precious jewels, etc. In Tibet this became known as 'giving an empowerment from the royal crown'. In a similar way, an authentic person who themselves has received the power of the kingdom of Dharma, in other words a qualified vajra master, having first given instructions of maturation and liberation, infuses with blessings a student, who is a worthy vessel and has complete conducive circumstances. This is the sacred ritual called 'empowerment'.

When you hear about an empowerment, images may come to mind of square mandalas with latticework of precious materials, and gold and silver vases etc. Basically, the empowerment vase is made from gold and silver beaten into shape by a smith, and the mixture of liquid and substances inside the vase is also nothing out of the ordinary. The presiding Lama, with some mantras and mudras, places the vase on the crown of your head and gives you liquid from the vase to drink. The ritual nature of this process may raise some questions, such as: "Where do the so-called blessings come from and how do I receive them?" or "I'm not sure what change has taken place in me, since having received empowerment." Such doubts are bound to arise for some.

To use doubts like these as a starting point, and then investigate them to come to a definitive truthful conclusion is termed 'research'. Through research we can learn in detail the reasons, key points and problems associated with a subject. Having understood this method, those then entering the path of the holy Dharma will avoid blind faith and join the ranks of those with sharp faculties who follow the Dharma.

In order to receive empowerment, two causes and four conditions must be fulfilled. The first cause is the concomitant cause. Each individual phenomenon which appears to the student's conceptual thought patterns, taken to its intrinsic nature is the nature of mind, self-arising wisdom ever-present within oneself; it is nothing other than that. There is nothing that was not there before and has been newly attained. This is the concomitant cause: our wisdom nature.

The second cause is the co-operating cause; this concerns the ordinary objects which comprise the empowerment articles, including the vase and deity icons etc. It is important to understand both the concomitant cause of individual empowerments, the wisdom blessings to be attained, and that which resembles this, the concomitant cause of the mind of the student, our mind of innate wisdom to which conceptual thoughts appear, are non-dual in every aspect with regard to their actual nature. The resultant state is blessed by the supreme wisdom and enlightened qualities of Buddha, and in this way therefore, the empowerment articles become accomplished and imbued with power.

Of the four conditions, the first condition is the causal condition: On the all-ground, the latencies of positive virtuous karma are able to become awakened by themselves and may also be awakened by conditions; so, according to the level of mind and faculties of the student, it is appropriate to give empowerment to one who is a fortunate *student*.

The second condition is the governing condition: From the perfect Buddha Lord Vajrapani up till now, the river of empowerment has flowed unbroken, and it is the *master* who has the capability of placing the potential of empowerment in the student's mind stream, to whatever degree is appropriate.

The third condition is the objective condition: The master and student, relying on a completely pure ritual assembly of articles, mantras and concentration to bring about that which is to be attained comprise the power of the *empowerment*.

The fourth condition is the immediate condition: By having purified the mind stream in the past, the door is open to make the mind stream suitably *mature* to empower in the future.

Those with sharp facilities attain empowerment all at once through their powerful potential. Those with duller faculties attain empowerment gradually by being granted successive empowerments. Of these two, at this time, giving empowerment into a mandala painted on cloth so a fortunate student may attain it, or by the exceptional representational mandala which is made from coloured sand, is the empowerment of the devoted student which matures the ability for potential to grow.

The qualities of a student who is suitable to be given empowerment should include: strong faith, diligence and wisdom, and eagerness for meditation and teachings. In addition, a suitable vessel for Dharma needs to be greatly generous for the sake of Dharma, and should protect their vows as they do their eyes, and so on. It is taught it is necessary to give students with faith outer beneficial empowerments and to give hard workers inner capacity empowerments. Those who can accomplish their own objectives receive listening and meditation empowerments, those who can accomplish benefit for others, teaching and activity empowerments, those who can accomplish their own and other's objectives, vajra king empowerments, and those with yogic discipline should be given profound empowerments. One who gives empowerments should be well learned, greatly wise, and always striving for the benefit of others, etc. They must be complete with all the general and specific good qualities.

How should empowerments be received? Receive an empowerment by means of an authentic ritual, so in this way, even if the wisdom of the empowerment does not obviously develop at the time, the stains of obscurations will be cleansed, and blessings to gain potential will be received. In the vehicle of individual liberation, if monks' vows are received by means of the ordination ritual, the wisdom of power to meditate on the path does not immediately develop, but conditions are granted by which the continuum of immoral ways is broken. Likewise, the mantra vows are received when empowerment is given, but if at the time of empowerment wisdom does not grow, it still causes maturation of potential power so later, as training in the path progresses, wisdom will certainly grow.

Fortunate students who are suitable vessels to enter the spiritual approach of secret mantra have attainment of the ordinary, and particularly the supreme, accomplishments as their ultimate goal, and this comes about through reliance on meditation of the path. The path itself is one of maturation and liberation, and the basis of this is the vows and sacred commitments with which it is linked. Similarly, the actualisation of maturation and liberation is also linked to empowerment; therefore the giving of empowerment is the entranceway to the path of the secret mantra spiritual approach. In the mantric spiritual approach, if empowerment is not received, the secret mantra will not be accomplished. This principal is referred to by the Buddha in the Tantras:

"Without relying on empowerment, no accomplishment can
be made in secret mantra."

For example: "A boatman without an oar is unable to be freed to the
other side of a river. If empowerment is received, though nothing of the
secret mantra is practised, still accomplishment will come about."
Additionally, it is taught in the root Tantra of the Illusory Display:
"Without pleasing the master or obtaining empowerments, to begin
attending and practising Tantric teachings will be fruitless and lead to
ruin."

Whichever empowerment is received, the recipient is then allowed to
study and practise that particular section of Tantra and mantra. The
giving of empowerment is not only the entrance to the path, but it is also
the main body of the path. The entire path of the secret mantra spiritual
approach is subsumed within two aspects: maturation and liberation.
Having received empowerment, someone whose vital sacred
commitments have not become impaired will generally actualise the
supreme accomplishment within seven or sixteen lifetimes, and there
also exist a few who possess great fortune and excellent faculties, who are
liberated at the time of empowerment.

Generally, the nature of empowerment is as follows: The giver of an
empowerment, a properly qualified vajra master, undertakes the
preparatory phase to purify and prepare the mind stream of the student.
The action, the empowerment itself, is then given to this worthy
recipient by the appropriate ritual assembly of articles, mantras and
meditative concentration. The object of the empowering action is the
student's aggregates, constituents and sources, together with sense
objects. What is wholly to be attained is the mandala of the complete
three seats of Buddhas, Bodhisattvas and wrathful deities, or the mandala
of primordial Buddha bodies and wisdom. This is introduced as the
actual wisdom which already dwells within oneself, whereby one's share
of obscurations is purified in fitting proportion, or becomes weakened;
thereby wisdom of the two stages of development and perfection is
manifestly developed, or maturation of a suitable capacity for certain
development of this wisdom occurs. The seed of the resulting four
Buddha bodies, which is timelessly present, is once again brought to
maturity.

'Empowerment' or 'wong' in Tibetan is called 'abhisheka' in Sanskrit,
which means to engage in eliminating, cleansing and imbuing. This

refers to the elimination and cleansing of all the stains, subtle and gross, of the body, speech and mind of the student who needs to be purified and accomplished, in order that the mind stream, which has become clear, can be established or imbued with extraordinary and unceasing suitable capacity to meditate on the path and attain the result. This is what is called an empowerment.

There are as many empowerments for maturing that which is immature as there are mandalas of the four or six great classes of Tantra, and those rituals which depend on them: the different rituals of the canonical, revealed treasure and pure vision scriptures. Of all these, in the pinnacle vehicle, the supreme yoga of Dzogpa Chenpo, the student's mind stream is purified by means of the elaborate, unelaborate, extremely unelaborate, and utterly unelaborate empowerments. Having received this kind of empowerment, guarding the sacred commitments is the life force of the empowerment.

The vows of the mantric spiritual approach are received during an empowerment. Having entered this path, the situation resembles that of a snake which has entered a bamboo tube. Except for going straight up or directly down, there is no third place to go. It is a situation with huge benefit and risk, so great care is needed. The heart of all sacred commitments is the body, speech and mind of the Lama, which can be differentiated into the multiplicity of ancillary sacred commitments. There are sacred commitments without guarding, binding, or restraint from the beginning, also 'not existent', 'openness', 'spontaneous presence', 'solely', and other such detailed classifications in which to train.

The benefits of receiving empowerments are as follows: Long life, plentiful wealth, and everything you wish for accomplished as desired. In addition, conditions opposed to practising Dharma are pacified, and conducive conditions are amassed. Later, because karmic obscurations are exhausted or have become attenuated, you will not fall down to the lower realms, and you will always enjoy the happiness and wealth of the upper realms of gods and humans. Further, however the empowerment has matured you, through following this by meditating on the appropriate path, now or in a future life, you will attain the ordinary and supreme accomplishments, perfect the two benefits, and attain the unexcelled level of enlightenment without difficulty.

THIRTY

EPILOGUE: A LOOK AT THE FUTURE LANDSCAPE
OF THE NEW MILLENNIUM

Counting in years from the birth of Christ, this is the beginning of the twenty first century, the eve of the year two thousand in the general western calendar. It is therefore of concern to all of us what unforeseen events may arise from this point in the transitions and changes of the world.

Regarding this, some people hazard a guess that the changes this century brings will be like flicking over the page in a magazine and seeing a brand new picture, entirely different from the one before; as if we will suddenly arrive in a completely new world, but this is a childish way of thinking. Some people are terrified, because previous changes in the world caused them to experience terrible suffering of body and mind, and so in their eyes the path in front of them will continue to be totally frightening; they anticipate events from a weak and helpless point of view. Others with huge expectations create effects without causes in their minds, building castles in the air, and so envisage a pure realm and cherish unrealistic hopes of enjoying future happiness and comfort. Still others have no thoughts or ideas apart from the here and now, and give no consideration to tomorrow or the future.

These various ways of looking at the future inspire many different hopes, but in essence everyone shares the same desire for happiness in the future. However, what we call past and future centuries are merely divisions of the continuum of time into consensually designated parts. From tiny fractions of one previous moment to the next, to slightly grosser divisions of today and tomorrow, and so on like this; in truth, except for the aspect of a change in the mere classification of the length of time's continuum, there is nothing distinctive or special whatsoever about a new or old century.

This being the case, throughout the arrival of a great many new centuries, the sun and moon have kept rising and setting just as they have always done. Rivers continue to flow downstream. The oceans continue to swell. Fire is hot, water is wet etc. Even with the dawning of a new century, the individual actions and qualities of the four elements do not change into something new. Similarly, wandering humans experience periods of comfort and dissatisfaction in unequal measure as before. All living creatures in our environment, together with everything else, are born, age, become sick and die, afflicted unchangingly as before by the four great sufferings. Each time a pleasant experience occurs and we feel happy, this is also impermanent; pleasure and suffering are of an alternating nature, and our experience reverts to how it was before.

Even that which seems to be unchanging, relying on time and continuity is of the nature of change. For example, if we investigate this great river in front of us which has been flowing for thousands of years, in actual fact the river of a previous moment is not the river of a subsequent moment. Similarly, the entire world and everything in it has this nature of change, subtly in moments and grossly in their continuum. The change between white-toothed youth and white-headed old age is a continuous one, moment by moment, certainly not a change to sudden old age in one day.

However, the causes of our mistaken perception: our inner habit of grasping at permanence and the apparently unchanging external similarity of what appears to our senses, meet, and we become confused. In this case there is nothing wrong with saying the 'you' of yesterday and the 'you' of today are different. Except for merely changing physical basis, consciousness which connects the gap between past and future lives depends on a single continuum. This being the case, how feeble and powerless are humans whose consciousness depends on a material body! The same is true of all wandering living beings, and they are certainly objects of compassion. If we think and investigate, all things we see are forms of miserable suffering. All that we hear are sounds of lamenting cries. If we look at tiny insects and so on, each lives no longer than a day, and we see species of fish and birds and other small living creatures, close to being slaughtered, feeble and powerless. If a being with more strength and power than us, and possessing great lifespan and merit, took a look at us, we humans would certainly also appear in the same way.

To give a simple illustration of this: if we consider our individual situation as a drama in a film, with this life edited and made shorter in every respect, then a life of one hundred years would amount to just one day. Of this, time spent in enjoyment would be only a few minutes. In addition, if the human body were only the size of a thumb, we could imagine enjoyable experiences arising from happiness would have no real savour, in just the same way as we regard the experiences of insects and small birds.

Despite the advance of modern sciences in fields such as manufacturing and health care, reliance on science alone will never produce a formula to totally prevent suffering from occurring. Just as there is no way of making the nature of fire not hot, there is no way of making the nature of samsara not unsatisfactory.

Building on the foundation of today's scientific achievements, the human race has certainly excelled, making great progress to reach a current pinnacle of achievement. However, to attempt such feats as measure the full extent of the universe or calculate the total number of sentient beings, we would need to rely on faculties other than the ones we have now, faculties which are exceptional. Also, it is imperative we find means to end suffering of old age and death, a method more effective than those offered by current medicine and pharmacology. For example, I think current experiments to freeze human bodies so they may live again in the future are nothing but games played by credulous children!

In the context of scientific progress, research in the field of psychology is a difficult area, involving many subtleties and unknown factors. Despite this, if the human psyche can be thoroughly explored and understood, I believe the root of all suffering, the underlying flaw of our very existence, can be conclusively identified. If this fundamental issue is comprehended, then pioneering means to address it can be sought. If ultimately we can attain a state in which we encounter the great enemy of death without fear, than all other methods of finding contentment will simply follow.

In the order of the new millennium, the four seasons follow in sequence as before, and there is no way of changing things to ensure it is not hot in summer, nor cold in winter, that both day and night have equal daylight, and there is no suffering of old age, sickness and death. Threats such as wars, weapons, conflicts and terrorism are all caused by human activity; consequently human beings themselves have the power to change and eradicate them. Society does not exist independently, it comes into being by means of each of us private individuals, just as a yak's tail is made of many strands of hair and a forest consists of many trees.

Theoretically, if each person were to begin working for the common good, because the whole is formed from individuals, then eventually everyone would do the same; after which time, however extensive the search, a deliberately antagonistic person could not be found. In terms of problems in society, it is of no benefit to observe from a distance and say, "This is the bad behaviour of a degenerate time." This behaviour is carried out by individual people among a population of a few tens of hundreds of millions. If each individual worked towards positivity, then it follows the entire population could do the same.

People relate to each other through physical and verbal expressions, but it is the mind which controls both body and speech, and so the manner with which it directs actions. Whether behaviour is called 'good' or 'bad' has its root in the mind, so ultimately it is good or bad thinking that is important. In the new millennium, whether or not peace and happiness comes to the world depends on mind. That is to say, it depends on your own mind.

To summarise: if everyone on earth with the label 'I' from their own viewpoint, and the label 'you' from the viewpoint of others, were to have a totally good heart, all the expenditure on armies and weapons could be used for relieving poverty, protection of the environment, improvement in education and scientific advancement; thereby it would be easy to achieve new happiness and comfort in the new millennium for everyone collectively.

However, the opposite of a good heart is bad intent. The cause of bad intent in Buddhist terms is the afflictive emotions, particularly aggression. If we wish to expel afflictive emotions from their very core, we can find detailed methods in the Buddhist scriptures to abandon, transform and even take afflictive emotions onto the spiritual path. I am not saying this in order to persuade you into entering a religious scripture house, but to encourage your exploration into methods to bring forth increased happiness and fulfilment.

Among all beings, there is never one person who is without feelings of attraction or aggression, and so on; the only difference is the severity of feeling. If there existed a person without any afflictive emotions, they would be someone with very different sensory perceptions from ours, and would not be counted among the ranks of ordinary people. We desire instant happiness and fulfilment but have no quick method of ridding ourselves of the cause of dissatisfaction: aggression and so on, so we are unable to find happiness free from afflictive emotions. However, if we can restrain these afflictions and exercise control over them, then we will be able to limit our suffering to some extent. When violent afflictive emotions develop, we should recognise our feelings and thereby face up to them, fighting against them so they do not become victorious. If we yield the victory to afflictive emotions, they will control us, and we will certainly be tormented by experiencing all kinds of dissatisfaction.

The extent of the harm that losing control to afflictive emotions brings depends on the capacity of the individual. If someone with immense power falls under the influence of violent afflictions like aggression, they may not give themselves time to consider the future consequences of their actions. Under command of the malevolent mind of aggression, with just the movement of a finger, savage nuclear or chemical weapons capable of destroying many lands are deployed. In a moment, the treasured lives of many people and property gathered over many years of hard work become completely annihilated.

Under the influence of violent emotions, someone with a measure of power abuses those under them, making their lives a misery. Deprived people take the lives of their adversaries at the slightest provocation. Those worse beat or kill their own parents, siblings and friends. At the very least some smash crockery and household possessions. Having done these things in anger, once they have calmed down, they are sure to develop regret for their previous actions. But at that time, regret cannot change actions which have been committed, and there is no way to recall negative actions once they are complete. These examples illustrate the basis of ruin for self and others, and are experiences of losing the battle against the enemy of the afflictive emotions,

This being the case, when we encounter them, the method for pacifying the enemy of violent afflictions is by relying on the weapon-like remedy. Alternatively, the means to convert an enemy into a friend and thereby gain control is a method used to transform afflictive emotions into something useful. At the time, at the very least, if we do not avoid or limit afflictive emotions, on a large scale it will certainly become the basis for global discontent. On a middling scale, afflictive emotions can cause a country's ruin and on a small scale, conflict and imprisonment, each bringing their respective sufferings.

In the new future millennium, through clear awareness that everyone cherishes self as much as everyone else, if aggressive verbal abuse is not met with retaliatory verbal abuse, aggressive mistreatment is not met with retaliatory mistreatment, aggressive blows are not met with retaliatory blows, aggressive exposure of faults is not met with retaliatory exposure, and each individual takes responsibility for upholding a good heart and behaviour indivisible from gentle compassion, then no one person will harm another, and a new previously non-existent happiness can certainly be established.

Since the human race evolved, all kinds of religions have come into being. The origin of these religions is similarly diverse. Some of them derive from the summation of an ordinary person's deliberations. After the passing of many centuries, scholars and devotees supplement the original teachings with their commentaries, complete with contemplations and tracts. Other religions are taught by extraordinary teachers who have outstanding minds and possess wisdom knowledge. In addition, a few religions are fabricated by plagiarising those already in existence, or making slight alterations. Except for those which consider harming others an act of faith, I believe all the diverse traditions that are actually benevolent bring benefit to human society and are without harm. However, those which make use of a system of religious belief, controlling it for ulterior aims, are exceptions. The Enlightened Bhagavan said: "For as long as the mind has not ceased engaging, there will be no end to the infinite numbers of vehicles." Accordingly, there is no end to the varieties of religious traditions fabricated by mind.

If a modern scientifically-minded person has need of a religion, we can see Buddhism is closely related to science in many areas. Ultimately, however close to the pinnacle of understanding science gets, that is how much closer it will get to Buddhist understanding of the nature of reality. Furthermore, the Buddha taught the ultimate definitive meaning of the mysteries of life; permanent satisfaction, the path of no death, and so on, together with many more extremely abstruse topics. Of all these, the teachings of highly esoteric unexcelled Dzogpa Chenpo reach the innermost point of investigation without exception, something to which I can personally attest. These words may provoke some critics to shoot angry glances, and speak words of rebuke; however, when you come close to the path of death, or when you meet with other less conducive circumstances, I hope you will be able to form a genuine understanding of this analysis from its foundation. If you were able to live for a long time without dying, many decades, or for so much as several hundred years, then I think you could witness clear confirmation of this, universally agreed, in connection with the development of science.

In a time past, in a secluded area where many forest animals grazed, a Bodhisattva took the form of a deer called Sharaba. He was physically powerful and skilful. His strength of mind was also excellent and he had true compassion, so never brought harm to other living beings. He survived on just grass, leaves and water, living comfortably. At one time, the king of the land, together with four troops of soldiers from his army led by the most skilful archers, came to hunt wild animals. The king rode a swift horse and outpaced the rest of the company. Carrying a bow and arrow, he chased the deer Sharaba, king of wild creatures, galloping very fast.

The deer had the capacity to retaliate, but he did not attack and raced ahead. Before them was a huge gorge which the deer leapt across, escaping by means of his strength and speed. When the king of the land suddenly arrived on the edge of the gorge, his horse was unable to jump and reared up, so the king fell from his horse into the gorge. No longer hearing the sound of horse's hooves following him, the Bodhisattva who had taken the form of the deer stopped and looked back. He saw the horse had lost his rider and was standing, empty-saddled, on the edge of the gorge. The deer knew the king must have fallen into the gorge and this aroused his great compassion. "If this is someone of royal descent who enjoys perfect wealth and pleasures, falling into this terrifying ravine must be causing him overwhelming suffering," he thought. "If he still has any spark of life in him, it's not appropriate to abandon him there to die." Even though he knew the king might attack or kill him, the mind of great compassion was aroused by the king's plight and the deer went to the edge of the ravine to take a look.

He saw the king in the dust, writhing in pain from the fall. Tears filled the king of wild creatures' eyes and, speaking to the king in human language, he said, "Great king, has your body sustained any injury? I'm a wild animal living in your land and I survive by eating your grass and drinking your water. If you could allow me to continue to live a carefree life, I will rescue you from the gorge. Give me your permission to do so." When the king heard these gentle and respectful words, feelings of amazement, embarrassment and delight arose all at once, and he thought, "Can this be true?" He said, "The herds and wild animals I own are all equally mine, but I was an enemy trying to kill you! How is it you're compassionate towards me? I can bear my slight injuries, but falling into a ravine is nothing compared with the regret I'm suffering for the limitless negative karma I've accumulated in relation to a being with such a virtuous mind as yours. I'm confessing my faults to you, so remember this!"

Then the deer, having tested his strength on a stone the weight of a person, entered the gorge and approached the king. "Climb onto my back and hold on firmly," he requested respectfully. The deer then leaped vigorously into the air, and they arrived safely at the top of the gorge. Having shown the king the path out of the forest, the deer went to leave, but the king tightly grasped the deer who had saved his life, and said, "You, deer, have given me a second life. It wouldn't be fitting for me to leave you in this forest with its extremes of heat and cold. Let's keep company and return home together," he said.

Sharaba spoke with a gentle voice: "Great One, your qualities are worthy of my admiration. If you wish to be of benefit, have compassion for the herds of wild beasts, creatures whose natural stupidity causes them suffering, and don't hunt them in future. All sentient beings are the same in their desire for happiness and their dread of suffering, so it's unacceptable to inflict on others what you do not wish for yourself. Give up actions which bring you into disrepute, or which disparage holy beings. Work again to increase the particular merit which gained you your kingdom, founded on glory and excellence.

We're wild animals, we don't live in towns or houses; we're suited to living in the hills and forests and don't share the same objects of happiness as humans, so I won't go to your home. You should return home and, with the mind which abandons harming others entirely and works solely to accomplish benefit for yourself and others, train in the conduct of a Bodhisattva in order to accomplish happiness and increase repute and merit." So the deer instructed. The king listened to this and, looking back in devotion, left the forest.

It is impossible that ordinary beings with unrealised or unknowing minds, regardless of their status, never make any terrible mistakes. However, if we train through many progressive stages of investigation and analysis, we will no longer make big mistakes, and can progress in the direction of making no mistakes at all.

When we subject the Dharma the Buddha taught to careful analysis, first we need to investigate whether Buddha's holy Dharma teachings are immaculate and true, or a false doctrine confused and adulterated by others. If they are truly the teachings of the Conqueror, we need to be aware that he also taught all kinds of teachings with provisional and definitive meaning, in accordance with the minds of beings to be subdued. Therefore, to start with, we at least need to identify the distinction between teachings of provisional and definitive meaning, so we may begin to investigate from the fundamental points upwards.

Alongside this, in accordance with the need to understand that distinction, we consider the ultimate result desired in Buddhism, aspired to according to the general tradition of the Mahayana. This is as follows: Through the power of the force and aspiration of previously accumulated virtuous merit, not only is a precious human body complete with the freedoms and advantages attained in this life, but the Dharma of the Mahayana is encountered. Disenchanted with cyclic existence, and with tremendous strength of mind to accomplish benefit for both oneself and others, merely making a start in the tremendous training of the Bodhisattva has boundless benefit. You will be totally victorious over the hoards of Mara and you will become worthy of the worship of gods and humans.

Gradually, as meditative concentration becomes supreme, you will come to possess the qualities of the ten strengths, the four fearlessnesses, and the eighteen distinctive qualities. By attaining a supreme body adorned with the major and minor marks, you attain the state of buddhahood. This is the dharmakaya, completely pervading samsara and nirvana, ever-present great eternal bliss, primordially abiding, and the sambhogakaya, unconfined great enjoyment abiding throughout the three times. Possessed of the twofold knowledge and working for the benefit of sentient beings of samsara, the state of the nirmanakaya is actualised. Currently we train in accumulating the causes whereby ultimately the result is actualised. The conclusion of the bhumis is the rupakaya, and the conclusion of the paths is the dharmakaya.

To be more specific is difficult. This subject is so profound and vast it cannot be summarised in just a few words, and this is not the time to do so. However, if there is a need to speculate about the future of the new millennium, and investigate from this, then it is just as the Buddha taught: The sum total of suffering of beings who are degenerating in this aeon of decline is boundless. For humans, in this sometimes pleasant, sometimes miserable world, a life without suffering is just not going to happen. However, I do think, if at some stage all humanity adopted the same language upon which to base a shared policy for governing society with which the majority of people were content, then happiness would occasionally occur.

It is taught, in the degenerate aeon, the size of the human body when the average lifespan is only ten years, will be the same as one span of a finger in our present aeon. As well as the longest lifespan being ten years, disease, wars and famine are predicted to bring destruction and harm. At that time, one Rigden king from Shambhala will come to this world, and the holy Dharma will spread once again. This is how it is taught in the scriptures. However, if you do not take a too literal, narrow-minded view of these teachings, and know how to comprehend the significant meaning as it was intended to be understood, I think it is possible to come to a clear understanding of the true intended meaning.

Some religions which have gained a following are close to Buddhism, while others seem to follow along similar lines. Devout people with faith in religion maintain and protect their own traditions from contamination by the falsifications of others. However, as well as doing this and trying to live in harmony, everyone who professes to follow a religion should avoid being sectarian, and never grasp or snatch from each other, uniting together to demonstrate their ability to bring happiness and benefit. In addition, if all those with political power worked solely to achieve benefit for all humanity, doing everything they pledge to do, peace and happiness would come to the world as a matter of course.

It is very important for spiritual people to set an example to others by being good followers of religion, and for everyone else to maintain pure mind and conduct, abandoning bad intentions and deception. In this way, we come to the ultimate aim of undertaking all this research and investigation: To enable us to offer all gain and success to others and carry any loss and defeat ourselves. If approximately eighty percent of the general populace aroused this kind of bodhichitta mind to benefit others, a change would take place in the world making it akin to heaven. The mind and behaviour of people of that time would be extremely close to the Buddhist ideal.

So, to speak clearly about the connection between a good heart and happiness, by knowing the wisdom of how to bring about happiness for self and others, we can lessen and reduce the basis for everything undesirable, which is ignorance. With little attachment to self-centred desires, the bonds of self-grasping loosen. By this power, afflictions of attachment and aggression can be limited and subdued, by which obscurations become thinned out. With a good heart and behaviour which brings benefit to others, completely virtuous actions are accomplished, and also merit is accumulated in this way.

Because all wishes of someone in possession of merit are accomplished; by the power of communally-accumulated merit, harm caused by the four elements: earthquakes, fires, floods, and so on, is lessened. By abandoning unmeritorious actions, ordinary individuals experience less sickness and problems. Even if, because of irreversible previously accumulated negative karma, sickness and problems do occur, these can be taken as the path as methods to accumulate merit. In a world where a good heart is commonplace, everyone would be happy because there would be no one to cause harm, such as murderers and thieves. Harmful intentions would be few and people would live side by side like parents and children, and brothers and sisters. Armies, weapons and borders between countries would become legends of ancient history. Because outer wealth would be plentiful, everyone would strive solely for methods to achieve inner happiness, and to remove the suffering of old age, sickness and death.

In such a world, people would strive towards a path which is actually the ultimate definitive meaning of the Buddhist teachings today; however, by the time such harmony became possible, the examples, continuum of instruction, practice and experience of today's Buddhism will have become extremely rare. Because of this, currently those of us who are aware of its value, hold Buddhism as singularly important, seeing it as crucial among hundreds of alternative pursuits. Accordingly, it is important to understand now, by the conduct aspect of means: generosity, ethical discipline etc., and the wisdom accumulation of knowledge, the two accumulations of merit and wisdom are gathered, which results in undefiled inner joy. Old age, sickness and death then entail no suffering, and some of us will actually attain the realisation of a master of awareness with power over life and freedom from death. Of this we can be sure.

If we use the example of a school, at this time most of humanity, judging by the material objects we possess, and our inner mental motivation, behaviour and learning, are still only in the lower stages of primary school. Alternatively, taking the example of a nine-storied house, most people have only arrived at the first or second stories, and some are still left even lower than this. As I have said before, most peoples' first priority is filling their own bellies. Then we need clothes to protect us from the cold. If we have enough food and clothes, we start thinking about acquiring more and better-quality possessions. Very few people actually strive for the means to help others. Most continue working towards acquiring more goods and valuables. They envy those in a superior position, worry they have not piled up enough wealth and hatch schemes to accumulate even more. So their lives pass in this way, they reach death and finally buy into defeat.

If you ask what defeat means, running around endlessly for the sake of comfort and then dying before experiencing any satisfaction is defeat.

We are always meeting with many undesirable circumstances. Never finding inner satisfaction, we have none. We sometimes manage a little outer happiness, but by having one but not the other, outer and inner happiness are never in balance, and so we end up defeated.

Even if we reach a time when we have more than enough worldly wealth, if our inner mental state remains poor, fixated attachment will become that much greater, and there is a danger that lying, deceit and even theft will lead us down a ruinous path of unhappiness, now and in the future. This being so, in conjunction with seeking to establish agreeable conditions in our outer circumstances, if we can steer ourselves in the direction of methods to reduce the extent of the disease of afflictions in our inner mind, we will find outer and inner satisfaction can develop mutually. By these means, regardless of external comforts, we will reach a stage where we become satisfied, with true inner happiness. At that stage, unlike now, signs of inner qualities, like a measure of miraculous power will be manifested.

In this case, directing an advancement of understanding in the areas of psychology and mind science, to enable humanity to travel the path which leads to happiness and comfort, is an extremely important need. Everyone has their individual hopes. If all their hopes were combined and summarised, that hope would be for happiness and comfort. Currently people have the simple desire for happiness, but they do not know what true happiness and comfort is. Who can blame them? It is because up to now they have never experienced it.

To demonstrate this with a brief example: When we are hungry, if we have some delicious food we consider that to be happiness. Having eaten the delicious food, once our stomach is full, we are not as eager for food as we were. If we do not become hungry again, we will not want food and we will not seek it. In this case the real happiness is not the food, and it is also not the having eaten it. Happiness is the absence of the suffering of being hungry, the no hunger that is satisfaction. Similarly, if there were no inner afflictions then there would be no discomfort. The absence of discomfort is satisfaction.

To use another example, scratching an itch is considered comfortable, but more comfortable than scratching an itch is the comfort of not itching. A hundred times more satisfying than gratifying ourselves with sensory enjoyments like food or clothes is to find satisfaction within. Once this is attained, the pleasure of external objects no longer satisfies the mind, and is seen as suffering. This being so, according to our inner perception and point of view, our outer perceptual experience changes. On a day when your mind is happy, even if you travel to a place full of treacherous ravines, it will still seem pleasant. On a day when you are feeling unhappy, you can walk through meadows of flowers in beautiful parkland and you will not become filled with joy; the park will not seem attractive. In this case, if all humanity, at the same time as acquiring external objects brought progress to their inner thinking, and acquired material objects encouraged and lead by a good heart, then the whole world would become united, happy and comfortable.

If, from now on, each of us strive together to actualise a joyful pure realm, just as we have discussed; then, as described in the example of the nine-storied house, as if arriving at the very top floor, we can arrive at achievement without doubt.

Yogis perceive worldly happiness, the deceptive seductions of sensory enjoyments, as being like a conjuror's illusions without any essence; therefore they meditate one-pointedly on profound meaning and achieve attainment. There are also many others who enter the path by developing renunciation through perceiving the inherent fault of existence, which is that desire for sensory enjoyments is insatiable. Like drinking salt water, our thirst only returns and increases.

As is clearly indicated in the Buddhist teachings, when virtue increases fortune correspondingly increases. So, in the future, when Lord Protector Maitreya teaches Dharma, the length of life of sentient beings will increase in what is considered a fortunate aeon. Before this, everyone accumulates non-virtue, so lives are short, disease is rife and physical bodies are small and sickly. Alongside this, wars, natural disasters and famines occur. Subsequently, by the power of the Buddha Maitreya's compassion and by the force of sentient beings' virtue increasing, the aeon evolves positively, at which time disease and harmful occurrences are few. People become stronger and healthier and, in addition, their enjoyments become equal to those of the gods. Because cause and effect is infallible, the ten year lifespan of the bad times can undoubtedly be increased by practical methods.

It is an unfortunate fact that if the holy Dharma taught by the Buddha, and the teachings given by other genuine teachers to benefit sentient beings, are fabricated or mixed with falsifications or adulterations, it will be a tremendous loss for future generations. Because of this, we see that protecting ancient teaching traditions is even more important than protecting one's own life, as I have repeated over and over again.

In all these pages I have tried to write from the viewpoint of an unbiased investigator. I have prioritised investigation behind closed doors which conceal some difficult issues people of today are not so aware; including the hidden secrets of lifespan and vital energy, past and future rebirths, karmic cause and effect, methods to increase happiness, and so on. In the manner of a rough guide to the holy Dharma, the nectar of mind which establishes self and others in lasting contentment, I have set forth the methods of how to cure the root source of all suffering, the ignorance of unawareness which gives rise to the illnesses of confused afflictive emotions, and the specific key points of the path of gathering accumulations and purifying obscurations by offering forth some of the immaculate vajra speech of the Buddha.

Alongside this, you can also see a brief section which introduces the snowy land of Tibet, roof of the world; at this time Tibet is the place where the complete teachings of Buddha have spread in their entirety. Sometimes I have illustrated the writing with amazing authentic legends to please the reader, and needless to say, at the same time, this book is completely filled with my, the author's, world view.

Although I have received the name of a holy incarnate master, like a donkey covered by a leopard skin, it is not hidden from my mind that I am an ordinary average person. However, those who gave me the crown of a holy name were great masters possessed of the ornaments of Dharma and wisdom; there is no confusion in their words and they never happened to say anything baseless or false. So, just from the aspect of positive latencies, the karmic propensity of previous aspirations and the highest intention that desires to benefit others, I may come to perform activities which fulfil the aspirations of those great masters. I merely hold the crown of a holy master's name, but the hopes of sentient beings who make a connection with me can still be fulfilled, like a wish-fulfilling gem or a wish-granting tree, by the power of aspirations made by the holy masters of the past.

"May all those who see me, just hear my name, or make a positive or negative karmic connection with me, by my compassion, be established in a state of temporary and ultimate sacred happiness, never to return to suffering. May I in the future become food for those who are hungry, water for those who are thirsty, clothes for those tormented by cold, cooling wind for those tormented by heat, a friend for those without companions, a refuge for those without refuge, protection for those without a protector, even so far as becoming a boat, a bridge, or medicine, and so on, to bring benefit to all sentient beings without distinction!"

Thus I pray throughout the six periods of day and night, continuously arousing bodhichitta and making prayers of aspiration, together also with the aspirations of this work.

This text was written using a few intervals at an extremely busy time filled by activities, working to revive the teachings in various ways. I leave it for unseen friends to be, people of future generations, with the thought it may be of benefit.

A Shakya Shramana (virtuous student of Buddha) of the snowy land on the roof of the world, Thupten Longdok Tenpe Gyatsen or Pema Kalsang, offers this on the first day of the first month of the year two thousand beginning the twenty-first century, in the manner of a gift to every single person.

INTRODUCTION TO DZOGCHEN MONASTERY

Dzogchen is a renowned monastery, a major Buddhist university, a secluded retreat centre and a holy pilgrimage destination, all enshrined within a stunningly beautiful valley. For the casual visitor, the valley of Dzogchen provides a haven of peace and quiet, with the natural beauty of snow-mountains, verdant forest, a winding river and cascading waterfall, abundant wild flowers, and tame wildlife, including rare birds. For the pilgrim, Dzogchen is the home of a profound tradition of realised masters and their enlightening teachings. The monastery valley is full of holy sites which confer tangible blessings, and those with pure perception see Dzogchen as a true pure realm, a temple and mandala of the enlightened ones.

Numbering among the twenty-five key pilgrimage sites in the Kham region of Tibet, Guru Rinpoche personally retreated in Dzogchen and blessed it as a place of his enlightened qualities. It is the site of many revealed treasures, and masters have noted that all eight auspicious symbols are naturally present within the valley. Guru Rinpoche prophesied that anyone who so much as sets foot in the valley, will not fall down to the lower realms. Spend more time in Dzogchen and realisation will naturally arise.

It is taught that hundreds of years before the monastery was founded, Guru Rinpoche himself miraculously travelled to the Dzogchen valley. He undertook retreat, concealed a number of profound treasures and conducted powerful rituals to bless the valley as a truly exceptional place of spiritual attainment.

At that time, the valley was flooded, forming a lake where nine demon brothers lived. In order to make the area conducive to the practise of Dharma, Guru Rinpoche opened up the south bank of the lake, allowing the water to drain away. As the lake water emptied, the demon brothers tried to escape, but Guru Rinpoche brought down a rain of rocks to trap them as they fled. Thus the demons were imprisoned and subdued. To this day in the village below Dzogchen Monastery there are nine small hills of large boulders under which the demons remain; stupas were built upon each hillock to ensure they will never escape. The original name of the Dzogchen valley is Rudam Nukpo, which is understood to mean "dark valley of demons bound".

Subsequently, in Dzogchen Pema Tung, Guru Rinpoche conducted rituals to produce Dharma medicine which rained down throughout the valley. The medicine took the form of the medicinal fruit myrobalan which is normally only found in India. In most places the fruit perished, but on the glacier at the top of the valley the seed of the fruit has been preserved. Even now, if one goes up to the glacier line when all the winter snow has melted, the seeds can be collected from the freshly melting ice. Dzogchen's retreat centre, Pema Tung or Lotus Ground, is named after Guru Rinpoche, the Lotus Born Master. Guru Rinpoche's blessings and the prayers of aspiration he made can still be strongly felt throughout the valley, and even a brief visit can bring lasting peace of mind and spiritual fulfilment.

Many years later, His Holiness the Great Fifth Dalai Lama instructed his teacher, the outstanding Dzogchen master Pema Rinzin, to travel to the Kham region of Eastern Tibet and found a monastery.

His Holiness prophesied:

> "As prophesied by Guru Rinpoche,
> You, the mighty yogi named Pema,
> Will establish a seat in eastern Dhokham,
> At Gye, Rudam or Rawaga, whichever is best.
> Then the general decline in teachings and people will be restored,
> And Dharma will tame the folk of the borderlands."

Following His Holiness's instructions, at the age of sixty-one, Dzogchen Pema Rinzin travelled on foot to the Kham region of Tibet with his two main students, Ponlop Namkha Osal and Rabjam Tenpe Gyaltsen. Having arrived close to the Rudam valley, the masters stopped to have some tea. Pema Rinzin made an offering of the tea and placed the offering cup on a nearby stone. Then, as the masters watched, an emanation of the Dharma protector Pehar Gyalpo, in the form of a crow, flew down and picked up the cup in its beak, carrying it off. They saw the crow disappear into the adjacent valley. Considering this an auspicious sign, the masters followed in the direction the crow had flown. After a short time, Pema Rinzin found the offering cup sitting on a rock in the Rudam valley. It was on that spot he founded Dzogchen Monastery, in the year 1685.

Once Dzogchen monastery had been established, more than one thousand, five hundred practitioners gathered to practise there. At first there were no buildings, so these dedicated students camped out on the grassy slopes to receive teachings and empowerments from the master Pema Rinzin. Engaging in Dzogchen meditation, they would stay out throughout the night, completely covering the monastery hillside.

Following this, with the king of Dege as patron, temples and shrine rooms were constructed. The monastery expanded in both size and reputation, and large numbers of masters trained and became realised in the enlightening Dzogchen teachings. Many of these went on to found their own monasteries, and before the 1950s it is no exaggeration to state that Dzogchen had close to three hundred branch monasteries in the Amdo, Central and Kham regions of Tibet. Included among these are the great monasteries of Dodrupchen and Nyidruk Gon, the monastery of Terton Nyima Drakpa, both of which have over twenty branch monasteries themselves, as well as the famous monastery of Shechen.

In the years following 1959, the entire monastery of Dzogchen was razed to the ground, leaving not one single building standing, and the valley of Rudam remained dark and empty of Dharma for a full twenty years. However, due to the remarkable efforts of the thirteenth throne holder, Kyabje Pema Kalsang Rinpoche, and under the current abbotship of the seventh Dzogchen Rinpoche, Dzogchen Monastery is flourishing once again. It is currently home to a number of senior and highly respected Lamas and around two hundred and fifty exemplary monks.

The tradition of monastic ordination has also been fully revived, and is once again strictly maintained in Dzogchen. Historically, the Vinaya lineage of ordination was not widespread among monasteries of the Nyingma tradition in Eastern Tibet. Later however, the Dzogchen master Gyalse Shenpen Thaye brought the lineage from Central Tibet, and from Dzogchen proceeded to promote the ordination of monks in the region. He also introduced the three bases of ordination, the practice ceremonies of restoring the vows and entering and releasing summer retreat, to the Nyingma monasteries of Kham, where it flourishes once again to this day.

A number of grand temples have recently been rebuilt to inspire devotion and accommodate the extensive programme of regular spiritual services. The traditions of major annual prayer festivals have also been revived, and these include the Great Vase Consecration Ceremony held every Tibetan New Year. Also, during the same month the rite of the Heart Essence of Kilaya Tantra System is held, which concludes with five days of amazing ritual dancing, including the ritual dance of King Gesar. These ceremonies attract thousands of devoted pilgrims, and Dzogchen

Monastery is once again the spiritual centre of a wide community of people, further inspiring them to live happily in the holy Dharma.

DZOGCHEN SHIRA SING BUDDHIST UNIVERSITY

Praised as "the second glorious Nalanda", Shira Sing Buddhist University, fountain of wisdom and learning, is the most historic and influential university in Eastern Tibet. Many highly learned and renowned masters have presided over the university, including Patrul Rinpoche, the Great Khenpo Pema Banza and Mipham Rinpoche. Shira Sing has attracted large numbers of excellent students, including the well known Jamyang Khyentse Wangpo, Shechen Gyaltsab Pema Namgyal, Mura Rinpoche Pema Daychen Zangpo, Nyoshul Longdok, Khyentse Chokyi Lodro, Dilgo Khyentse Rinpoche, Khunu Lama Tenzin Gyaltsen, Ajon Dokden Rinpoche, Jigme Phuntsok Rinpoche, and the current masters Dodrup Rinpoche and Alak Zenkar Rinpoche.

Many important Buddhist universities of the Sakya, Kargyu and Nyingma traditions in Tibet, Bhutan, Sikkim, India and Nepal were founded by masters who graduated from Shira Sing, including the Buddhist Universities of Dzongsar, Gatok, Shechen and Palyul Monasteries. As well as this, a number of key texts which form the core curriculum of Buddhist universities around Tibet and India were written in Dzogchen.

Founded in 1848 by the fourth Dzogchen Rinpoche Migyur Namkhai Dorje, the Great Khenpo Sengtruk Pema Tashi and Gyalse Shenpen Thaye, the university is named after the great Dzogchen master Shira Shigha, one of the principal lineage holders of the Dzogchen tradition. He was seen miraculously, sitting next to a rock, by Gyalse Shenpen Thaye, indicating where the college should be built. The master left an imprint upon the stone he leaned against, and this can still be seen today enshrined on the north-west corner of the university quadrangle. The reincarnation of Jigme Lingpa, Dho Khyentse Yeshe Dorje, personally tamed and consecrated the ground, outlining with his dagger the site where the university was to be built.

The university curriculum runs for twelve years and specialises in the Sutric system, covering the thirteen fundamental texts on Buddhist philosophy, including the Vinaya, Bodhisattva trainings, Maitreya's five treatises of Prajnaparamita and so on, as well as Abhidharma and Madhyamaka. In addition the works of Ronzompa, Je Tsongkhapa, Longchenpa and Jigme Lingpa are studied, together with the writings of masters who actually taught in the university, including Gyalse Shenpen Thaye, Patrul Rinpoche, Great Khenpo Pema Banza and Mipham Rinpoche.

Historically, Shira Sing Buddhist University played a pioneering and exemplary role in the preservation and propagation of the Buddhist teachings, spreading them far and wide, both at home and abroad. This tradition has currently been re-established, with the continuing education of new generations of Khenpos and masters to ensure the accuracy of the teachings and availability of teachers for the benefit of future generations.

DZOGCHEN'S RETREAT CENTRES

Dotted throughout the valley of Dzogchen are many secluded and idyllic dwellings for practice and retreat. Most well known of these is the practice cave of Guru Rinpoche, which overlooks the second of three holy turquoise lakes. Here Guru Rinpoche stayed in retreat, blessing the area with his practice and enlightened presence. As well, hidden in the forest above Dzogchen are the retreat caves of Patrul Rinpoche, including the Yamantaka cave where he wrote his much loved 'Words of My Perfect Teacher'. The Nagchung retreat cave, located in a beautiful sunny spot high above the Dzogchen valley, is the retreat cave of Mipham Rinpoche where he wrote some of his most important texts. In addition, there are the practice caves of Dodrup Rinpoche, Dho Khyentse, Nyoshul Longdok and Ajon Dokden Rinpoche, secluded around the Dzogchen valley.

Traditionally, it was in the larger Dzogchen practice centre that practitioners undertook intensive three year three month group retreats, beginning with completion of the full five hundred thousand repetitions of the Preliminary Practices in just three months. This centre is renowned for the large number of practitioners who demonstrated the ultimate level of attainment, with no less than thirteen yogis attaining full enlightenment in the rainbow body. Nowadays, the beautiful and peaceful long life retreat centre of Tsering Jong remains a key centre for long-term retreat, where dedicated Lamas undertake secluded meditation practice, some for their entire lives.

More recently, Dzogchen Pema Tung Great Perfection Retreat Centre was founded by Kyabje Pema Kalsang Rinpoche, in the heart of the Dzogchen valley. This centre was built on the foundations of Great Khenpo Pema Banza's original retreat centre and continues to focus on the practice and realisation of the profound Dzogchen teachings. Every summer, Kyabje Rinpoche leads large group retreats, offering students the opportunity to join in intensive programmes of instruction and practice on the most profound Dzogchen teachings. Teachings and empowerments are also given to the lay community, and huge prayer festivals involving many thousands of Tulkus, Khenpos, monks and nuns are held on important dates, bringing together people from the whole region in prayer and practice.

With the establishment of Pema Tung Great Perfection Retreat Centre, the gradual progression of spiritual development is fully complemented. Following fundamental training of the monastic tradition in Dzogchen Monastery, the student then progresses onto intensive study of the Buddhist scriptures in Shira Sing Buddhist University. When a wide theoretical basis is established, experiential training, contemplation and meditation is undertaken in Pema Tung Retreat Centre. Eventually, the practitioner enters long term retreat to realise the ultimate meaning of Dharma.

Dzogchen Monastery shines brightly as a beacon of holy illuminating light. The great Jamyang Khyentse Wangpo stated that all the large and small monasteries of the Nyingma tradition are the result of the activities of just two key monasteries: Gatok and Dzogchen. Dzogchen Monastery continues to be an incomparable model of sacred Buddhist glory and serves as an inspiration and focus of devotion and practice for tens of thousands of Tibetans, Chinese and Western students worldwide.

> *An impeccable lineage of monastic ordination,*
> *upheld purely and proudly.*
> *The scholastic excellence of unrivalled teachers*
> *faithfully expounded and debated.*
> *Living examples of genuine compassion and wisdom:*
> *incomparable holy masters.*
> *Ultimate realisation of perfect enlightenment,*
> *true Dzogpa Chenpo!*